# LEADERS AND LEGACIES:

## CONTRIBUTIONS TO THE
## PROFESSION OF COUNSELING

Edited by
John D. West, Cynthia J. Osborn, and Donald L. Bubenzer

Brunner-Routledge
New York and Hove

Endorsed by
Chi Sigma Iota
Counseling Academic and
Professional Honor Society
International

Published in 2003 by
Brunner-Routledge
29 West 35th Street
New York, NY 10001

Published in Great Britain by
Brunner-Routledge
27 Church Road
Hove
E. Sussex, BN3 2FA

Copyright © 2003 by Taylor & Francis Books, Inc.
Brunner-Routledge is an imprint of the Taylor & Francis Group.

Photography credits: Mary Thomas Burke, *photograph by Wade Bruton*; Roger F. Aubrey, *photograph property of Vanderbilt University Alumni Publications Archives, Archive Photo*; Samuel Templeman Gladding, *photograph by Ken Bennett*; Judith Lewis, *photograph by Richard Burd*; John McFadden, *photograph by Phil Sawyer, Jr.*, George E. Hill, *photograph property of Ohio University*; Joe Wittmer, *photograph by Herb Press*; Courtland C. Lee, *photograph by Alexia A. Martinez*; Theodore P. Remley, *photograph by Vicki Stanwycks*; Harold F. Cottingham, *photograph by Harris & Ewing, Washington, D.C.*; Merle M. Ohlson, *photograph by Indiana State University Audio-Visual Center*

Printed in the United States of America on acid-free paper.

10 9 8 7 6 5 4 3 2 1

Library of Congress Cataloging-in-Publication Data

Leaders and legacies : contributions to the profession of
counseling / contributing authors, Michael C. Altekruse . . . [et al.] ;
edited by John D. West, Cynthia Osborn, and Donald L. Bubenzer.
p. cm.
Includes bibliographical references and index.
ISBN 0-415-94458-9 (alk. paper) — ISBN 1-58391-089-1 (pbk. :
alk. paper)
1. Counseling. 2. Leadership. I. Altekruse, Michael C.,
1966– II. West, John D. III. Bubenzer, Don. IV. Osborn, Cynthia J.

BF637.C6 L39 2003
361′.06—dc21

2002014087

# LEADERS AND LEGACIES

# Contents

# Preface

It is from a writer's anxiety, anxiety about being able to say something of value, that we begin this book. And, as with many efforts, we take some comfort by starting with a bit of an overview of what is to follow.

## CONTEXT

The impetus for editing this work on leadership, leaders, and their legacies came from many sources. For example, we have marveled at the leadership exhibited by our own students as they raise money for travel to conventions, provide services within our program, and plan for convention presentations or writing projects. We have also puzzled over how to cultivate living with a focus on contributions. We have appreciated the work of our sister counseling programs and their intentional efforts to cultivate leaders. Discussions with colleagues throughout the country have helped us to widen and sharpen our understandings of leadership. These conversations also led us to realize that the profession of counseling is maturing and that we could benefit from greater documentation of the dimensions of leadership in the history of the counseling profession.

Perhaps foremost in the context of pulses urging us to organize this publication was a profound appreciation for those who have provided leadership to us in our own professional development. Some of these folks are among those honored on these pages, others are among the various authors, and still others are unrecognized here but held in our hearts as people who made a difference.

## VISION

This book was born from a desire to record an appreciation for the many who have contributed to the counseling profession and a belief in the value of documenting the dreams, the work, the disappointments, and the accomplishments of some of those who have been intimately and intricately involved in the growth of the profession. Thus, it is our hope that the book will provide a basis for appreciation of some of the dimensions of leadership and of the people who have helped the profession develop. We also hope that the writings will serve as a source of encouragement for the visioning and actions needed to maintain the vitality of the profession of counseling in this new century.

## ACTION

As we began our work, we focused on stimulating thought about leaders and leadership and on documenting a record of significant leadership contributions made to the profession. Further, we wanted to explore the leadership opportunities that are available to students and to professional counselors. Finally, we wanted to recognize some of those who have made significant contributions to the profession.

The authors of the first chapters of the book discuss dimensions of leadership and document some of the nodal actions of leadership within the profession. These chapters offer thoughts on leadership opportunities within the counseling profession and on how leadership may be nurtured. The chapters on leadership are followed by 23 short writings that serve to share the lives and works of some of those who are considered to have made noteworthy contributions to the profession. The book closes with a chapter that uses a "leadergram" to illustrate how, within the dimensions of context, vision, and action, counselors might express their leadership potential.

To choose a select group of counselors who have been leaders of note is a humbling experience. As the book's editors, we wanted to develop a selection process of integrity. Thus, an Academy of Advisors was formed to evaluate the records of those counselors nominated by their colleagues for inclusion in the book. Three criteria were developed for selection of the Academy Members: (a) that the Academy comprise counselors who had occupied significant leadership positions within the American Counseling Association (ACA), its divisions, or related accrediting bodies; (b) that they be distributed across the geographical spectra of the United States; and (c) that the diversity of backgrounds of counselors be respected. We then solicited nominations for leaders of note through a professional print publication and through a recognized electronic listserv. Material collected included a letter of nomination and a curriculum vita. We repeated the call for nominations a second time to help ensure that all who had made significant contributions to counseling over the years would be given consideration. All of those eventually included as noteworthy leaders were nominated by their peers.

We then developed a rating grid whereby Academy members assigned overall points of merit to nominees, with attention given to leadership in the American Counseling Association and its divisions, leadership of scholarship, and leadership to universities and other communities. The materials of all nominees were then mailed to the eight members of the Academy for independent rating. Academy members were eligible for nomination; however, where a rater might have been asked to rate themselves, or where a rating was not provided for a nominee, the mean rating from the other Academy members was used. At least six Academy members rated each nominee. Selection of the noted leaders was made by visual inspection of the mean number of points received by nominees. An observable dividing point in the ratings of nominees was discerned, and 23 individuals were selected for their contributions as leaders. Finally, those selected were notified and authors of the biographical chapters were selected through conversation among nominators, honorees, and the editors.

We are pleased to share these ideas and witnesses of leadership. Our lives have been touched by those who have contributed and continue to contribute to the well-being of the profession of counseling and the larger society. All involved—the honored, those who provided nominations, the nominated, the Academy members, and the writers—expressed a deep commitment to the mission and work of counselors. We realize there are many more who on a daily basis contribute and over a lifetime have contributed significantly to the profession and deserve to be honored. It would, of course, be impossible to include all such persons in one volume. We want to say "thanks" to all of you, and we regret that some who are deserving are not included in these pages. We are grateful to you, our colleagues.

By way of closing this preface, we would also like to offer a special message of appreciation to three who have been our partners during this as well as many other projects. Eileen, Dick, and Nancy have made it possible for us to experience rewards in our professional service. They have been by our sides and participated with us as possibilities and projects have taken shape, and they have provided needed support during periods of disappointment along the way. As our respective life partners, they continue to offer us a life of special meaning.

# Academy of Advisors

Loretta J. Bradley, Ph.D. is Coordinator of the Counselor Education Program at Texas Tech University in Lubbock, Texas. Loretta has been President (1998–1999) of the American Counseling Association (ACA) and President (1995–1996) of the Association for Counselor Education and Supervision (ACES). She has also served as Chairperson of the ACA Executive Committee and the ACA Governing Council, and she has been an ACES National Conference Chairperson and Chairperson of a Search Committee for an Editor of the *Journal of Counseling & Development*.

Mary Alice Bruce, Ph.D. is Head of the Department of Counselor Education at the University of Wyoming in Laramie, Wyoming. Mary Alice coordinates the school counseling program and enjoys working with many dedicated and creative colleagues. She has served as Membership Chairperson for the Association for Counselor Education and Supervision (ACES) and as President (1993–1995) of Wyoming ACES. She has also served as a member and as Chairperson of the Council for Accreditation of Counseling and Related Educational Programs (CACREP).

Stephen S. Feit, Ed.D. is a Professor and Chairperson in the Department of Counseling at Idaho State University in Pocatello, Idaho. He has also served as the Chairperson of the Program Committee for the 2002 Association for Counselor Education and Supervision (ACES) National Convention in Park City, Utah.

Thomas W. Hosie, Ph.D. is a Professor and Department Head of Counselor Education and Educational Psychology at Mississippi State University in Starkville, Mississippi. He is also a Professor Emeritus from Louisiana State University in Baton Rouge, Louisiana. Tom has served as ACES President (1989–1990), Treasurer, and Editor of *Counselor Educa-*

*tion and Supervision*; ACA Governing Council member; Council for Accreditation of Counseling and Related Educational Programs (CACREP) member; and Chairperson and member of the Louisiana Professional Counselors Board of Examiners.

Joseph R. Kandor, Ed.D. is a Distinguished Services Professor Emeritus at the State University of New York College at Brockport in Brockport, New York. He has served as President (1996–1997) of the Association for Assessment in Counseling, as Chairperson of the Council for Accreditation of Counseling and Related Educational Programs (CACREP), and as a member of the American Counseling Association (ACA) Governing Council.

Don C. Locke, Ed.D. is a Professor of Counselor Education at North Carolina State University in Raleigh, North Carolina, and he is Director of the North Carolina State University Doctoral Program in Adult & Community College Education at the Asheville Graduate Center. He has served as President (2000–2001) and Secretary of the Association for Counselor Education and Supervision (ACES), as President (1988–1989) of Southern ACES, as a member of the American Counseling Association (ACA) Licensure Committee, and as a member of the ACA Governing Council.

Jane E. Myers, Ph.D. is a Professor of Counselor Education at the University of North Carolina at Greensboro. Jane has been President of the American Association for Counseling and Development, now the American Counseling Association (ACA) (1990–1991). She has been president of two ACA divisions, the Association for Assessment in Counseling (1987–1988) and the Association for Adult Development and Aging (1986–1987), for which she served as Founding President. Jane has served as President of Chi Sigma Iota (1987–1988), the Counseling Academic and Professional Honor Society International, as well as Rho Chi Sigma (1979–1983), the rehabilitation counseling honor society. She has also been Chairperson of the Counseling and Human Development Foundation, the ACA Executive Director Search Committee, and the Council for Accreditation of Counseling and Related Educational Programs (CACREP).

Thomas J. Sweeney, Ph.D. is a Professor Emeritus of Counselor Education at Ohio University and he is the Founding President (1985–1987) and Executive Director of Chi Sigma Iota Counseling Academic and Professional Honor Society International. Tom has served as President (1980–1981) of the American Personnel and Guidance Association, now the American Counseling Association (ACA). He has also served as Chairperson of the ACA Southern Region Branch Assembly,

President (1976–1977) of the Association for Counselor Education and Supervision (ACES), President (1972–1973) of Southern ACES, and Founding Chairperson of the Council for Accreditation of Counseling and Related Educational Programs (CACREP). He authored the adopted position papers of ACA on both licensure (1975) and accreditation (1981).

# Part I

# Perspectives on Leadership

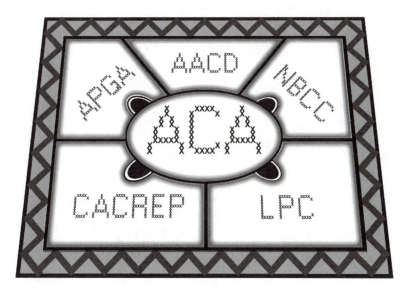

# CHAPTER 1

# Dimensions of Leadership in the Counseling Profession

John D. West, Cynthia J. Osborn, and Donald L. Bubenzer

It is certainly difficult to imagine any community of people or any organization surviving without leadership, and, of course, a central concern for those in a community or organization focuses on the quality of leadership. The counseling literature appears to offer limited discussion pertaining to leadership. We see leadership as consisting of attitudes and behaviors that can be developed in counselors, and in this chapter, we have made an effort to discuss three dimensions of leadership (dimensions of context, vision, and action). In preparation for this discussion, however, we take a moment to reflect on the counseling profession, to consider how it is that its members are drawn to the profession, and to consider the importance of participation in professional organizations.

## HEEDING THE CALL

Those who are drawn to counseling as a profession are likely to report a fascination with people and their stories about human behavior. "People watching" at an international airport, a shopping mall, an amusement park,

3

or at various sightseeing attractions such as Niagara Falls is perhaps not an uncommon activity among many counselors.

Those who explain their selection of counseling as a profession may also refer to their sensitivity to human emotion and a natural or unencumbered empathy for the disenfranchised. In a national survey of major value orientations among American Counseling Association (ACA) members, Kelly (1995) noted that of 10 values represented, the value of benevolence, or the concern for the welfare of others, was rated highest by respondents. He concluded that "a strong core value of holistic-humanistic empowerment for personal development and interpersonal concern" (p. 652) reflected a predominant value system among counselors. Similarly, counseling students often report both an interest in people and a desire to help others as primary motivations for entering the profession. Ninety-one counseling students at various levels of program completion in the Community Counseling master's degree program at Kent State University were surveyed regarding their entry into the counseling profession (Mason, 1998). In response to the question, "What draws you to this work?" the majority of respondents cited a desire to help and a genuine interest in people, regardless of their level of program completion (i.e., first four weeks of the program, completion of one practicum, completion of two practica, currently enrolled in internship).

It appears that the experience of being drawn into the profession for many counselors reflects a genuine desire to help people and to provide meaningful and useful services to others. A primary focus on service, rather than self-interest, and the social value provided by such service, represents an important professional criterion that counseling fulfills (Hosie, 1991; Ritchie, 1990). This commitment to benevolence is typically not a random decision, but one born of a sense of calling, a summons to a lifelong career. Indeed, professionalism has been described as a lifelong process, rather than a product (Spruill & Benshoff, 1996), and those "who do not possess a strong commitment or calling do not last long as counselors" (Ritchie, 1990, p. 222).

## A PLACE FOR EXPRESSION

Once the desire to work with others in some meaningful fashion has been acknowledged, the intended professional begins searching for an appropriate avenue of expression. That is, one considers how and in what ways to pursue his or her intentions to become a helping professional. This entails finding people with whom to associate and carefully selecting a place in which one can belong. Entering a graduate degree program in counseling represents a mechanism that those would-be helping professionals can and do utilize to "announce" themselves as potential providers of services intended to offer hope, possibilities, and positive change for clientele. In a document that described eight different mental health disciplines, West et al. (2001) stated that,

> counseling can be distinguished by its developmental and preventative orientation as well as its focus on the individual within an environmental context. Counseling thus takes a broad view of mental health care, emphasizing the developmental, preventative, and educational aspects in addition to the traditional focus on the remedial treatment of illnesses. (p. 303)

Establishing connections with those who share similar commitments may be helpful and one of the most important steps that an emerging counselor undertakes. In a very real sense, professional identity requires and entails affiliation with a specific group of people, people whose employment and lifestyles resonate or are compatible with one's own values, ideals, and goals, or, as Vacc and Loesch (2000) underscored, one's orientation to the kind of work desired and intended. This implies that professional practice is not an isolated endeavor, but rather a dynamic activity that is experienced and carried out interactively and collaboratively. It may be that upon graduating, finding a setting or an arena in which to practice, and a company of people with whom to surround oneself, becomes the hinge pin for one's professional counselor identity.

Membership and active participation in a professional counseling organization at the local, state, regional, and national levels not only furthers one's professional growth, but also defines one's professional identity and integrity. Collison (2000) regarded active membership as an obligation for counselors who continue to benefit in meaningful and very concrete ways from the work of professional associations (e.g., obtaining counselor licensure, publication opportunities in counseling journals, employment opportunities as counselor educators, and benefiting from legislative lobbying efforts). He stated that refusal to join a professional counseling organization "is rejection of the professional colleague group of which one is a part" (p. 21). Echoing Collison's observations, Weinrach, Lustig, Chan, and Thomas (1998) forthrightly asked, "Do not those who derive enormous personal benefit from ACA have a professional obligation to join?" (p. 434). Indeed, it would seem that to be identified and to practice as a counselor, an individual must surround him- or herself with other counselors and actively participate in counseling associations at the local, state, regional, and national levels. Such involvement is an important mark of professionalism (Spruill & Benshoff, 1996) and represents pride in one's professional identity (Remley & Herlihy, 2001).

This is a good time to be a counselor and there is reason for optimism regarding the identity of professional counselors (Smith, 2001). Indeed, the counseling profession represents an impressive movement in that:

- 45 states and the District of Columbia currently have some form of counselor licensure,
- 31,756 counselors are certified with the National Board of Certified Counselors (Pam Leary, personal communication, July 26, 2000),
- ACA boasts 51,200 members (Janice MacDonald, personal communication, July 21, 2000),
- approximately 108,104 clinically trained counselors practice in the United States (West et al., 2001),
- approximately 490 departments in higher education offer one or more graduate-level programs in counselor preparation (Hollis, 2000),
- 331 counselor preparation programs are accredited by the Council for Accreditation of Counseling and Related Educational Programs (CACREP) (Hollis, 2000), and
- the *Journal of Counseling & Development*, the flagship journal of ACA, has one of the highest circulations of any scholarly journal (Weinrach et al., 1998).

Yet, despite this impressive level of activity, Smith (2001) noted, "The identity of professional counselors must be built on professionalism . . . [requiring] active participation in the ongoing life of the profession" (p. 578). We have interpreted this type of remark to suggest the importance of counselors becoming involved with professional leadership.

Chi Sigma Iota (CSI; CSI Academy of Leaders for Excellence, 1999) has recognized a philosophy of leadership built on service. Indeed, the first principle of CSI's 10 "Principles and Practices of Leadership Excellence" states that "service to others, the profession, and the associations are the preeminent reasons for involvement in leadership positions." One of the requirements of this form of leadership, according to CSI, is "acceptance of leadership positions primarily for the purpose of service rather than personal reward." It would seem that leadership in this direction consists of at least an appreciation for the *context* in which leadership originates and is practiced, and an understanding of the importance of a *meaningful vision* or dream for the future, as well as a willingness to *act* on this vision or dream in order to help it come to life.

## DIMENSIONS OF LEADERSHIP

### Context

Leadership begins with an appreciation of one's context, past and present. This means that those who become leaders are mindful of their current surroundings and know their heritage. They are able to identify and make use of resources within their environment and opportunities within their reach, and they do so in a manner that exemplifies and honors the wisdom of their past. An awareness and use of one's context suggests that leaders are industrious, resourceful individuals.

### *Historical Hindsight*

Leaders within the counseling profession are those who know and value the history of the profession (CSI Academy of Leaders for Excellence, 1999)—the context of the past—and view themselves as privileged members of and contributors to the profession's lineage. They have studied the timelines and tributaries of the profession and are familiar with its pioneers, their predecessors who comprise the profession's "family tree."

Heppner et al. (1995) stated that studying the history of a profession provides several benefits for students: (a) the ability to critically evaluate current work in light of historical roots and build on past accomplishments rather than reinventing conceptualizations or methods; (b) the ability to anticipate how current and future events will affect the field's developments (i.e., prepares students for the future); and (c) the ability to establish a greater sense of identity with the profession. Granello, Hothersall, and Osborne (2000) described the academic genogram as an opportunity for counseling students to situate themselves within the counseling profession. The project entails identifying one's mentors and tracing their academic and professional lineage. Students new to the field may benefit from the discovery of intergenerational themes and may gain a greater perspective on the profession and their place in it.

Maintaining such historical hindsight is vital for effective leaders. Their work has been shaped and influenced by the founding and early counseling practitioners. Without regard for the work and accomplishments of their predecessors, leaders fall out of context and lose their footing, their foundation.

This is not to say that leaders merely "step in line" and blindly perpetuate the views and actions of their forebears, without regard for their relevance to the present. Rather, leaders are students of their history who maintain a judgment about applying the fundamental values and practices of the profession to today. Leaders take their past with them in order to fashion new futures. As an illustration, counselors may participate in professional discussions about psychopathology yet they are also able to understand the counseling profession's historical interest in developmental issues and, for example, they can consider the relevance of developmental issues even when in conversations about psychopathology.

Although written in reference to friendships, Kundera's (1997) words might be applied to the importance of remembering the history of counseling and those who were active in it (i.e., the present counselor's predecessors):

> Remembering our past, carrying it with us always, may be the necessary requirement for maintaining, as they say, the wholeness of the self. To ensure that the self doesn't shrink, to see that it holds on to its volume, memories have to be watered like potted flowers, and the watering calls for regular contact with the witnesses of the past . . . They are our mirror; our memory; we ask nothing of them but that they polish the mirror from time to time so we can look at ourselves in it. (pp. 45–46)

The "witnesses of the past" continue to be our teachers and, as leaders in the counseling profession, we all must nurture and cultivate what they have bequeathed to us as a way to "polish the mirror" that reflects our worth, legitimacy, and relevance as a profession.

## *Peripheral Vision*

Not only are leaders familiar with the context of the past, they also situate themselves in the present. They not only have historical hindsight and a vision for the future, they also cultivate what we refer to as peripheral vision. This means that they are keenly aware of their surroundings, mindful of current events and trends, and perceptive to shifts in the landscape. They are alert.

Kouzes and Posner (1995) referred to this type of peripheral vision as "outsight," meaning that leaders are sensitive to external realities, keeping their antennae tuned to such things as census results, changes in the stock market, supreme court rulings, and the effects of natural disasters. They suggested that good leaders "do not turn their back on the ocean," a phrase attributed to a pamphlet they came across on a vacation to northern California that cautioned visitors about a particular stretch of the Pacific Ocean. This is evident in Smith's (2001) discussion of three external domain issues relevant to the counseling profession: (a) identity of counselors in relation to other mental health care providers, (b) recognition of counselors in state and federal legislation, and (c) increased consumer knowledge of health care. Without being attentive to these and other external forces, leaders place their profession on shaky ground. As Kouzes and Posner noted, "when we take our eyes off the external realities, turning inward to admire the beauty of our own organization, we may be swept away by the swirling waters of change" (p. 47).

An illustration of this peripheral vision might include those individuals who first considered accreditation for graduate programs in counselor education. While being committed to their goal (establishing a procedure for accreditation in counselor education), they had to reflect on the perspectives of other professional accrediting groups, the views of university administrators, the opinions of university faculty, and the benefits of such an action for the public when formulating guidelines and standards for what was to become the Council for Accreditation of Counseling and Related Educational Programs (CACREP).

Peripheral vision also entails and implies an intentional connection with others. Leaders are fellow members of an organization or profession. As a leader, therefore, "I am one of you; indeed, I need to be one of you if I am to represent your interests and the welfare of the organization." An example of this needed connection is evident in the numerous travels made by ACA presidents. In their active presidential year, these leaders are typically on the road and raking up frequent flyer miles as they meet at the state and regional levels, attend ACA organizational activities, and represent ACA at meetings of related organizations (e.g., The Education Trust). Such visibility and involvement in the concerns of the association are expected of the ACA president, who is regarded by ACA as a full-time leader and representative of the association for one year. As an example, the ACA 2001–2002 President, Jane Goodman, reported (personal communication, December 29, 2001) her commitment to attend all divisional conferences during her presidential year.

We believe that leaders need to consistently interact with the persons they serve and to whom they are accountable, displaying an ability to relate well to others, considering their needs, and engaging them in conversations about their work and goals. This entails maintaining regular contact with colleagues and constituents, preferably in face-to-face interaction that encourages a consideration of mutual goals and long-term benefits (Kouzes & Posner, 1995). Examples of this might include making a point to stop in the offices of all staff members on a somewhat regular basis for a few minutes, scheduling a semiannual or annual planning retreat with colleagues that includes a meal and informal discussion, establishing an electronic listserv for student officers of a CSI chapter, and inviting members of the county mental health board to visit a local agency and meet with counselors and support staff.

In this manner, leaders can be likened to circuit riders, those early Methodist clergy who were responsible for a number of parishes, not just one, and rode their "circuit" on horseback (Norwood, 1974). By remaining on the go, these traveling preachers became familiar with the terrain of their assignment and gained an appreciation for the daily tasks and challenges of their "flock." Indeed, some might claim that helpful, relevant sermons are those born of pastoral calling. That is, the messages proclaimed on Sunday mornings take their shape and are formed from interactions and conversations with parishioners throughout the week. Similarly, in order to be effective, the message or vision conveyed by a counseling leader to students, colleagues, university administrators, legislators, and other constituents needs to be the product of "riding the circuit," reflecting the leader's familiarity with and appreciation of the needs and hopes of the persons he or she serves.

Counselors appear to prefer this style of leadership (i.e., exhibiting strong relationship skills). Rehabilitation counselors reported greater job satisfaction when their supervisors displayed high levels of consideration and supportive behavior (Packard & Kauppi, 1999). Employee satisfaction, however, should not be the only impetus for this type of interaction and cooperation. Bemak (2000) stated that a collaborative style of leadership (i.e., interacting and cooperating with multiple entities, e.g., school counselor graduate training programs, school personnel, communities, and families) is essential for the future of the school counseling profession and he noted that school counselors who are committed to addressing the complex needs facing today's youth must adopt such an approach. Part of this, he stated, includes the practice of "de-expertizing," wherein the school counselor shuns the notion that he or she is an "expert," preferring to recognize and promote the specialized knowledge of multiple parties. In this manner, school counselors initiate interagency cooperation and interdisciplinary collaboration, a leadership style necessary for school reform.

Various leaders have themselves conveyed the importance of their involvement and collaboration with those they serve and represent. Although leadership per se was not the focus of their study, Niles, Akos, and Cutler (2001) interviewed 14 "prominent counselor educators" (most of whom had served in counseling leadership positions) about their professional roles and strategies for successfully managing role expectations. When asked to comment on recommendations to new counselor educators concerning the successful management of their careers, the majority of responses referred to participation in professional growth activities and, in turn, nurturing and developing professional relationships. It can be inferred from the select group of individuals included in this study that maintaining close relationships with peers and other members of the counseling profession, that is, appreciating and making full use of their present context, has contributed to and enhanced their leadership efforts.

From numerous interviews with successful leaders from various disciplines around the globe, Kouzes and Posner (1995) heard a style of leadership far different from a traditional management model. Those who participated in their study refuted one of the myths of leadership that "it's lonely at the top" (p. 16). To the contrary, "The most effective leaders we know are involved and in touch with those they lead. They care deeply about others, and they often refer to those with whom they work as family" (p. 16). Leaders actively interact with and listen to stories from their clients and colleagues. They use peripheral vision, as well as historical hindsight, to stay aware of the context and to help generate a vision for the future.

## Vision

Leonard Bernstein (1973), the noted composer and conductor, in adapted remarks from the funeral service of singer Jennie Tourel, wrote, "Wherever she stood to sing, that stage was the Holy of Holies. And [when] she opened her mouth in praise of music, she was a High Priestess, and each phrase was the Name of God; and that moment was the Sabbath of Sabbaths" (p. D19). Bernstein's words create the image that when Tourel sang she was attentive and cared for the words, the melodies, the composers, and the listeners. She demonstrated the possibilities of the music in ways that fired the imaginations (myths) of those who were assembled. Bernstein was able to represent Tourel in the same caring way. They were visionaries who inspired visions.

Although perhaps not on such an emotional scale as that referred to by Bernstein, leadership has the same qualities as those exhibited by Jennie Tourel in her singing and by Leonard Bernstein in speaking of her life. We see leadership as an action, or actions, taken by a person in a defined context at a particular moment of time to stir imagination in ways that move people to create or realize a vision. But, leadership is not a solitary act. Rather, it is a part of an ongoing conversation among people that enables people to establish and move toward their goals.

In ancient Greek culture there were people, most notably Hecataeus and Herodutus (Walter, 1988) and Solon (Jones, 1952), who traveled the known world seeing the sites and describing a worldview or vision of the world. The Greek word describing this process was *theoria*, an ancient way of grasping a worldview from a holistic perspective using one's mind, senses, and passions (Walter, 1988). Both the word *theory* and the word *tourist* are derivatives of the word *theoria*. These wise men, visionaries, were assisted in this process by *periegetes* or local guides (Walter, 1988). It was the local guides who showed the learned ones and helped them to see. They showed them what they considered to be the notable sites, described the local rituals, explained the customs, and told of the historical stories and mythical events. From their travels, guided trips, and reflections, the *theoria* (tourists) were involved in a complex process of active observation, asking questions and listening to stories and myths and feelings. Walter indicated that this visioning encouraged a receptiveness to emotional, cognitive, sensory, and imaginative experiences, a holistic practice of thoughtful awareness. From this wealth of input and information these visionaries created the myths (realities) by which people lived. And so, it has appeared to us that people can be moved more by visions of possibilities that arise from social dialogue than by moral promptings or objective understandings.

In the ancient world these theorists who traveled to strange places and the local guides who showed them around might be called the *therapeutae*, the close attendants of places or those who care for something. They assessed the world through their focus on events, places, stories, and meanings, and they represented these understandings through conversations that evoked visions with an awareness of possibilities for the future. These conversations of possibilities were then the basis for further conversations about action, the doing. Our own word *therapy* is a derivative of this word, *therapeutae*, and hence counseling comes from the concept of being a close attendant of a person and of caring for them. The *therapeutae* of a profession are the ones who care for it with close attention, and the 23 persons honored in this book are some of those who have cared for the profession of counseling with close attention. They all had the ability to pay close attention from a holistic perspective in creating their visions. Perhaps an example of this visionary aspect of leadership will help us in describing how the visionary part of leadership works and how it is related to the dimension of action.

Susan Jones Sears at Ohio State University is a visionary, pulled by possibilities. We've seen her work; participated in it, and benefited from it. Her latest gambit (actually she has been pursuing it for 15 years and now it is finally coming to fruition) is the reforming of school counseling, at least in Ohio:

> I just thought if school counseling has a future, and it needs one for the sake of kids, then there have to be changes; changes in what counselors do with kids and parents, changes in how they are seen by and work with teachers and administrators, changes in their skills and in how they see themselves.

And in her typical way, Susan began to generate the vision by conversing with many *periegetes*, that is, school counselors, teachers, children, parents, colleagues, state department of education personnel, and professional association members. She has noted that this vision indicates that school counselors need to offer leadership where they collaborate with others in the school and community in order to create learning environments that instill hope and a sense of purpose for the youth they serve. To achieve this vision, she believes school counselors must engage in creative problem-solving with students and staff, and have the courage to advocate for all of these students. Attached to this vision were sequential and simultaneous actions that included:

- cultivating a university and faculty with an increased interest in school counseling, including mentoring younger faculty, by developing grants with them;
- getting herself elected to an office in the state school counseling association;
- garnering a three-year grant that involved eight universities in a statewide planning effort and eventually over 1,000 school counselors (to reform school counselor preparation);
- obtaining a large grant to reform school counseling in a major urban district that included development of an evaluation process that was appropriate and specific to counselors (as a way to alter the very work of the school counselor); and
- being involved in a legislative process that resulted in expanding the criteria by which one could become a licensed school counselor.

Susan's leadership style is one of developing a vision and a strategy (a set of related actions) to accomplish the vision. It involves broad and targeted input from others in ongoing conversations about both vision and action. By paying close attention to context, visionaries are able to exercise their imaginations in ways that discern or create meaningful possibilities. Karl Tomm, noted psychiatrist, in speaking of the dynamic character of these visionary aspects of clinical work, stated, "I'm trying to engage in a social dynamic to create or to open space for something to emerge that would be healing if it were there" (Bubenzer, West, Cryder, & Lucey, 1997, p. 87). In a similar manner, visionary leaders are involved in a social dynamic that opens space so that new myths (stories) of possibility might emerge in a selected context (e.g., the counseling profession).

## Action

Regarding the dimension of action, there are undoubtedly more aspects to this component of leadership than can be covered in any one chapter. Here, however, we share some thoughts on the action dimension that have added to our understanding of leadership.

### Communicating a Vision as Well as Steps Toward a Vision

With regard to vision, action, and leadership, it has been pointed out, "Leaders draw upon the wisdom of the past and challenges of the future to articulate a vision of what can be accomplished through imagination, collaboration, cooperation, and creative use of resources" (CSI Academy of Leaders for Excellence, 1999, Practice #4). Bennis (LearnCom, Inc., 1989) also appears to have been speaking of the vision and action dimensions when he mentioned that leaders need to "constantly and consistently **communicate** their vision in word and action" (p. 2; boldface in original).

We believe that acting in a reflective manner can be helpful when considering a vision, as well as steps toward a vision, when pondering how to make the vision and its steps intelligible. Speaking of reflexivity in clinical practice, Zimmerman and Dickerson (1996) noted that it is "a process in which ideas can bounce off other ideas; aspects of experience can come to the fore, so that persons can begin to notice and examine previously held assumptions" (p. 101). Zimmerman and Dickerson mentioned that reflexivity "is more than 'reflecting'," and yet for us reflexivity appears similar to our understanding of reflective thinking (p. 101). They seemed to suggest that this process might be more likely to occur when the individual can find some psychological distance from whatever has been the traditional perspective on an issue. So, for example, when reflecting on ways to make the vision intelligible, one might create some of this distance by considering the benefits of the vision for the profession as well as for a larger community. Zimmerman and Dickerson appeared to suggest a type of inquiry similar to this in clinical practice in order to help "clients to begin to reflexively notice their own preferred possibilities" (p. 102). Finding a quiet place to think from the perspective of colleagues and/or of members in a particular community might facilitate reflective thinking. As an illustration, "How might the portability of licensure benefit clients as well as counselors?" and "Why might some challenge this portability and, also, what might they see as benefits to be derived from the portability of licensure?" Finding ways to think from additional perspectives may make room for views that are not dominated by tradition and may facilitate reflective thinking.

## *Creating a Space for People to Make a Contribution*

Individuals become committed to a vision by participating in its formulation and implementation, and participation should allow for diversity of involvement, such as diversity of gender, age, culture, and so on. As part of an interview on leadership, Frances Hesselbein (former National Executive Director of the Girl Scouts of the U.S.A.; Polk & Rodgers, 1989) noted that, rather than tolerating differences, she has learned to "appreciate" diversity. Likewise, as mentioned by the CSI Academy of Leaders for Excellence (1999), "Leaders assure that members are provided with opportunities to develop and apply their unique talents in service to others, the profession, and association" (Practice #8). Hesselbein also noted that, when working with others, she tries to focus on their "strengths" and "on what they do uncommonly well." Max DePree (Chairperson Emeritus and former Chief Executive Officer of Herman Miller, Inc.; Polk & Rodgers, 1989) made a similar comment when he mentioned,

> I continue to believe that the greatest untapped resource that we have in business . . . is the potential of a person. By and large we still . . . do not capitalize on the gifts that most persons bring to the work place. So we have to learn how to deal . . . both more innovatively and more authentically with the human spirit. See, that's one of the big problems in American corporate life. . . . You have leaders who . . . in effect limit the quality of the corporation to their personal talent.

We believe that, while DePree was speaking of corporate life, similar comments could have meaning for the leadership efforts of counselors. Indeed, the feeling of participation can be empowering and recognizing others for their contributions can be encouraging. Kouzes and Posner (1995) noted that, "If you're not involving people in planning and problem solving and in the execution of their responsibilities, you're underutilizing the skills and resources in your organization" (p. 175). Moreover, the recognition of such efforts does not need to be withheld until the project is completed but can be offered while efforts are under way to reach a vision. People certainly feel recognized and supported in different ways: some folks feel recognized by privately or publicly receiving acknowledgment for their contributions, some feel recognized by having their views seriously considered and, if appropriate, included in steps toward a vision; and some feel recognized by receiving additional opportunities to make contributions. Recognition from others for services offered can help to open space (or serve as an incentive) for additional contributions.

### *"Getting Dirty" and Working Alongside Others as a Leader*

As part of the previously noted video on leadership (Polk & Rodgers, 1989), mention is made of the importance of "getting dirty" with the folks with whom one works. It is important to not only lead by creating a vision and delegating responsibilities, but also to lead by participating in those steps that implement the vision. For example, rather than announcing that "I'm not a details type of person," leadership requires that one realize that the job has not been done until the details are completed, and leadership requires that one demonstrate this philosophy by working alongside others. These actions show to others that the vision is indeed important; that is, "It's important enough that I'm willing to expend my effort to make it happen." Kouzes and Posner (1999) noted,

> When it comes to deciding whether a leader is believable, people first listen to the words and then watch the actions. They listen to the talk, and watch the walk; then they measure the congruence. . . . If people don't see consistency, they conclude that the leader is at best not really serious about the words, and at worst is an outright hypocrite. (p. 133)

At the same time, one wants to be cautious that she or he does not become the only one "helping to make something happen." Delegating, by asking who would like to assume responsibilities, or by approaching particular people for contributions, may be valuable. When working with others, part of "helping to make something happen" depends on valuing tenacity. This includes moments of self talk where one reminds oneself of the value of a particular project and what needs to occur in order to accomplish smaller aspects of the vision, so that eventually the larger vision or dream might be realized. Working alongside others, "helping to make something happen," and demonstrating tenacity can become components of action in the service of leadership.

### Receiving Feedback and Evaluating Progress Toward a Vision or Dream

Senge (1999) noted that there are two parts to the assessment of results (i.e., the measurement of results and the interpretation of the information from the assessment) and that these assessments are hopefully directed toward helping people learn more about how to proceed. The interpretation of information requires a culture in which people can share their perspectives without fear of punishment for opinions that may differ from the dominant story (Senge). Although the purpose of continuous evaluation is to help us think about progress toward a vision, Drucker (1999) noted that one must be willing to let go of what isn't working. Within committee work, this review and evaluation of progress toward a vision or dream can occur as the committee members are asked for feedback on efforts toward the vision. During these points of feedback, we believe that it is important for those in leadership positions to listen carefully to the perspectives of committee members and to be cautious about their own voices becoming too dominant. In a committee, the leader may want to facilitate conversation by using questions designed for clarification, questions designed for considering alternatives, or possibly summarizations designed for helping to open discussions around possible futures.

Regarding the process of helping people stay informed about progress, Kouzes and Posner (1995) noted, "We can't imagine any sports team that would wait until the end of the game for some official to tell them the score" and they suggested scheduling "regular opportunities for people to meet to discuss progress and problems" (p. 263). If, for example, the vision includes the development of a new unit in a mental health center, a new academic degree in a university, or a new program in a public school system, there will undoubtedly be opportunities to receive feedback from committee members on efforts toward the vision. Kouzes and Posner (1995) also mentioned that failure to meet objectives might be discussed "as only a temporary lack of success" (p. 289), and, as a solution-focused approach to therapy (Walter & Peller, 1992) might suggest, those wanting to offer leadership may ask, "What will we be doing as we get 'back on track'?" (p. 152).

There is frequently a need for numerous opportunities to review and evaluate progress. It may, for example, be useful to wonder with committee members whether steps toward a vision have been clearly articulated, whether they have been helpfully sequenced, and whether progress toward the vision is occurring in a timely fashion. Those in a leadership position can consider, with committee members, when it might be appropriate to receive feedback and evaluate progress toward a specific objective. Ensuring that committees engage in the review of progress toward a vision is an action-oriented dimension of leadership.

### *Celebrating Small Changes*

Whereas a vision may capture one's heart and passion, the initial size or extent of the vision may at times seem so overwhelming as to discourage action toward the vision. When involved with helping to bring a vision into action, one may want to view the path toward the vision as being comprised of a series of successive steps. Again, counselors may want to consider comments from a solution-focused approach to therapy (Walter & Peller, 1992) as they deliberate on developing steps that might move the committee toward a vision or as they work at changing problems into goals. Such a perspective may be reflected in the following questions:

- How will we know when we are making progress toward our vision?
- What will we see ourselves accomplishing as we progress toward this vision?
- Rather than focusing on this problem, how would I prefer to see the issue?

Kouzes and Posner (1995) noted, "Leaders help others to see how progress can be made by breaking the journey down into measurable goals and milestones" (p. 244). They went on to suggest that focusing on major advances limits leadership to a small number of distinctive individuals, noting that

> progress *today* is more likely to be the result of a focus on incremental improvements in tools and processes. . . . And a focus on one-hop-at-a-time leading will enable more of us ordinary mortals to take part in the joys of transforming our schools, congregations, communities, agencies, hospitals, corporations, governments, or small businesses into high-performing [preferred] organizations. (p. 245)

Progress toward a vision not only deserves celebration but may also benefit from such recognition. As Kouzes and Posner (1999) noted, "When you have a high level of participation not just in the work itself but in the celebration of achievements, you reinforce people's common stake in reaching their goals" (p. 121).

Recognition of others becomes a basic principle and practice of leadership (CSI Academy of Leaders for Excellence, 1999): "Exemplary leaders assure that all who devote their time and talents in service to the mission of the organization receive appropriate recognition for their contributions" (Principle #9). Communicating a vision, creating space for contributions toward a vision, working alongside others, obtaining feedback on the group's progress toward a vision, and recognizing and celebrating important steps toward the vision can all be representative of the action-oriented dimension in leadership.

## CONCLUSION

In this chapter we have discussed three dimensions of leadership: the context in which leadership occurs, the importance of a vision for leadership, and the need for action in leadership. This is not to say that there are not additional dimensions of leadership nor that there are not additional aspects to these three dimensions. Certainly, as one continues in her or his career as a counselor, further study of leadership may take on additional meaning. It is also important to mention that we have been trying to talk about leadership as a process or a verb rather than as a noun where someone is described as a leader. This is because we believe that many counselors will have opportunities at various points in their careers to offer leadership, and leadership then becomes a role that one takes on for a particular period of time rather than a title or position that is held interminably.

We hope that this chapter has stimulated a consideration of leadership for counselors, as they either envision what the process might be like or reflect on their own experiences with leadership. The counseling profession can only benefit from thoughtful and ongoing discussions about leadership, and it is our hope that these conversations will consider various aspects of helpful leadership.

## REFERENCES

Bemak, F. (2000). Transforming the role of the counselor to provide leadership in educational reform through collaboration. *Professional School Counseling, 3*, 323–331.

Bernstein, L. (1973, December 9). Jennie Tourel—1910–1973. *The New York Times*, p. D19.

Bubenzer, D. L., West, J. D., Cryder, A. P., & Lucey, C. F. (1997). Karl Tomm: Threads to his work. *The Family Journal: Counseling and Therapy for Couples and Families, 5,* 84–97.

Chi Sigma Iota Academy of Leaders for Excellence. (1999). *Principles and practices of leadership excellence.* Retrieved December 29, 2001, from http://www.csi-net.org/ty

Collison, B. B. (2000). The counselor's professional identity. In H. Hackney (Ed.), *Practice issues for the beginning counselor* (pp. 9–22). Boston: Allyn & Bacon.

Drucker, P. F. (1999). The discipline of innovation. In F. Hesselbein & P. M. Cohen (Eds.), *Leader to leader: Enduring insights on leadership from the Drucker Foundations Award-Winning Journal* (pp. 53–56). San Francisco: Jossey-Bass.

Granello, D. H., Hothersall, D., & Osborne, A. L. (2000). The academic genogram: Teaching for the future by learning from the past. *Counselor Education and Supervision, 39,* 177–188.

Heppner, P. P., Kivlighan, D. M., Wright, G. E., Pledge, D. S., Brossart, D. F., Bellatin, A. M., Wang, L., Kinder, M. H., Hertel, J. B., Hendricks, F. M., Kim, H., Durham, R. J., Berry, T. R., Witty, T. E., & Krull, L. A. (1995). Teaching the history of counseling: Training the next generation. *Journal of Counseling & Development, 73,* 337–341.

Hollis, J. W. (2000). *Counselor preparation 1999–2001: Programs, faculty, trends* (10th ed.). Philadelphia: Accelerated Development/Taylor & Francis.

Hosie, T. W. (1991). In F. O. Bradley (Ed.), *Credentialing in counseling* (pp. 23–51). Alexandria, VA: American Association for Counseling and Development.

Jones, W. T. (1952). *A history of western philosophy.* New York: Harcourt, Brace, and World.

Kelly, E. W., Jr. (1995). Counselor values: A national survey. *Journal of Counseling & Development, 73,* 648–653.

Kouzes, J. M., & Posner, B. Z. (1995). *The leadership challenge: How to keep getting extraordinary things done in organizations.* San Francisco: Jossey-Bass.

Kouzes, J. M., & Posner, B. Z. (1999). *Encouraging the heart: A leader's guide to rewarding and recognizing others.* San Francisco: Jossey-Bass.

Kundera, M. (1997). *Identity.* New York: Harper.

LearnCom, Inc. (1989). *The leader within with Dr. Warren Bennis: Leader's guide* [Brochure]. Bensenville, IL: Author.

Mason, M. J. (1998). *The development of counselors: A study of professional socialization through graduate school.* Unpublished doctoral dissertation, Kent State University, Kent, OH.

Niles, S. G., Akos, P., & Cutler, H. (2001). Counselor educators' strategies for success. *Counselor Education and Supervision, 40,* 276–291.

Norwood, F. A. (1974). *The story of American Methodism*. Nashville, TN: Abingdon.

Packard, S. H., & Kauppi, D. R. (1999). Rehabilitation agency leadership style: Impact on subordinates' job satisfaction. *Rehabilitation Counseling Bulletin, 43*, 5–11.

Polk, V., & Rodgers, J. (Executive Producers). (1989). *The leader within with Dr. Warren Bennis* (Distributed by LearnCom, Inc., 714 Industrial Drive, Bensenville, IL 60106).

Remley, T. P., Jr., & Herlihy, B. (2001). *Ethical, legal, and professional issues in counseling*. Upper Saddle River, NJ: Merrill/Prentice Hall.

Ritchie, M. H. (1990). Counseling is not a profession—yet. *Counselor Education and Supervision, 29*, 220–227.

Senge, P. M. (1999). The practice of innovation. In F. Hesselbein & P. M. Cohen (Eds.), *Leader to leader: Enduring insights on leadership from the Drucker Foundation's Award-Winning Journal* (pp. 57–68). San Francisco: Jossey-Bass.

Smith, H. B. (2001). Professional identity for counselors. In D. C. Locke, J. E. Myers, & E. L. Herr (Eds.), *The handbook of counseling* (pp. 569–579). Thousand Oaks, CA: Sage.

Spruill, D. A., & Benshoff, J. M. (1996). The future is now: Promoting professionalism among counselors-in-training. *Journal of Counseling & Development, 74*, 468–471.

Vacc, N. A., & Loesch, L. C. (2000). *Professional orientation to counseling* (3rd ed.). Philadelphia: Brunner-Routledge/Taylor & Francis.

Walter, E. V. (1988). *Placeways: A theory of the human environment*. Chapel Hill, NC: The University of North Carolina Press.

Walter, J. L., & Peller, J. E. (1992). *Becoming solution-focused in brief therapy*. New York: Brunner-Mazel.

Weinrach, S. G., Lustig, D., Chan, F., & Thomas, K. R. (1998). Publication patterns of *The Personnel and Guidance Journal/Journal of Counseling & Development*: 1978 to 1993. *Journal of Counseling & Development, 76*, 427–435.

West, J., Kohout, J., Pion, G. M., Wicherski, M. M., Vandivort-Warren, R. E., Palmiter, M. L., Merwin, E. I., Lyon, D., Fox, J. C., Clawson, T. W., Smith, S. C., Stockton, R., Nitza, A. G., Ambrose, J. P., Blankertz, L., Thomas, A., Sullivan, L. D., Dwyer, K. P., Fleischer, M. S., Goldsmith, H. F., Henderson, M. J., Atay, J. E., & Manderscheid, R. W. (2001). Mental health practitioners and trainees. In R. W. Manderscheid & M. J. Henderson (Eds.), *Mental Health, United States, 2000* (pp. 279–315). Washington, DC: Center for Mental Health Services [DHHS Pub. No. (SMA) 01–3537].

Zimmerman, J. L., & Dickerson, V. C. (1996). *If problems talked: Narrative therapy in action*. New York: Guilford.

# CHAPTER 2

# Counseling: Milestones and History Makers

Thomas J. Sweeney

Counseling is a relatively young profession in numbers of years. While our historical roots are traced back to the late 19th century, the last decades of the 20th century are the most significant in defining what we now call the profession. These have been exciting times for those who have participated in the evolution of the profession. In fact, we may be too close to our most defining moments to fully appreciate their significance. Likewise, individuals who have sacrificed financial rewards, time with families, and leisure pursuits to further the profession are too numerous to adequately include in a brief history.

There is a need to acknowledge at the outset that there are many individuals who use counseling in their work, who refer to themselves as "counselors" in directories or as "counselor educators" because they indeed prepare counselors. Such "counselor educators" may hold professional counselor credentials because of the political and legal constraints of credentialing boards, *but their professional preparation and identity, principal credentials, and professional affiliations* are not in counselor education. The confusion resulting from these circumstances is substantial and at times the usage of "counselor" and "counseling" in our society is so common as to discourage all but the most ardent advocates for the profession (Chi Sigma Iota [CSI], 1998a, 1998b).

Historically, doctoral graduates in counselor education had been required to obtain credentials, for example, from state psychology boards, often under "grand-parenting provisions," in order to continue working. This was true until counselor licensing laws were passed. In some cases, the names and emphasis of the programs in which individuals were educated changed from "counselor education" to titles such as "counseling psychology." This has lent much confusion to the preferred identity of many who use both titles. Quite often in discussions about such matters, confusion surfaces as those who are graduates of these different preparation programs are unaware of the underlying, fundamental differences in the disciplines. Although we have much in common with other disciplines, the counseling profession is unique and, as history will show, the distinctions are notable. In this chapter, I hope to help professional counselors understand something more about these distinctions while highlighting the leaders who advanced the professionalization of counseling as a discipline.

In his book on leadership, John Gardner (1990) offered:

> All too often when we think of our historic leaders, we eliminate all the contradictions that make individuals distinctive. And we further violate reality by lifting them out of their historical contexts. No wonder we are left with pasteboard portraits. As first steps toward a mature view of leaders we must accept complexity and context. (p. 5)

Likewise, the leaders of the counseling profession have influenced and been influenced by a variety of internal and external forces. Many of these are a result of societal events and conditions, including legislation, economic conditions, military needs, and social change. There are textbooks that provide excellent overviews of historical events that have helped to shape the profession (e.g., Gladding, 2000). The following sections, therefore, will focus principally on antecedents to and major factors impacting our professionalization, and the individuals associated with them.

Hallmarks of a profession (e.g., standards, accreditation, credentialing, associations, and advocacy) will be used in this chapter to provide structure, but it will be the events, personalities, and contexts that will provide substance. As the title of this book suggests, there are leaders and there are legacies. Not all elected leaders are able to leave a legacy. Likewise, not all who leave a legacy have held elected offices. Leaders who have left a legacy will be the focus of this chapter. The chapter will conclude with principles and practices of exemplary leadership developed by past leaders. With the conviction that leaders are developed, "not born," the wisdom of earlier proven leaders can be instructive in mentoring those who are yet to create legacies for the future.

## HISTORICAL ANTECEDENTS TO PROFESSIONALIZATION

### Philosophical Roots: Education and Educators

Most accounts of the history of the profession begin with Frank Parsons (1909), Clifford Beers (1908), and Jesse B. Davis (Brewer, 1932). These icons of the early days represent vocational guidance, mental health, and school guidance. Gladding (2000) recounted in detail the social, educational, legislative, and world events that helped to shape the early history of counseling as practiced principally in schools and colleges, subsequently in rehabilitation, and finally in community settings.

The literature reveals that "counseling" as an activity and identity evolved over time (Sweeney, 2001). "Guidance and personnel workers" were the titles used most commonly during the first half of the century. School teachers were the first-line guidance workers, and it was school guidance that was first introduced on any system- or schoolwide basis (Aubrey, 1977; Brewer, 1932; Hoyt, 1974). Community guidance centers also were introduced in the industrial cities of the north. Whereas the predominate emphasis in our counseling literature has been on the vocational influences and early guidance efforts, there are clear signs that the true potential of the profession was more broadly conceived by its chief advocates.

Philosophically, counseling had its earliest roots in a developmental and holistic value for human growth. This may be best illustrated by one of the most cited authors of the day. Arthur J. Jones (1934), Professor of Secondary Education at the University of Pennsylvania, published the second edition of what has become a classic text, *Principles of Guidance.* He stated his view on the need for guidance:

> Guidance is based upon the fact that human beings need help. To a greater or lesser degree we all need the assistance of others. The possibility of education, as well as the necessity for it, is founded upon the essential dependence of people upon one another. Young people, especially, are not capable of solving life's problems successfully without aid. Many critical situations occur in our lives, situations in which important and far-reaching decisions must be made, and it is very necessary that some adequate help be provided in order that decisions may be made wisely. (p. 3)

These simple and yet profound statements were consistent with the Progressive movement of John Dewey, whom the *New York Times* called "America's Philosopher," and the statements are consistent with our current philosophical positions in counselor education (Hickman & Alexander, 1998, p. iv). Jones's statements addressed the pragmatic nature of all human existence. Everyone at every stage of life must make decisions. With help, they can make them more "wisely." Although Jones (1934) notes that children "especially" need help, implicit in his statements is the need for some assistance throughout our lives. Human development, therefore, facilitated throughout the life span by deliberate, positive assistance is needed and normal in the course of human existence. Indeed, there is ample evidence that a preventive, developmental philosophy of helping was integral to the origins of counseling as an outgrowth of its close association with education (Cottingham, 1956; Gladding, 2000; Hamrin & Erickson, 1939; Hickman & Alexander, 1998; Hill & Luckey, 1969; Hutson, 1968; Miller, 1961; Peters & Farwell, 1967; Shertzer & Stone, 1971).

In education, human development is expected to take place over time. Educational experiences including guidance and counseling are most effective when they anticipate, facilitate, and enhance the learners' capacity to change and grow. This is a fundamental belief of counseling that predates others who have since embraced its value. For example, Hamrin and Erickson (1939) noted:

> Like many other movements, guidance has passed through various stages of emphasis in its development. In the earliest stage it was looked upon as a cure for much of the maladjustment evident in school life of the pupil and in his later vocational life. Soon, however, the emphasis was changed from that of cure to that of prevention. Much failure, it was found, could be averted by preparing the pupil both for the present and future adjustment. The highest stage, and one which is being accepted increasingly, is that the goal of guidance should be not only to cure and to prevent maladjustment but also to make it more nearly possible for every pupil to achieve the most complete, satisfying life possible, both in school and in post-school days. *The all-round wholesome growth and development of every pupil is a real challenge to those interested in guidance and personnel work.* (author's emphasis) (pp. 2–3)

Unknown to some even in counselor education, the leaders of the mental health counseling movement of the 1970s ascribed to the same philosophical position as school counseling; that is, to define the essence of mental health counseling as that of promoting healthy lifestyles, eliminating stressors that detract from such lifestyles, and preserving or restoring positive health (Seiler & Messina, 1979). Adherence to this philosophical position is one of the defining distinctions that mental health counselors bring to any community or interdisciplinary team. Professional counselors are not alone in this position now, however, as others embrace the value of prevention and enhancement of optimum health. Counseling psychology, for example, set out to establish its place among psychologists in the same way (Super, 1955; Wright, 1980).

Although vocational guidance and those associated with measurement, theory, and practices of vocational guidance are often cited as the pioneers of present day counseling, a careful review of history reveals that educators working under vocational education funding had the most direct impact on professionalization. Without such efforts and more, counseling could be a specialty in psychology or teacher education.

## Professionalization Roots: Vocational Education

Hoyt (1974) reported that prior to 1938, the counseling and guidance movement grew slowly and principally at the local level. The George-Deen Act of 1936, however, created the Vocational Education Division of the U.S. Office of Education and an Occupational Information and Guidance Service headed by Harry A. Jager, a former high school principal. This, in turn, led to the creation of State Supervisor of Guidance positions in state departments of education throughout the country. All of these positions were located within divisions of vocational education. The National Association of Guidance Supervisors (NAGS) was likewise established in 1940. This was the forerunner of the present Association for Counselor Education and Supervision (ACES).

After World War II, the George-Barden Act of 1946 provided vocational education funds through the U.S. Office of Education (USOE) for partial support of state supervisors of guidance as well as counselor educators in universities. Jager then moved to encourage the state certification of school counselors through his network of state supervisors. For this reason, state school counselor certification preceded other forms of counselor credentialing. Unfortunately, there were no national preparation standards to help create uniformity from state to state. Acceptance of national standards was still three decades in the future.

Eighty colleges and universities were training school counselors in the late 1940s. Half of the programs were at the undergraduate level. Jager sought to increase both the status and number of counselors as rapidly as possible. Borrowing from a strategy used by the school principals' movement 20 years earlier (i.e., to portray the school counselor as a "teacher plus" specialist in the schools), he wanted to convince school boards that this was a position worthy of financial support. Therefore, Jager decided not to fund undergraduate programs under the George-Barden Act (Hoyt, 1974). The result, no doubt, had a profound effect on the university undergraduate programs at the time. Most institutions moved toward graduate-level preparation for counselors thereafter.

Professionalization had another major boost from Jager's unit between 1949 and 1952. His office published a series of eight reports on counselor preparation, six on course content, and two on in-service education. The last report was entitled, "Supervised Practice in Counselor Preparation." State supervisors of guidance and counselor educators were reimbursed by the USOE for developing these reports. Hoyt (1974) attributed great importance to these reports. They set the pattern for school counselor education and heavily influenced other forms of counselor education from 1946 to 1958.

Hoyt (1974) recalled, for example, that when federal legislation provided for the preparation of vocational rehabilitation counselors in 1955, those responsible decided it was more appropriate to train rehabilitation counselors at the same level and in ways analogous to school counselor training rather than at the undergraduate level. As a result, most vocational rehabilitation programs were placed in colleges of education, where the master's degree was considered an appropriate entry-level degree. Likewise, Jager's and the USOE's influence on content and clinical courses appropriate for counselor preparation helped shape preparation for the rehabilitation counselor (Hoyt, 1974). World events, so often important in the profession's development, became a major factor once more in the late 1950s with another new piece of federal legislation.

## Professionalization Roots: School Guidance

Public Law 85–864, the National Defense Education Act of 1958, changed the fate of counselor education and those associated with it in a few short years. It was the single most important legislation to the counseling profession's ascendancy on university campuses. This act provided funds for guidance and counseling graduate institutes, fellowships in counselor preparation, and expanded guidance and testing programs in schools. The origin of the legislation and its intended purposes are important. In 1957, the Soviet Union launched a successful space capsule. American leadership in rocket and space technology was in serious question. Whereas national defense was the stated issue against the Communist Soviet Union missile research, national pride was uppermost in the minds of Congress.

Congress decided that schools needed to identify, prepare, and "guide" the most gifted and talented youngsters into engineering and other technical careers important to our "space race" with the Soviets. Testing programs were quickly assembled and put into schools throughout the country. Teachers were identified by their principals as promising guidance counselors and sent off to summer or academic-year institutes with full stipends for living expenses and tuition.

Beginning in 1958, the number of counselors in schools would quadruple and the ratio of counselors to students would decrease from 1:960 between 1958 and 1959, to 1:450 by 1966 and 1967 (Shertzer & Stone, 1971). The number of universities training counselors and the number of counselor educators also increased dramatically.

In 3 years, from 1958 to 1961, Dugan (1961) reported that the number of counselor education *programs* grew from 175 to 475. In 1964, the Department of Education, *Directory of Counselor Educators*, listed 706 counselor educators and 327 preparation *institutions* (Hollis, 1997). By 1967, this same directory listed 1,119 counselor educators (58% increase) and 372 institutions offering programs (14% increase). The stage was now set for a shift in the initiative of advancing the profession from the government to the professionals themselves. Those who did so were products of this explosive era of growth, optimism, and hope for the future of counseling.

## DEFINING THE PROFESSION

### National Standards for Preparation

National standards for preparation are essential to defining a profession. They were and remain today controversial because they set forth the *minimum* standards by which what is acceptable for preparation of a professional entering the field is defined. Robert Stripling of the University of Florida, one of the first NDEA institute directors, was among those who insisted on the need for national standards of preparation. He and others in key positions at the time realized that without such standards, many universities and colleges were relegating counselor preparation to "cash" curricula taught by part-time staff whose commitment to counseling was minimal or nonexistent. Although Stripling was criticized by some in counselor preparation for his staunch advocacy for national standards, he was not alone in this cause.

Bill Dugan (1961) of the University of Minnesota and George Hill (Hill & Green, 1961) of Ohio University were among the strongest supporters and leaders for this effort. With their support (Stripling & Dugan, 1961), ACES made a decision to adopt national standards for the preparation of secondary school counselors in 1964 (Hoyt, 1991). It was Stripling, especially, who advocated for 2 years of graduate study in counselor preparation. This was a major issue in the 1960s (Hoyt, 1991). To understand the magnitude of such a proposal, it is necessary to note that most school counseling programs required 30 semester hours of preparation at the time. More than a few people disagreed with Stripling's position. It was almost two decades before ACES adopted his proposal in 1982. Stripling later chaired the ACES committee on doctoral standards that also were adopted by the Council for Accreditation of Counseling and Related Educational Programs (CACREP) during its formative stage.

Dugan was the first president, from 1961 to 1962, of what is now the Association for Counselor Education and Supervision (ACES). The ACES forerunners, the National Association for Guidance Supervisors (NAGS) from 1940 to 1952 and the National Association for Guidance Supervisors and Counselor Trainers (NAGSCT) from 1952 to 1961, reflect the evolution of counselor education from only comprising state supervisors of guidance to including university counselor educators (trainers) and, finally, local supervisors of guidance (Sheeley, 1977).

Dugan first chaired the North Central NAGSCT Committee on Criteria, Policies and Procedures for Analysis and Review of Counselor Education from 1959 to 1960 and then cochaired the NAGSCT Committee on Counselor Education Standards from 1960 to 1962. Throughout his many years of leadership, as ACES president and as president and later executive director of the American Personnel and Guidance Association (APGA, and now ACA), Dugan helped support the standards movement.

Under George E. Hill's mentorship, Ohio University faculty developed and implemented one of the first institutional self-studies in counselor education (Hill & Green, 1961). These early experiences resulted in a prototype for later use by ACES and CACREP (Sweeney, 1992). He also chaired the ACES subcommittee that made the recommendations for secondary school guidance counselor preparation standards. These standards became the basis of all future standards. In addition, Hill was reported in the ACES journal anniversary issue to be the single most prolific contributor in its first 25-year history (Hosie, Poret, Lauck, & Rosier, 1986). In addition to standards and accreditation, one of Hill's many professional concerns was the need for better selection and retention policies and practices in counselor education. Students and faculty today may find it hard to believe that issues like these needed advocates in order for universities to establish criteria suitable for individuals being admitted to the field for practice.

The late 1950s through the 1960s were critical years in the process of establishing national standards for counselor education for at least three reasons. First, the leadership shifted from educators at the federal level to state supervisors and counselor educators. Second, leadership within ACES began to move from state and school system supervisors to counselor educators. Finally, there was the initiative by counselor educators whose background was in education to ensure that school counseling was not a specialty within psychology nor an extension of teacher education (Peters, 1977, p. 20).

With the funneling of NDEA federal funds into school counselor education at the end of the 1950s, counseling psychologists sought to establish standards for the preparation of school counselors. ACES leaders with a strong identity in education, however, succeeded in winning the collaboration and adoption of standards by the American School Counselors Association (ASCA), and these standards became the forerunners of all subsequent standards for counselor preparation (Sweeney, 1992). To this day there continues a tension with counselor education by psychology departments and to some degree teacher education in colleges of education.

For teacher education, however, the tension was more a result of shift in emphasis in counselor education from primarily school counseling to community, mental health, rehabilitation, and marriage and family counseling after the 1960s. This is especially so in programs where nomenclature such as "therapy," "therapist," "treatment," and "patient" was used to describe counselors, what they do, and with whom. Such language is contrary to the educational philosophy and developmental approach of not only educators in general but, historically, counselors in particular (Brewer, 1932; Jones, 1934; Myers, Sweeney, & Witmer, 2000; Peters & Farwell, 1967; Seiler & Messina, 1979; Shertzer & Stone, 1971; Sweeney, 2001). So it was that the movement to implement preparation standards through national accreditation would have tensions related to this history.

## Pathways to National Accreditation

There were multiple early developments of national accreditation. The first efforts at counselor education accreditation began at the state level. However, national accreditation was in place in school counseling through the National Council for Accreditation of Teacher Education (NCATE) long before CACREP came into being. The Council on Rehabilitation Education (CORE) also preceded CACREP.

CORE had federal funds to create its process for rehabilitation counselor education in the 1970s and has continued to do so. CORE, like NCATE, has constituent members whose primary identity is not with counseling. As a consequence, they have chosen to cooperate with CACREP on institutional visits when desired by the faculty and administrators, but they have remained separate as an organization. They also have a different self-study and review process than is traditionally used (Linkowski & Szymanski, 1993). Two of CORE's past presidents also served as representatives for the American Rehabilitation Counselors Association (ARCA) on CACREP: Don Linkowski of George Washington University and John Thompson of the University of Seattle. Thompson also served as CACREP's second chair. In spite of both leaders' strong preference and sincere efforts for closer working relationships between CACREP and CORE, the noncounseling sectors of rehabilitation prevailed in the policies of CORE.

In 1973, Earl Stahl (University of Wisconsin-Oshkosh) provided leadership for an effort toward accreditation of counselor education programs, sponsored by the Wisconsin ACES. His colleague Pete Havens, also from the Oshkosh campus, helped as president of ACES to further the efforts of ACES toward national accreditation. By the late 1970s, California ACES also instituted a statewide accreditation effort, with Bill Evraiff (San Francisco State University) chairing the committee. As president of ACES (1976–1977), I appointed Robert Stripling to chair a committee to develop doctoral level preparation standards. I also appointed Bill Van-Hoose of the University of Virginia to chair a committee to move ACES into the accreditation of programs. Both committees successfully completed their charges and the shape of counselor education took on new form (VanHoose, 1978). As a consequence, CACREP inherited both master's degree and doctoral degree standards and a roster of institutions already recognized by state and national ACES efforts.

Stripling was appointed in 1978 to chair the ACES Committee on Accreditation. While ACES was moving forward with its initiative, I became president-elect of APGA/ACA and carried the standards and accreditation agenda to its Governing Council. ACES leaders generally agreed that accreditation should be a responsibility and source of pride for the profession, not just one of its divisions. Equally important was a concern that practitioners, in addition to counselor educators and supervisors, have a stake in both standards and preparation program assessment. It was considered professionally responsible that ACES encourage APGA and its constituent divisions to adopt the standards and take the initiative for national accreditation of counselor education.

APGA adopted the ACES Standards in 1979 and I was appointed to represent APGA to the NCATE as an associate member to explore the possibility of NCATE assuming the accreditation of all counselor education programs, not just school counseling. NCATE at that time had become equally represented by deans of education and National Education Association (NEA) appointees. The political climate was professional but tense whenever there were discussions of additional accreditations taking place, especially by "specialty" organizations such as APGA and ACES. Even Stripling had doubts about our efforts succeeding unless we first went through NCATE (Stripling, 1978). After three years of participation in NCATE, however, the APGA Governing Council accepted the recommendations of its accreditation committee, which I chaired, to establish what became CACREP in 1981.

The first executive director of CACREP was Joe Wittmer of the University of Florida. Working from a university office with a staff of one graduate assistant and a secretary, CACREP picked up the torch from ACES with modest but important financial support from APGA, the divisions who paid for representation, and modest institutional fees. Wittmer's stewardship helped win over deans, department heads, and presidents to the integrity of the CACREP accreditation process. This was a critical time of close scrutiny by university administrators and any misstep could have been used to discredit our efforts.

I was engaged in the political arena of university accreditation and helping CACREP during its first 6 years as its first chairperson to establish policies, procedures, and cooperation on a number of fronts. One of our major tasks was to convince the Council for Postsecondary Accreditation (COPA) that we were needed, that our scope of accreditation was not duplicating others, and that we would be good partners with others in higher education (Sweeney, 1992; Sweeney & Wittmer, 1984). The process took the better part of 6 years but CACREP was accepted as an equal participant.

An immediate effect of this success was that some deans or presidents could no longer use CACREP's lack of COPA recognition as an excuse for thwarting a counselor education program's desire to have CACREP accreditation. At one time, some states would not permit state funds to be used for accreditation purposes without COPA recognition. Early in our efforts, the American Association of Colleges of Teacher Education (AACTE) executives wrote to college of education deans urging them not to have any non-

COPA-approved accreditation teams on their campus. CACREP was the most obvious target for this request.

With the advent of CACREP into the accreditation community, standards of preparation became all the more important. In fact, specialties within counseling, including gerontological (Myers, 1995a) and marriage and family counseling (Smith, Carlson, Stevens-Smith, & Dennison, 1995), were added to those in school, career, mental health, and college counseling.

## Distinctive Features of Counseling

Where did the road to national standards and accreditation lead us as a profession? First, the national standards codified the historical origins and philosophical orientation of counseling as a profession. Our standards reflect a strong identification with prevention, human development over the life span, and interventions designed not only to remediate but also to enhance the length and quality of life for all persons living in a diverse society and world. Second, they delineate the core and clinical requirements for counselors in any setting while providing specialty guidelines as well. Finally, the standards also affirm the adequacy of preparation at the master's degree level as sufficient for entry into the profession.

Accreditation, on the other hand, represents the collaboration of educators and practitioners in the process of ensuring not only the adequacy of present preparation, but also the necessity of continually moving toward change in keeping with societal needs. Although these are notable and essential accomplishments toward professionalization, they are not sufficient (Hosie, 1991).

## Credentialing: The Necessity of Legal Identity

In the early 1970s, counseling faced a real threat of being marginalized by other helping professions (Sweeney & Sturdevant, 1974). School counselors had succeeded in helping establish state certification in most states, principally through state boards of education, although the requirements still varied considerably among them (Forrester & Stone, 1991). Rehabilitation counselors were soon to establish a national certification process but it would be decades before its criteria would approach the effect desired by its advocates (Leahy & Holt, 1993). At this same time, psychology, social work, and marriage and family practitioners were more attuned to the implications of state and national credentials than were counselors. Psychologists, in particular, caught many counselors unaware when they relegated all other mental health providers to an "assistant" status. The consequences were substantial for those caught in the field without the benefit of fore-warning (Sweeney & Sturdevant, 1974).

Culbreath Cook of Cuyahoga Falls, Ohio, learned of the consequences when he was arrested and booked for committing a felony by the City of Cleveland prosecutor on behalf of the Ohio State Board of Psychology (*City of Cleveland* v. *Cook*, 1975). His private practice stopped immediately. His neighbors and church members were in shock, unable to know what to think about an otherwise responsible citizen and friend. His charge was practicing psychology without a license. He did not claim to be a psychologist, although he repeatedly attempted to contact the state board to learn of its implications for him, as the law had only recently been enacted in 1972. A reading of the definition of what constituted the practice of psychology left little doubt that virtually everything that counselors were prepared to do was considered within its practice (Sweeney, 1991).

The fact that there was a court decision in Virginia that "the profession of personnel and guidance counseling is a separate profession (from psychology) and should be so recognized" suggested to me that, as chair of the newly established APGA Licensure Commission, we should intervene on APGA member Cook's behalf (*Weldon* v. *Virginia State Board of Psychological Examiners*, 1972). Carl Swanson, a counselor educator at James Madison College who also was an attorney, prepared a brief on behalf of APGA in support of Cook's right to practice (Cottingham & Swanson, 1980).

After hearing the attorneys' arguments, the judge decided that the prosecution had not presented a case warranting further deliberation. In short, the judge agreed with the defense that the board of psychology had overstepped its authority by trying to regulate another equally competent practitioner. In point of fact, psychology boards have fared badly in more than one instance, but their influence can extend far beyond the legal realm (Cottingham & Swanson, 1980). State agencies often rewrote their administrative personnel guidelines simply assuming that they should employ only licensed psychologists based upon psychologists' lobbying efforts. Counselors, therefore, could take little comfort in such victories as Cook's.

For these and related reasons, the APGA's Governing Council had earlier adopted a position in favor of vigorously pursuing licensure in every state on behalf of professional counselors (APGA, 1974). As author of the licensure position paper and first chair of the Licensure Commission, I was able to help see that a variety of positive and significant steps were taken to move the initiative forward. One early goal was to establish model legislation for use by state committees. In addition, a legal defense fund for counselors allegedly practicing psychology without a license was established. Among the other national leaders for this effort were Carl Swanson, Harold Cottingham, and David Brooks. All three served on and as chairpersons for the APGA Licensure Commission during its early years. Swanson, in addition to his efforts nationally as noted in the Cook case, helped to gain the first regulation in1975 and subsequent state license in 1976 for professional counselors in the state of Virginia.

Harold Cottingham was a professor in counselor education at the Florida State University. He served as president of the National Vocational Guidance Association (NVGA) (1962–1963) and APGA (1964–1965) and was a prolific author. Not content to rest on his earlier contributions, he first served on and then chaired the licensure committee with his characteristic intensity and commitment to doing any task well (Cottingham & Warner, 1978). One of Cottingham's graduates, J. Melvin Witmer of Ohio University, served with Cottingham on the licensure commission. Witmer, however, did not stop there.

Witmer was the Ohio Personnel and Guidance Association's (OPGA) first licensure committee chair for what became one of the strongest licensure laws in the nation. Beginning in 1974, Witmer began the 75-mile trip between Athens and Columbus, Ohio, that ended in 1984 with the passage of the Ohio law. Later in this initiative, Bill Nemec at the University of Akron and Susan Sears at Ohio State University were key members of the delegation for counselors and subsequently served on the State of Ohio Counselor and Social Worker Board during its formative years of reviewing thousands of applicants and setting board rules and policies that shaped the true nature of the legislation. One of the notable features of this Ohio law is the clear provision that counselors can diagnose and treat mental and emotional disorders. This was unprecedented at the time, as stated in the law. What is notable, too, is not just the length of their service but the fact that a less substantial law could have been passed earlier. Witmer, Nemec, Sears, and their supportive colleagues, however, chose to continue lobbying until Ohio counselors got what they needed and deserved.

Another leader who devoted years of his life to the profession was David Brooks. Brooks served on the APGA Licensure Commission in 1975, first as a student representative with me, then with Cottingham; finally, Brooks chaired it after becoming a counselor educator at Syracuse University. During these early years, the commission worked hard on debating and recommending "model" legislative language and effective lobbying methods. Fretz and Mills (1980) reported that they viewed the

*Licensure Committee Action Packet* (APGA, 1979) as the "most thorough set of preparatory materials that any professional organization of counseling or psychologists has made available to its members" (p. 84).

Brooks became president of the American Mental Health Counselors Association (AMHCA) and continued his efforts to advance counselors' services through legislation, including licensure. He also served as a representative for mental health counselors on the CACREP Board. While on the counselor education faculty at Kent State University, his premature death in 1997 deprived us of one of the most eloquent and devoted members of the profession.

Licensure efforts also resulted in some leaders anticipating the challenges of administering state licensing boards. Issues of board rules related to grandparenting, supervision, reciprocity (portability of one's license from one state to another), and related matters take enormous amounts of time and consideration. Ted Remley of the University of New Orleans has both a law degree and a doctorate in counselor education. He recognized early in his own state board tenure that all boards would benefit mutually from sharing information and ideas on how to meet common issues. As a result, he helped found and served as first chair of the Association of American State Counseling Boards (AASCB). Susan Sears was its second chair and was active in helping the group establish working relationships and an agenda for future work. Other leaders in the initiative for counselor identity through credentialing, however, sought other means to meet the profession's goals.

Whereas state licensure was considered the preferred credential for protecting the practice of counselors, voluntary professional certification was viewed as the unifying credential for counselors nationally. State legislation on title and practice varies from state to state, as is the nature of all legislation. Profession-generated credentials, however, provide a means for defining the profession without the same degree of political influence from nonprofessional or opposing professional groups.

## From Registry to National Certification

Certification is a process by which a professional body grants formal recognition to individuals who meet certain standards. APGA leaders realized shortly after adopting the licensure initiative that most counselors would be without an official title until state licensure laws were passed or unless another alternative was available to them. As a consequence, an APGA Registry Committee was appointed in the late 1970s with the charge to investigate the possibility of a professional registry for counselors such as existed for other disciplines in mental health. Lloyd Stone of Emporia State University chaired this committee at a time when the APGA Governing Council was unaware of the interest in national certification by its members (Stone, 1985). As a result, funding for this initiative was tentative at best and even questioned as a needed item.

In order to convince others of the need, Stone conducted a survey of members in 1980 that resulted in one of the most dramatic responses in comparison to any prior APGA survey. The members' strong support for a national certification was compelling. The APGA Governing Council members determined that it was essential to devote the resources needed to start what became the National Board for Certified Counselors, Inc. (NBCC). NBCC subsequently repaid APGA for its start-up funding. Stone also became the NBCC chairperson during its formative years. However, APGA's effort was not the first initiative into national certification by counselors.

Rehabilitation counselors have had the opportunity to be certified by the Commission on Rehabilitation Counseling Certification (CRCC) since 1973 (Leahy & Holt, 1993). In addition, before APGA agreed to establish NBCC as a separate agency, the AMHCA started its own agency (Messina, 1979). The National Academy of Certified Clinical Mental Health Counselors was established in 1979 as a separate specialty agency but it merged with NBCC in 1993 to provide a unified certification program (H. B. Smith & Robinson, 1995).

Contrary to what many thought regarding the staying power of national certification when state licensure was in place, professional counselors continue to value identification with their national credentials even though it is the state license that secures their employment. The practitioners' need for a strong, positive professional identity seems to be a part of why this is true. Even when the leadership lacked the understanding or vision of what its membership needed and wanted in professional identity and advocacy, practicing counselors never had doubt. Given the opportunity to voice their opinion, as they did through the survey by Stone, members made it clear that they belonged to APGA/ACA for its potential to act on their behalf in matters of advocacy.

## Associations and Advocacy: A Professional Imperative

APGA was the creation of four organizations in 1952. APGA was preceded by the American Council of Guidance and Personnel Associations

(ACGPA), a confederation of organizations "concerned with educational and vocational guidance and other personnel activities" (Harold, 1985, p. 4). Although an organization since 1935, it lacked authority to act on behalf of its membership. Therefore, a new coalition was formed. Constituents included the American College Personnel Association (ACPA), composed principally of university deans of students and related administrators; NAGSCT, composed of state department of education state supervisors of guidance and university counselor educators; the National Vocational Guidance Association (NVGA), with membership from both schools and community settings; and the Student Personnel Association of Teacher Education (SPATE), comprised of teacher education student services personnel.

Although economy was an important factor (i.e., combining resources to provide better and more cost-effective services to their memberships), a major interest was for greater influence on legislation in Washington, DC, and advocacy for their collective memberships. By today's standards, even combined membership numbers of the organizations were modest. ASCA joined APGA in 1953, resulting in a total APGA membership of 6,089 (Romano, 1992). Name changes over the years also reflected the changing nature and needs of the membership as a shift in demographics and size of the organizations took place.

Membership in APGA and its divisions grew to 40,000 in the 1970s. The membership demographic changes in the parent association went from personnel administrators, vocational educators, and counselors in the 1950s, to multiple divisions of APGA concerned with the issues of professional counselors, including preparation standards, accreditation, state and national credentials, and advocacy for the right of clients to choose a counselor for mental health counseling (Myers, 1995b). In 1983, after much debate, APGA changed its name to the American Association for Counseling and Development (AACD).

Not incidental to this debate was the omission of "guidance and personnel" in the new name. "Development" was still considered essential because of its association with counselors as human development specialists who facilitate well being over the life span. Sadly, the first appointed APGA/AACD committee on advocacy for counselors languished from 1980 to 1990 with no notable success or support. This was due in part to a lack of understanding among some members of the APGA Governing Council that without strong support for professional counselors in the marketplace, clients' rights to our counseling services were academic so far as employers and third-party payers were concerned.

By the late 1980s, greater concern about advocacy for counselors had resulted in a much sharper focus on the desirability of "professional counselor" versus the older nomenclature of "guidance worker," "guidance counselor," and similar references that hardly fit the competence and skills of counselors working in a variety of settings. In 1991, when ACPA decided to leave what had become AACD, another change was already in the making. By this time, membership had grown to over 58,000 and there were 16 divisions made up of special interests in counseling and counseling populations. In addition, AACD President Jane E. Myers of the University of North Carolina at Greensboro appointed the organization's first Professionalization Directorate (later a committee) to establish a unified plan for promoting counselors and those they serve. The first meeting of counseling division representatives and agencies, including CACREP, CORE, NBCC, CRCC, and the AASCB, was so successful that the participants requested that AACD continue to bring these groups together in the future. The AASCB, however, as a body composed of representatives for public interests, declined the invitation to participate further. Advocacy for the profession would be a conflict of interest for its members and that was one of the outcomes desired from these meetings, as was clear in the conference report and the subsequent AACD professionalization plan of action.

A number of positive outcomes resulted from this meeting, including (a) the employment of more staff at AACD to address advocacy issues on behalf of counselors; (b) dialogue between NBCC and the mental health certification academy that resulted in the merger of mental health into NBCC; (c) initiatives toward better definitions of professional counseling and specialties within counseling; and (d) attention to greater support for the national accreditation of preparation programs. Unfortunately, due to ACA's financial difficulties in the 1990s, these meetings were discontinued. Subsequently, two national invitational meetings were sponsored by Chi Sigma Iota, the international counseling honor society, under the leadership of President Bill Nemec of the University of Akron in 1998. Representatives for the organizations invited to the 1990 Professionalization Conferences were among the participants.

Substantive recommendations were made by those in attendance, including a proposal for continuing the joint professionalization initiative. The report of the meetings and their recommendations were endorsed by ACES, International Association of Marriage and Family Counselors (IAMFC), and CSI (CSI, 1998a, 1998b). Efforts by the various organizations continue, but at present there is no coordinated, comprehensive professionalization effort under way and no new plans proposed to start one.

Although eligibility for membership in the parent association, AACD/APGA, traditionally had been available to anyone interested in counseling, guidance, personnel work, or the clients they served, in 1991 the Governing Council, under the leadership of Jane Myers, adopted professional criteria for membership. For the first time, AACD became a professional association in keeping with the criteria for a profession (i.e., requiring professional qualifications for membership). The new criteria stated that membership required a master's degree in counseling or a closely related field. The following year, the Governing Council voted to have the association known simply as the American Counseling Association (ACA). The operative term in the name is "counseling" and not "counselors." The criteria are, therefore, still inclusive of individuals not prepared in counselor education but in a "related field."

## Client Advocacy

Advocacy increasingly has been balanced with attention to those whom counselors serve. While human growth and development has always been a part of counselor education, in 1986 a new division of AACD was approved under the leadership of Jane Myers (1995a): the Association for Adult Development and Aging (AADA). In addition, Myers, also a prolific scholar, has advanced the case for counselors to be at the forefront of prevention and wellness as a remedy for a health system that is itself dysfunctional. This was her ACA presidential year and convention theme in 1990 and it is her chief research and writing topic in the new millennium (Myers, Sweeney, & Witmer, 2000). As developmental counseling across the life span was being emphasized in the literature, attention to issues of gender, particularly feminist theory and sexual preferences, was forthcoming. In addition, there was renewed interest in moral development, and multicultural dimensions of counseling were also being highlighted.

Perhaps the most notable of developmental and multicultural efforts was that associated with what had been known as "nonwhite concerns." The forerunner of the Association for Multicultural Counseling and Development (AMCD) was the Association for Non-White Concerns in Personnel and Guidance, which was established as a division of APGA in 1972 (McFadden & Lipscomb, 1985). Even the choice of terms is indicative of the changes that inevitably took place. The first African American president of APGA was a school system counseling supervisor, past president of ASCA, Thelma Daly. Not unlike other organizations in our society, APGA was in serious need of greater cultural sensitivity and the courage to face its various prejudices, not the least of which was racism. Thelma Daly's presidency from 1976 to 1977 was the first occasion for APGA to acknowledge the competence, dignity, and strength of one of its African American members. Daly subsequently served APGA/ACA in a variety of capacities as Governing Council parliamentarian, treasurer, and foundation chair. Her part in challenging racial stereotypes has been invaluable not only to furthering the cause of respect and equity for ACA members but also to advocating for the recipients of counseling services.

The third African American president of ACA from 1997 to 1998 was Courtland Lee at the University of Virginia. He was a past president of AMCD and Chi Sigma Iota before being elected president of ACA. A prolific scholar and statesperson not only in this country but abroad, Courtland Lee's leadership reaches across elementary school education to graduate counselor education. He continues his active role in both Chi Sigma Iota and ACA, in addition to his scholarly works. His identity with multicultural theory and methods in counseling has made him a dynamic force not only in counseling but in education in general.

Another force for multicultural advocacy and counseling within the ranks of leaders has been Don C. Locke of North Carolina State University. Don C. Locke's work within ACA includes multiple leadership roles. A past president of the North Carolina Counseling Association, ACA regional association chairperson, president of both Southern ACES and ACES, and past president of CSI, he also served on the ACA Governing Council and was its parliamentarian. In addition, his publication activities extend from publishing on multicultural techniques for teachers and diversity issues for counselors to being senior editor for *The Handbook of Counseling* (Locke, Myers, & Herr, 2001).

## Leadership for the Future

Issues for leadership in counseling are too vast to respond to adequately in this chapter. By addressing only major issues related to professionalization, the chapter necessarily omitted leadership in other areas. The many individuals working toward passage of state and federal legislation for schools or mental health counseling or for specialty standards and certifications, for example, are leaders not identified in this chapter. As a consequence, some of those who were leaders in career development and counseling, for example, were omitted in this chapter, although some will be addressed in later chapters (i.e., Aubrey, Bradley, Gladding, Hosie, Ohlsen, and Shertzer).

Edwin Herr of Penn State University, for example, has been a prolific scholar and generous leader in career counseling and guidance as well as the profession as a whole. As past president of ACA, ACES, NVGA/NCDA, and CSI, his leadership is matched only by his contributions to the counseling literature over a span of more than four decades. Kenneth Hoyt of the University of Iowa and the University of Maryland, also past president of ACES, NVGA/NCDA, and ACA, served as head of federal career education programs when a voice in Washington, DC, was critical to the success of such programs. Hoyt's passion for career education is his most enduring legacy.

Likewise, individuals who were not in multiple roles or nationally elected positions, whose positions were as paid staff or whose publications were not as extensive as some of those mentioned in this book, may have been overlooked. Hopefully, a future edition of this work will permit inclusion of more of these individuals in the portrayal of our leadership history. New leaders will also emerge whose contributions will be shared.

Perhaps the most important matter before us is related to how we encourage new leadership. As our history shows, leadership emerges from among our ranks related to matters of the heart for those who come forth to truly lead. When an individual is new to the profession, it is through local and state organizations that he or she is introduced to the power of one: one vote, one voice, and one vision. Whether that person learns to use it wisely is often a matter of mentoring and ethical guidance.

CSI's Academy of Leaders for Excellence developed a set of Principles and Practices of Leadership Excellence (CSI, 1999) with the expectation that new leaders can be educated and encouraged to serve at the chapter level in preparation for future service to the profession at the state, regional, national, and international levels. What follows are recommendations by the CSI Academy of Leaders for consideration by those who aspire to lead or mentor those who express a desire for leadership (CSI, 1999).


## PRINCIPLES AND PRACTICES OF LEADERSHIP EXCELLENCE[1]

### *Principle #1:* Philosophy of Leadership

Exemplary leaders recognize that service to others, the profession, and the associations are the preeminent reasons for involvement in leadership positions.

---

[1]Copyright 1999 by Chi Sigma Iota. Reprinted with permission. Full document accessible from http://www.csi-net.org/ty

### *Practice:*

Leaders recognize that service to others is a hallmark for effective leadership that requires:

    a. careful consideration of the magnitude of their commitment prior to accepting a nomination for a leadership role;

    b. acceptance of leadership positions primarily for the purpose of service rather than personal reward; and

    c. willingness to seek counsel prior to decision making that affects others.

### *Principle #2:* Commitment to Mission

Exemplary leaders show evidence of a continuing awareness of and commitment to furthering the mission of their organization.

### *Practice:*

Leaders maintain a continuing awareness of and dedication to enhancing the mission, strategic plan, bylaws, and policies of the organization throughout all leadership functions. They work individually and in teams to fulfill the objectives of the organization in service to others.

### *Principle #3:* Preservation of History

Exemplary leaders respect and build upon the history of their organization.

### *Practice:*

Leaders study the history of their organization through review of archival documents (e.g., minutes of meetings, policies) and other resources, and discussions with current and former leaders, and they act to build upon that history through informed decision making.

### *Principle #4:* Vision of the Future

Exemplary leaders use their knowledge of the organization's history, mission, and commitment to excellence to encourage and create change appropriate to meeting future needs.

### Practice:

Leaders draw upon the wisdom of the past and challenges of the future to articulate a vision of what can be accomplished through imagination, collaboration, cooperation, and creative use of resources.

### Principle #5: Long-Range Perspective

Exemplary leaders recognize that service includes both short- and long-range perspectives.

### Practice:

Leaders act to impact the organization before the year of their primary office, during the year of their primary office, and beyond that year, as appropriate, to assure the ongoing success of the organization.

### Principle #6: Preservation of Resources

Exemplary leaders act to preserve the human and material resources of the organization.

### Practice:

Leaders assure that policies and practices are in effect to assure financial responsibility and continuing respectful treatment of human and other material resources of the organization.

### Principle #7: Respect for Membership

Exemplary leaders respect the needs, resources, and goals of their constituencies in all leadership decisions.

### Practice:

Leaders are deliberate in making decisions that are respectful of the memberships' interests and enhance the benefits to them as active members in the organization.

### *Principle #8:* Mentoring, Encouragement, and Empowerment

Exemplary leaders place a priority on mentoring, encouraging, and empowering others.

### *Practice:*

Leaders assure that members are provided with opportunities to develop and apply their unique talents in service to others, the profession, and association.

### *Principle #9: Recognition of Others*

Exemplary leaders assure that all who devote their time and talents in service to the mission of the organization receive appropriate recognition for their contributions.

### *Practice:*

Leaders maintain records of service to the organization and provide for public recognition of service on an annual basis, minimally (e.g., letters of appreciation, certificates of appreciation).

### *Principle #10: Feedback and Self-Reflection*

Exemplary leaders engage in self-reflection, obtain feedback on their performance in leadership roles from multiple sources, and take appropriate action to better serve the organization.

### *Practice:*

Leaders seek feedback, for example, from members of their leadership team, personal and leadership mentors, and past leaders of the organization. Exemplary leaders experiencing significant life transitions or crises actively and regularly seek consultation from such mentors regarding their capacity to continue the work of the organization during such duress. Leaders take action congruent with that feedback, which reflects their commitment to these Principles and Practices of Leadership Excellence.

## CONCLUSION

The leaders featured in this chapter and book exemplify the principles of leadership noted previously. In fact, by practicing as they did—selflessly, with passion, and in service to others—much was achieved. By nurturing new leaders with such principles, we can secure an even better future for professional counselors and those whom they serve.

## REFERENCES

American Personnel and Guidance Association. (1974). *Counselor licensure: A position statement*. Falls Church, VA: American Personnel and Guidance Association.

American Personnel and Guidance Association. (1979). *Licensure committee action packet*. Alexandria, VA: Author.

Aubrey, R. F. (1977). Historical development of guidance and counseling and implications for the future. *Personnel and Guidance Journal, 55*, 288–295.

Beers, C. (1908). *A mind that found itself.* New York: Longman Green.

Brewer, J. M. (1932). *Education as guidance*. New York: MacMillan.

Chi Sigma Iota. (1998a). *Counselor advocacy leadership conference report: I.* Greensboro, NC: Author.

Chi Sigma Iota. (1998b). *Counselor advocacy leadership conference report: II.* Greensboro, NC: Author.

Chi Sigma Iota. (1999). *Principles and practices of leadership excellence*. Greensboro, NC: Author.

*City of Cleveland* v. *Cook,* Municipal Court, Criminal Division, No. 75-CRB 11478, August 12, 1975. (Transcript dated August 19, 1975)

Cottingham, H. F. (1956). *Guidance in elementary schools*. Bloomington, IL: McKnight & McKnight.

Cottingham, H. F., & Swanson, C. D. (1980). Recent licensure developments: Implications for counselor education. In R. W. Warner, D. K. Brooks, & J. A. Thompson (Eds.), *Counselor licensure: Issues and perspectives a book of readings* (pp. 47–51). Falls Church, VA: American Personnel and Guidance Association.

Cottingham, H. F., & Warner, R. W. (1978). APGA and counselor licensure: A status report. *Personnel and Guidance Journal, 56*, 604.

Dugan, W. (1961). Critical concerns of counselor education. *Counselor Education and Supervision, 0*, 5–11.

Forrester, D. V., & Stone, L. A. (1991). Counselor certification. In F. O. Bradley (Ed.), *Credentialing in counseling* (pp. 13–21). Alexandria, VA: Association for Counselor Education and Supervision.

Fretz, B. R., & Mills, D. H. (1980). *Licensing and certification of psychologists and counselors: A guide to current policies, procedures, and legislation*. San Francisco: Jossey-Bass.

Gardner, J. W. (1990). *On leadership.* New York: Free Press.

Gladding, S. T. (2000). *Counseling: A comprehensive profession* (4th ed.). Upper Saddle River, NJ: Merrill/Prentice Hall.

Hamrin, S. A., & Erickson, C. E. (1939). *Guidance in the secondary schools.* New York: Appleton-Century-Crofts.

Harold, M. (1985). Council's history examined after 50 years. *Guidepost, 27*(10), 4.

Hickman, L. A., & Alexander, T. M. (1998). *The essential Dewey pragmatism, education, democracy: Volume I.* Bloomington, IN: Indiana University Press.

Hill, G. E., & Green, D. A. (Eds.). (1961). *Appraising a counselor education program: The cooperative approach.* Athens, OH: Center for Educational Service.

Hill, G. E., & Luckey, E. B. (1969). *Guidance for children in elementary schools.* New York: Appleton-Century-Crofts.

Hollis, J. W. (1997). *Counselor preparation 1996–98: Programs, faculty, trends* (9th ed.). Washington, DC: Taylor & Francis.

Hosie, T. W. (1991). Historical antecedents and current status of counselor licensure. In F. O. Bradley (Ed.), *Credentialing in counseling* (pp. 23–52). Alexandria, VA: Association for Counselor Education and Supervision.

Hosie, T. W., Poret, M., Lauck, P., & Rosier, B. (1986). Contributions to *Counselor Education and Supervision* for volumes 0–25, 1961–1986. *Counselor Education and Supervision, 25,* 284–288.

Hoyt, K. B. (1974). Professional preparation for vocational guidance. In E. L. Herr (Ed.), *Vocational guidance and human development* (pp. 502–527). Boston: Houghton Mifflin.

Hoyt, K. B. (1991). Concerns about accreditation and credentialing: A personal view. In F. O. Bradley (Ed.), *Credentialing in counseling* (pp. 69–80). Alexandria, VA: Association for Counselor Education and Supervision.

Hutson, P. W. (1968). *The guidance function in education* (2nd ed.). New York: Appleton-Century-Crofts.

Jones, A. J. (1934). *Principles of guidance* (2nd ed.). New York: McGraw-Hill.

Leahy, M. J., & Holt, E. (1993). Certification in rehabilitation counseling: Its history and process. *Rehabilitation Counseling Bulletin, 37,* 71–80.

Linkowski, D. C., & Szymanski, E. M. (1993). Accreditation in rehabilitation counseling: Historical and current context and process. *Rehabilitation Counseling Bulletin, 37,* 81–91.

Locke, D. C., Myers, J. E., & Herr, E. L. (Eds.). (2001). *The handbook of counseling.* Thousands Oaks, CA: Sage.

McFadden, J., & Lipscomb, W. D. (1985). History of the Association of NonWhite Concerns in Guidance and Personnel. *Journal of Counseling & Development, 63,* 444–447.

Messina, J. (1979). The National Academy of Certified Clinical Mental Health Counselors: Creating a new professional identity. *AMHCA Journal, 1,* 607–608.

Miller, C. H. (1961). *Foundations of guidance.* New York: Harper & Brothers.

Myers, J. E. (1992). Competencies, credentialing and standards for gerontological counselors: Implications for counselor education. *Counselor Education and Supervision, 32,* 34–42.

Myers, J. E. (1995a). From "forgotten and ignored" to standards and certification: Gerontological counseling comes of age. *Journal of Counseling & Development, 74,* 143–149.

Myers, J. E. (1995b). Specialties in counseling: Rich heritage or force for fragmentation? *Journal of Counseling & Development, 74* (2), 115–116.

Myers, J. E., Sweeney, T. J., & Witmer, J. M. (2000). The Wheel of Wellness counseling for wellness: A holistic model for treatment planning. *Journal of Counseling & Development, 78,* 251–266.

Parsons, F. (1909). *Choosing a vocation.* Boston: Houghton Mifflin.

Peters, H. J. (1977). In V. L. Sheeley (Ed.), *Presidential review: ACES leaders create ties, 1940–77* (p. 20). Falls Church, VA: Association for Counselor Education and Supervision.

Peters, H. J., & Farwell, G. F. (1967). *Guidance: A developmental approach.* Chicago: Rand McNally & Co.

Romano, G. (1992, Spring). AACD 40th anniversary. *American Counselor, 1,* 18–26.

Seiler, G., & Messina, J. J. (1979). Toward professional identity: Dimensions of mental health counseling in perspective. *AMHCA Journal, 1,* 3–8.

Sheeley, V. L. (Ed.). (1977). *Presidential review: ACES leaders create ties, 1940–77.* Falls Church, VA: Association for Counselor Education and Supervision.

Shertzer, B., & Stone, S. C. (1971). *Fundamentals of guidance.* Boston: Houghton Mifflin.

Smith, R. L., Carlson, J, Stevens-Smith, P., & Dennison, M. (1995). Marriage and family counseling. *Journal of Counseling & Development, 74,* 154–157.

Smith, H. B., & Robinson, G. P. (1995). Mental health counseling: Past, present, and future. *Journal of Counseling & Development, 74,* 158–162.

Stone, L. (1985). National Board for Certified Counselors: History, relationships, and projections. *Journal of Counseling & Development, 63,* 605–606.

Stripling, R. O. (1978). Standards and accreditation in counselor education: A proposal. *The Personnel and Guidance Journal, 56,* 608–611.

Stripling, R. O., & Dugan, W. E. (1961). The cooperative study of counselor education standards. *Counselor Education and Supervision, 0,* 34–35.

Super, D. E. (1955). Transition: From vocational guidance to counseling psychology. *Journal of Counseling Psychology, 42,* 132–136.

Sweeney, T. J. (1991). Counselor credentialing: Purpose and origin. In F. O. Bradley (Ed.), *Credentialing in counseling* (pp. 1–12). Alexandria, VA: Association for Counselor Education and Supervision.

Sweeney, T. J. (1992). CACREP: Precursors, promises, and prospects. *Journal of Counseling & Development, 70,* 667–672.

Sweeney, T. J. (2001). Counseling: Historical origins and philosophical roots. In D. C. Locke, J. E. Myers, & E. L. Herr (Eds.), *The handbook of counseling* (pp. 3–26). Riverside, CA: Sage.

Sweeney, T. J., & Sturdevant, A. D. (1974). Licensure in the helping professions: Anatomy of an issue. *Personnel and Guidance Journal, 52,* 575–580.

Sweeney, T. J., & Wittmer, J. (1984). *Council on Postsecondary Accreditation preapplication phase II: Demonstration of capacity.* Alexandria, VA: Council for the Accreditation of Counseling and Related Educational Programs.

VanHoose, W. H. (1978, March). *1978 Commission on Standards Implementation Report.* Report to the membership, American Personnel and Guidance Association Convention. Washington, DC: Association for Counselor Education and Supervision.

*Weldon* v. *Virginia State Board of Psychologists Examiners.* Corporation Court, Newport News, Virginia, 1972.

Wright, G. N. (1980). *Total rehabilitation.* Boston: Little, Brown, & Co.

# CHAPTER 3

# School Counselors: Leadership Opportunities and Challenges in the Schools

L. DiAnne Borders and Marie F. Shoffner

Historically, and consistently, school counselors have been extolled as natural and essential leaders in the school setting. The unique opportunities of school counselors to have a significant impact on the school environment and the people involved in that environment have been highlighted repeatedly. In this literature over the years, the school counselor as leader is often referred to as a *change agent*, *catalyst*, *advocate*, and even *social activist* (e.g., Allen, 1998; Bemak, 2000; Blocher, 1974; Dahir, 1998; Hansen, 1968; House & Martin, 1998; Menacker, 1976; Sheldon, 1998). Although these terms were particularly popular in the literature in the 1960s and 1970s, they are still common today (Baker, 2000). Indeed, the *opportunities*—the need—for leadership in the schools are greater today, and, at the same time, the *challenges* that detract from school counselors' abilities to provide leadership in the schools also have increased.

In this chapter, we will discuss the leadership opportunities and challenges facing school counselors today. First, we will summarize the view of school counselors as "natural" leaders, as found in the professional literature, and then highlight the social and political issues that create the need and opportunities for leadership in the schools. Third, we will report the results of an informal survey of school counselor leaders regarding their views of leadership and their efforts in the schools. Finally, we will discuss some aspects of school culture and preservice training for school personnel that challenge school counselors' ability to function as leaders in their schools, and offer some suggestions for addressing these challenges.

## NATURAL LEADERS

Why are school counselors seen as "naturals" for leadership roles? It is asserted that, because of their preparation, school counselors bring unique knowledge and skills to bear on issues affecting schools and students (Clark & Stone, 2000; Kern, 1999). The academic background particular to school counselors and valuable to their leadership functions covers many areas (e.g., Quigney & Studer, 1998; West & Idol, 1993).

First, school counselors typically are the only in-house school personnel who have had extensive training in human relations, communication skills, interpersonal relationships, problem-solving, and conflict resolution. Many also have had substantial training in systemic thinking. Not only are these skills important for working with student clients; they are also vital for facilitating communication among the various members of the school community. In addition, such skills are essential for understanding and working with the complex interpersonal dynamics within a school, including the competing expectations, demands, and priorities of counselors versus teachers versus principals versus parents versus students. Second, and relatedly, school counselors also have training in the dynamics of change, such as how change is encouraged, individual and systemic hurdles to change, and the overlapping processes that lead to real change. Thus, they are well equipped to foster change in the school environment.

Third, school counselors are seen as the developmental specialists in the school. Familiarity with a wide variety of developmental theories is perhaps the area most frequently discussed and promoted in discussions of the unique leadership contributions of school counselors. School counselors' training includes in-depth study of cognitive, social, psychosocial, and moral development theories of children and adolescents, giving them a comprehensive understanding of the evolving needs of their students. They have studied a variety of identity development theories, from general psychosocial maps (e.g., Erikson, 1963, 1968) to identity formation processes of particular populations (e.g., racial/ethnic groups, females, sexual minorities).

School counselors are acutely aware that students' needs in all of these areas must be recognized and addressed in their school through proactive and responsive efforts. In addition, school counselors are aware that the various areas of development are interactive and not isolated and that all influence the child's academic performance and success. Many also have studied stages of family development and its variations, with a focus on the family's changing needs and how these influence a child's presentation and performance at school. Using their knowledge of developmental theories, school counselors are able to provide preventive as well as remedial services, designed to be appropriate to a particular developmental level, that facilitate a student's mastery of the successive developmental tasks they necessarily face during their years of schooling.

Fourth, school counselors have extensive training in career development theories and processes, not only from a K–12 or K–16 perspective, but also as a lifelong process. They know the gender-related and social-economic influences on career choices, as well as the necessity of early interventions to broaden a student's career decision-making.

Fifth, school counselors have knowledge of learning theories and therefore understand how children learn, variations in learning styles and processes, and psychosocial challenges to optimal learning. This background makes them valuable resources for teachers, parents, and administrators concerning larger learning questions and when considering the needs of individual students.

Finally, school counselors also have been trained to conduct program evaluations and to value the role that evaluations play in maintaining an effective school counseling program (Baker, 2000). Program evaluation is critical due to increased accountability demands from school administrators, parents, and legislators. More importantly, however, school counselors understand that program evaluation results indicate program strengths as well as areas for improvement, and thus can be used intentionally in program planning and renewal as well as staff development (Borders & Drury, 1992).

These academic background areas are complemented by school counselors' training in the applied skills of counseling, consultation, and coordination (Borders & Drury, 1992). Their skills in individual, group, and family counseling approaches, as well as interventions particularly suited for their student populations (e.g., play therapy), enable them to address the wide variety of issues presented by their clients. They are able to help their clients deal with the academic, career, social, personal, and family issues that may be impeding students' success in school. Their coordination roles involve skills in organizing and managing the broad scope of school counseling program activities, including the testing program, as well as coordinating services provided for a student by other professionals within and outside the school setting. School counselors are the natural "brokers" for recent systems-of-care or wrap-around (Adams & Juhnke, 2001) approaches that involve a variety of professional and nonprofessional persons teamed to address the academic, clinical, and practical needs of children and adolescents.

Training in consultation skills is especially vital in terms of school counselors' leadership potential in the schools. By definition, consultation skills involve collaborative efforts with school staff and parents, and thus a role that involves providing direction, guidance, and support. As a result of their consultation training, school counselors know how to approach, bring together, and work with various school professionals, family members, and other adults in a child's or adolescent's life. As a consultant, the school counselor provides a range of services, from educational workshops to individual conferences, focused on helping consultees work more effectively with students.

## LEADERSHIP OPPORTUNITIES

The conditions, issues, and needs in previous decades requiring school counselors' unique knowledge and skills—and leadership—have not gone away; rather, they are more numerous, complex, and serious (Gysbers & Henderson, 2000). Students in the public schools are increasingly diverse, coming into school from a variety of cultures, countries, and challenging circumstances (Harris, 1999; Lee, 2001), including many with English as their second language (McCall-Perez, 2000). School counselors are still called upon to combat racism and gender bias and to be advocates for exceptional children and sexual minority youth (Baker, 2000; Cooley, 1998; Quigney & Studer, 1998). They also must deal with serious societal issues that affect students and schools, including increasing violence, substance abuse, sexual and physical abuse or neglect, divorce, and poverty (Keys & Bemak, 1997). Coupled with these changes are growing demands and pressures related to schools' accountability for student achievement. These conditions have both expanded and complicated the role of the school counselor, with students, parents, teachers, and administrators struggling to function successfully.

With this expanding role has come more ambiguity regarding how the school counselor should prioritize competing and often overwhelming demands. Stress and work overload caused by ambiguous role definitions and excessive involvement in administrative tasks, including rapidly expanding testing programs (Studer & Allton, 1996), seriously detract from a counselor's ability to act as a leader. In fact, it is these job expectations that comprise the greatest stressor impacting school counselors (Kendrick, Chandler, & Hatcher, 1994). Lack of adequate funding contributes to high school counselor ratios (Boyer, 1988), which in turn force counselors to spend more time on administrative and organizational tasks (Mustaine & Pappalardo, 1996). Clearly, the need for school counselors' unique knowledge and skills is as critical, or more so, than ever, while at the same time their ability to be leaders seems more limited than ever.

## Voices of School Counselor Leaders

How do school counselors see their leadership roles? We conducted an informal survey using a convenience sample to get some answers to this question. We asked colleagues (counselor educators and practitioners) to nominate school counselors whom they considered to be leaders. We defined leadership broadly, from being elected to an office in a professional organization to having had an impact on one's students, school, school system, or community. Our colleagues nominated 15 school counselors, whom we then surveyed by e-mail. The 6 nominees who responded reflected our broad definition of leadership and included system-level administrators as well as school counselor practitioners. The nominees responded to open-ended questions regarding their leadership activities (as defined by the respondent), their views of leadership, how they saw themselves as a "leader," and what had influenced them to take on a leadership role.

Most respondents reported that they had viewed themselves as a leader since early in their careers. For some, this response seemed to reflect a general view of self (e.g., "I'm not afraid to raise questions" and "I have always been a person who looked for different ways to solve problems and make things happen"). Others said they were prompted to take on a leadership role in response to an on-the-job challenge (e.g., "The job role was not very well defined. . . . School counselors performed whatever tasks were assigned by their individual principals. Working with the other counselors, we began to put together a job role and provide services, consistent with our training, and educate others about what we could do."). Overwhelmingly, however, respondents reported that they first began to see themselves as a leader in response to "being asked to be a leader": to run for an office in a professional organization, to help write a comprehensive school counseling curriculum, to serve on a school leadership committee, or to represent the school system at a workshop or meeting. Importantly, the respondents emphasized that their efforts were nurtured and encouraged by colleagues, principals, supervisors, and/or fellow officers who served as role models and mentors.

Respondents defined "leadership" using terms quite similar to those in the professional literature. Frequently listed terms included "taking initiative," doing things "above and beyond what is required," "taking some risks," and "being creative in problem-solving." Leaders, they said, motivate, pioneer, challenge, inspire, energize, support, and listen to others. One said, "Leaders are not selfish, but will devote time and energy to projects without thinking about what is in it for them. They don't always put their own comfort or well-being first."

Our school counselor leaders reported various actions they characterized as leadership activities. They included activities such as applying for grants, presenting workshops at conferences, supervising interns, serving as a mentor for a new counselor, working on collaborative projects with counselor educators, providing staff development, and other role-related activities. They listed numerous elected and appointed positions in professional organizations, from president at the state and national level to board member to committee chair or member. Some described community outreach activities, such as organizing after-school activities, providing parenting workshops, and involvement in community-based organizations. Many mentioned advocacy, for students and for the profession, although few offered examples of their advocacy acts. One reported, "I worked with a reluctant city council to encourage them to fund additional school counselor positions, inviting the most vocal, skeptical critic of school counselors to shadow me for a day so that he could understand the vital role we play. The next day, he voted passionately to fund additional counselors in the elementary schools."

Indeed, respondents often stated (or implied) that they got involved in leadership activities out of frustration or a desire to change a situation, typically one that involved what was viewed as a misuse of school counselors' training, skills, and time. They also reported discouragement at the lack of response of some school counselors to these situations. One stated, "I think some people perceive leadership as making more work for yourself, and I guess that's true." Another wrote, "It is quite a challenge being a leader in the profession of school counseling. Public perceptions of counselors are not often positive. Some counselors themselves are resistant to change. Roles and responsibilities become entrenched in a large school system, making even small changes seem daunting." Another stated, "I think each counselor needs to ask him/herself, 'What activities am I directly involved in that prove that I practice what I preach?'"

Although these school counselor leaders described a wide variety of actions as examples of leadership, there were several common themes in their responses. Perhaps most fundamentally, they *chose* to see themselves as leaders—as professionals who had the ability to make a difference or create change. They seemed quite aware of their deliberate choice, noting that some of their colleagues apparently had chosen *not* to act as a leader. It was not clear why our respondents had made this choice toward leadership, or why their colleagues chose otherwise. The act of a deliberate, conscious choice, in spite of the work and effort required as a result, however, was a strong theme.

A second theme was that leadership involved defying, in some measure, the status quo in their school or school system. These school counselors would not accept things as they were, but created, advocated, and pushed "outside the box." As a corollary, they seemed to imply that some of their colleagues chose to accept the status quo, perhaps even preferring the safety or comfort of the familiar—"the system."

What makes the difference between those who choose to be leaders and those who do not? What stands in the way of these school counselors who are not able, willing, or confident enough to move beyond the tasks and requirements of their position? What challenges serve as blocks to their choice for leadership?

## LEADERSHIP CHALLENGES

Despite the promotion of school counselors as leaders and natural change agents, it often appears that much of the potential for school counselors to be leaders within their schools, communities, and at the national level has not been realized. In addition, although many school counselors are involved in leadership, many others are not and/or they are frustrated in their attempts at leadership and change. As indicated earlier, there are many explanations for this situation: increased demands, limitations, and distractions that pull school counselors away from leadership opportunities. It seems, however, that there also are more basic issues, as suggested by the results of our limited survey, that need to be addressed if the gap between potential and actual leadership can be bridged.

In most public school systems, it is the administration, and usually the school principal, who decides on the role of the school counselor (House &

Martin, 1998; Paisley & Borders, 1995). Most administrators, however, have very little understanding of the training, unique skills, and leadership potential of a school counselor (Shoffner & Williamson, 2000; Studer & Allton, 1996) and make decisions based more on need (getting the task at hand accomplished) than on what might be the best utilization of a counselor's expertise. Although one might point to the differences in perspectives and roles of principals and counselors to explain principals' approaches to working with school counselors, it may be more fruitful to point to their training programs. The various professionals in the schools, including school counselors and principals, are trained separately with few opportunities to learn about the roles, responsibilities, and perspectives of one another (Shoffner & Briggs, 2001; Shoffner & Williamson). Although some counselor education programs provide interdisciplinary training for future school counselors, teachers, and administrators (e.g., Golston, Bernstein, & Forrest, 1995; Shoffner & Williamson), these programs are rare. Yet the need for collaboration, as one aspect of transformational and proactive leadership, is critical.

In addition, although school counselors often have the skills necessary for leadership roles, most training programs incorporate these skills into counseling roles and management responsibilities. School counselor training programs primarily teach students how to manage a counseling program, how to manage the demands on their time, how to manage a large client load, and how to manage all of the other day-to-day duties and responsibilities of a professional school counselor. Management, however, is not necessarily leadership. Training in leadership, as well as management, could do much for school counselors and for the profession.

For principals, educational leadership is seen as inclusive of management; this perspective is pertinent to school counselors as well. Clearly, good management is a necessity for the school counselor to work effectively. Leadership and management can work together for the benefit of all. Leadership that truly transforms other people and systems, however, moves beyond mere management toward the encouragement of effective and rejuvenating change. This requires the leader to move beyond fostering passivity toward inspiring action (Bosler & Bauman, 1992).

Added to all of the complexities of acting as a true transformational leader in the school environment is the observation that public schools tend to be organized and run like many large bureaucracies. As a result, the status quo is the rule, and challenging the status quo through proactive leadership that may lead to lasting change is not always easy; it may even be tacitly discouraged. According to Blasi (1996), public education not only tends to indoctrinate children into becoming "passive receivers of learning" (p. 130), but also may be guilty of encouraging and even rewarding a culture of passivity rather than proactivity. According to Bredo (1997), passivity and powerlessness are built into the basic assumptions of the current educational system. True leaders, then, are those who are willing to step outside the existing set of rules or culture in education, and facilitate the creation of a new culture. Challenging the current rules should not be confused with rebelling against them (Bredo, 1997), as rebelling stops short of productive action. The key, then, especially for beginning counselors, is to have a strong "resistance to erasure" and resistance to the pull toward passivity (Munro, 1996). This is not an easy or comfortable stance, as this likely will mean choosing to voice perspectives that differ from one's colleagues (i.e., teachers) and "boss" (i.e., principal); in schools where there is only one full-time counselor, this is a particular challenge.

## ENCOURAGING LEADERSHIP IN SCHOOL COUNSELORS

Given the long lists of both leadership opportunities and challenges, how do we help encourage so many "natural leaders" to see themselves as leaders and choose leadership roles of *change agent*, *catalyst*, and *advocate* for themselves? For counselor educators, a key may be to help aspiring school counselors create concrete images of themselves as active agents of change who successfully challenge the existing culture and resist the pull to passivity. In essence, school counselor training programs must provide a "context of possibility" within which school counselors construct "possible selves" (Markus & Nurius, 1986), cognitive representations of themselves as effective leaders in their schools. Such possible selves, if nurtured and reinforced, could serve as incentives for future behavior, motivating ongoing action even within difficult situations.

Possible selves cannot be encouraged, developed, and nurtured, however, until they are first presented. Once presented, students can begin to imagine themselves in a leadership role, as well as imagine the type of school counselor they do *not* want to become (feared possible selves). Then they can begin to see the leadership possibilities as worth moving toward. Brower and Nurius (1993) emphasized that to move forward, "specific procedural knowledge is essential. Procedural knowledge is very difficult to develop without actual experience and practices" (p. 68). Counselor educators, then, must help students see themselves as leaders in a more concrete sense by providing opportunities *within school systems* to practice minor leadership roles, and to initiate discussion with current school counseling leaders. Students, therefore, are able not only to envision themselves as change agents (a necessary first step), but to be successful as school leaders in small ways.

In terms of curriculum content, students first can be provided with basic instruction on organizational structure and behavior, which allows them a framework around which to develop their possible selves as school leaders and their vision of the possible school. Without this foundation, students cannot develop the skills to effect organizational change. Much like we train school counselors to understand individual and small group change processes in order to effect client change in individual and group counseling, we must also train them in organizational change processes in order to effect change in organizations, such as the schools.

Carefully designed collaborative training experiences with other school personnel (i.e., principals and teachers-in-training) may be one promising context for helping school counselors discover what is possible for them to achieve, as well as ways to achieve this view of self as a professional. These training experiences have been found to re-create, in a smaller sense, the large organizational dynamics in a school (Shoffner & Williamson, 2000), including where power is vested, how power is exercised, how resistance to change is manifested, and the critical importance of viewing these dynamics from multiple perspectives. Students are able to begin to address the question, "How do we understand one another so as to work together for the common goal of helping students to learn and meet their full potential?"

For practicing school counselors, counselor educators (and others providing professional development) may be able to draw on the school counselors' frustrations, energy, and visions of a school committed to the academic success and mental health of all students. This would be a vision of a "possible school" where school counselors put into action their unique knowledge and skills and where they are respected and effective leaders. Practicing school counselors, as well as those in training, can create a vision of a possible school, not only by envisioning what can be, but also by drawing on their frustration and their desire for something different.

## CONCLUSION

Although the literature has consistently and historically spoken of the school counselor as a natural leader in the schools, the opportunities to truly effect lasting change have been met with increasing challenges and societal complexity. The critical need for school counselors and what they have to offer has increased; at the same time, the demands on their time have proliferated. In spite of, and occasionally because of, the demands of the job, some school counselors are seeing themselves as leaders and envisioning the possible school that they could help create. Yet, with the full potential still unrealized, it is time to examine what encourages and prepares those going into the school counseling profession to become effective leaders. Effectively resisting passivity and "erasure" is something that can be taught through effective leadership training, advocacy training, and knowledge of organizational dynamics and change processes. Counselor educators can help aspiring school counselors create images of themselves as change agents, provide collaborative experiences and training with other school professionals such as school principals, and help students draw on their sense of frustration with the status quo, their energy, and their vision to lead others, while concurrently strengthening their professional development.

## REFERENCES

Adams, J. R., & Juhnke, G. A. (2001). Using the systems of care philosophy within counseling to promote human potential. *Journal of Humanistic Counseling, Education and Development, 40*, 225–231.

Allen, J. M. (1998). The politics of school counseling. In J. M. Allen (Ed.), *School counseling: New perspectives and practices* (pp. 155–160). Greensboro, NC: ERIC/CASS.

Baker, S. B. (2000). *School counseling for the twenty-first century* (3rd ed.). Upper Saddle River, NJ: Merrill.

Bemak, F. (2000). Transforming the role of the counselor to provide leadership in educational reform through collaboration. *Professional School Counseling, 3*, 323–331.

Blasi, M. J. (1996). Issues in education: Pedagogy—Passivity or possibility. *Childhood Education, 72*, 130–132.

Blocher, D. H. (1974). *Developmental counseling* (2nd ed.). New York: Wiley.

Borders, L. D., & Drury, S. M. (1992). Comprehensive school counseling programs: A review for policymakers and practitioners. *Journal of Counseling & Development, 70*, 487–498.

Bosler, R., & Bauman, D. J. (1992, June). *Meeting cultural diversity with personal conviction: The teacher as change agent and transformational leader.* Paper presented at the National Forum of the Association of Independent Liberal Arts Colleges for Teacher Education, Louisville, KY.

Boyer, E. L. (1988). Exploring the future: Seeking new challenges. *The Journal of College Admissions,* (1998, Winter) 2–9.

Bredo, E. (1997, March). *Passivity and powerlessness in educational thought.* Paper presented at the annual meeting of the American Educational Research Association, Chicago, IL.

Brower, A. M., & Nurius, P. S. (1993). Goal striving, possible selves, and possible niches. *Social cognition and individual change: Current theory and counseling guidelines.* Newbury Park, CA: Sage.

Clark, M. A., & Stone, C. (2000, May). Evolving our image: School counselors as educational leaders. *Counseling Today, 42*(11), 21–22, 29, 46.

Cooley, J. J. (1998). Gay and lesbian adolescents: Presenting problems and the counselor's role. *Professional School Counseling, 1*(3), 30–34.

Dahir, C. A. (1998). The development of national standards for school counseling programs. In J. M. Allen (Ed.), *School counseling: New perspectives and practices* (pp. 109–117). Greensboro, NC: ERIC/CASS.

Erikson, E. H. (1963). *Childhood and society.* New York: Norton.

Erikson, E. H. (1968). *Identity: youth and crisis.* New York: Norton.

Golston, S. S., Bernstein, B. L., & Forrest, L. (1995). Counseling faculty members' involvement in schools and school reform: A national survey. *Counselor Education and Supervision, 34,* 243–252.

Gysbers, N. C., & Henderson, P. (2000). *Developing and managing your school guidance program* (3rd ed.). Alexandria, VA: American Counseling Association.

Hansen, L. S. (1968). Are we change agents? *The School Counselor, 15,* 245–246.

Harris, H. L. (1999). School counselors and administrators: Collaboratively promoting cultural diversity. *NASSP Bulletin, 83*(603), 54–61.

House, R. M., & Martin, P. J. (1998). Advocating for better futures for all students: A new vision for school counselors. *Education, 119,* 284–291.

Kaplan, L. S. (1995). Principals versus counselors: Resolving tensions from different practice models. *School Counselor, 42,* 261–267.

Kendrick, R., Chandler, J., & Hatcher, W. (1994). Job demands, stressors, and the school counselor. *School Counselor, 41,* 365–369.

Kern, C. W. (1999). Professional school counselors: Inservice providers who can change the school environment. *NASSP Bulletin, 83*(603), 10–17.

Keys, S. G., & Bemak, F. (1997). School-family-community linked services: A school counseling role for changing times. *School Counselor, 44,* 255–263.

Lee, C. C. (2001). Culturally responsive school counselors and programs: Addressing the needs of all students. *Professional School Counseling, 4,* 257–261.

Markus, H., & Nurius, P. (1986). Possible selves. *American Psychologist, 41,* 954–969.

McCall-Perez, Z. (2000). The counselor as advocate for English language learners: An action research approach. *Professional School Counseling, 4,* 13–22.

Menacker, J. (1976). Toward a theory of activist guidance. *The Personnel and Guidance Journal, 54*, 318–321.

Munro, P. (1996). Resisting "resistance": Stories women teachers tell. *JCT: An Interdisciplinary Journal of Curriculum Studies, 12*, 16–28.

Mustaine, B. L., & Pappalardo, S. (1996). The discrepancy between actual and preferred time on task for Ontario school counselors. *Guidance and Counselling, 11*, 32–35.

Paisley, P. O., & Borders, L. D. (1995). School counseling: An evolving specialty. *Journal of Counseling and Development, 74*, 150–153.

Quigney, T. A., & Studer, R. (1998). Touching strands of the educational web: The professional school counselor's role in inclusion. *Professional School Counseling, 2*, 78–81.

Sheldon, C. B. (1998). School counselor as change agent in education reform. In J. M. Allen (Ed.), *School counseling: New perspectives and practices* (pp. 61–66). Greensboro, NC: ERIC/CASS.

Shoffner, M. F., & Briggs, M. K. (2001). An interactive approach for developing interprofessional collaboration: Preparing school counselors. *Counselor Education and Supervision, 40*, 193–202.

Shoffner, M. F., & Williamson, R. D. (2000). Engaging preservice school counselors and principals in dialogue and collaboration. *Counselor Education and Supervision, 40*, 128–140.

Studer, J. R., & Allton, J. A. (1996). The professional school counselor: Supporting and understanding the role of the guidance program. *NASSP Bulletin, 80*(581), 53–60.

West, J. F., & Idol, L. (1993). The counselor as consultant in the collaborative school. *Journal of Counseling & Development, 71*, 678–683.

# CHAPTER 4

# Community Counseling: Leadership Opportunities Today

Samuel T. Gladding and Laura J. Veach

A community is composed of "an interacting population of various kinds of individuals in a common location" (Merriam Webster's Collegiate Dictionary, 1993, p. 233). The community in which people reside affects them significantly. It is in this context that individuals gain a sense of self and connection to others. If a community environment is impoverished, hostile, or nonsupporting, people may develop in ways that are dysfunctional or inappropriate within society at large. For example, children raised in a violent culture may learn to be overtly aggressive in problem-solving attempts. On the other hand, if a community environment is warm, friendly, and supportive, members may develop characteristics that are social, productive, and wellness oriented. For example, children may learn how to trust and work cooperatively with one another, to relate positively to people and work, and to develop a spirit of altruism.

"Community-level interventions have been recognized as essential within the social work field for more than 100 years" (Carter & McGoldrick, 1999, p. 19). However, community counseling has been a specialty area in the profession of counseling only since the late 1970s (Gladding, 1997). Although this specialty is still somewhat in its infancy, it has grown considerably since its conception. In addition, community counseling has a bright future both because of its broad-based nature and because of its accreditation by the Council for Accreditation of Counseling and Related Educational Programs (CACREP).

In this chapter, the nature of community counseling will be discussed along with opportunities available for counselors to work in community settings. In addition, developing oneself as a practitioner and leader in community settings and at state and national levels will be explored.

## THE NATURE OF COMMUNITY COUNSELING

The term *community counseling* is one that carries with it both specificity and ambivalence. The idea of this type of counseling was coined by Lewis and Lewis (1977, 1989) to describe the work of counselors in a variety of environments. According to the original ideas of Lewis and Lewis, a community counselor could work in a broad range of settings, from primarily educational to those strictly involved in other types of human service activities, like community mental health centers. There were three common elements that such professionals were assumed to have:

- an awareness of the assets and liabilities of environments,
- a multifaceted approach to helping, and
- an emphasis on prevention as opposed to remediation.

Thus, the focus of counselors was more important than the settings in which they were employed.

However, without exploring the exact meaning of what Lewis and Lewis meant by the term, a number of counselors thought that a community counselor was one who was not a school counselor. It is understandable that this kind of thinking occurred given the atmosphere of the era. The 1970s was a decade in which community mental health centers, created by an act of Congress in 1963, were flourishing, and in which schools were the primary employers of counselors (Gladding, 1997). It was also a time when more attention was being placed on communities other than those intended for educational purposes. Therefore, the concept of "community counseling" was broadened inadvertently to be not only a philosophy but a practice. Thus, as graduate programs in counselor education developed, they often billed themselves as offering a degree in "community and agency counseling" with an emphasis on the word "agency."

## THE PRACTICE OF COMMUNITY COUNSELING IN AGENCIES

Given the dual emphasis that marked the beginning and early evolution of community counseling, it is not surprising to find that counselor educators and clinicians initially stressed three areas in regard to this specialty: the philosophy, the practice, or both the philosophy and practice of community counseling. More philosophic in their curriculum were those who believed that a community counselor worked with individuals, groups, families, and communities in a variety of settings, both educationally and agency-related. They emphasized the "Big Three" ideas of Lewis and Lewis (1977, 1989): the environment, a multifaceted approach, and prevention as well as remediation. A second group of counselor educators and clinicians believed community counseling emphasized working with any counseling agency other than schools. Their main focus was offering services in settings for clients with special needs, such as addiction, or particular concerns, such as entry to the work force. A third group combined the emphasis of the first two groups with a both/and approach. In this section, the concept that community counseling is a combination of philosophy and practice will be explored with various community settings serving as the backdrop for working with a variety of clients.

Before describing agencies and services, it should be noted that community programs are either "not-for-profit" (e.g., United Way agencies) or "for profit" (e.g., some managed behavioral health care organizations). Counselors must be aware that in working for a specific agency they are implicitly, if not explicitly, stating to others through their employment that they agree with the ethics as well as the practices of their employer (Corey, Corey, & Callanan, 1998). Thus, it is imperative that before accepting an employment offer, the philosophy and practices of the agency be researched so as to avoid later embarrassment or ethical quandaries for the community counselor. Services provided by agencies can range from a focus on housing and job training to a broad array of mental health services that include personnel needing to be on-call to provide emergency and crisis care. Agencies may also be invested in a particular or specialized treatment program, such as a token economy system in a residential setting.

Once such preliminary research is completed, individuals who identify themselves through education, philosophy, and practice as "community counselors" should be comfortable within their settings and should flourish within them as they make positive contributions in the process. Careful consideration to matters of professional training and identity and how these "fit" with a particular community counseling agency or setting is a mark of leadership.

Where do community counselors work and what do they do? An easier question would be: "Where *don't* community counselors work and what *don't* they do?" Indeed, it appears that as far as variety and scope of duties, community counselors are engaged in a plethora of activities with diverse populations. Community counseling is not confined to a location or group. Indeed, community counselors work in many settings such as prisons, businesses, rehabilitation facilities, mental health centers, and private practices. Their particular duties and responsibilities vary, too. Thus, in this chapter only some of the more popular and salient employee opportunities and duties of these counselors can be covered. These aspects of the profession will be examined in regard to specific settings. It is hoped, however, that comments pertaining to leadership in specific settings will stir the reader to reflect on leadership possibilities in numerous other environments where community counselors are employed.

## Agencies and Services for Children and Adolescents

Community counselors work directly and indirectly in agencies that serve children and adolescents and with members of this age group. Working with agencies that serve children may involve direct employment as a counselor or indirect involvement as a consultant. Both have their advantages and drawbacks. For instance, one of the authors' (Sam Gladding's) first positions as a counselor was in a mental health center as the director of children's services. In that position, I (Sam Gladding) saw a number of children each week who were referred by the schools, courts, and their families. I realized that in working with them, I must be less verbal and more active than with adults, so I became skilled in play therapy (Landreth, 2001) and innovative in what I did and how I did it. I played with the children, engaging in a variety of games from checkers to basketball. I was down on the floor with dolls and trucks as much as, if not more than, in a chair. By the end of most days I was physically as well as mentally tired (and sometimes dirty). However, I noted that many of the children improved because I was working with them on an appropriate developmental level.

A second thing I did, and that many community counselors also do, was to expand my services from working one-on-one with children to seeing them in groups and with their families (Gladding, 1997). By working with them in peer settings, I noted that they tended to help each other and that treatment was often more effective. The same kind of phenomenon occurred in family counseling, where different dynamics were present than when I counseled a child individually. Sometimes the child played the role of the family "scapegoat" and had difficulty improving until the family made some necessary changes.

Finally, I branched out and began working as a consultant to the schools and the social service agencies in the county in which I worked. My purpose was to work in the area of prevention and consultation. Thus, on some days I traveled from one educational institution or agency to another. On other days, I offered in-service education where an outside presenter or a group within the county who had expertise in a particular area would be invited to the mental health center along with counselors interested and involved in the particular topic, such as anorexia or depression. This type of structured activity kept me enthusiastic and refreshed as a counselor and provided much-needed leadership to the community.

It should be noted that children, like adolescents and adults, have developmental concerns and nondevelopmental (i.e., unpredictable) situations that impact them. Therefore, it is crucial that counselors who work with them be psychoeducationally astute as well as clinically skilled so that issues like self-esteem, abuse, and divorce are handled with the same proper care and competence as those situations that would otherwise be expected, such as boy–girl relationships and acquiring social skills.

Adolescence and youth (i.e., those who are ages 13 to 25) have their own special culture as well as concerns (Erikson, 1968). Adolescents and youth devote considerable attention to changes in their bodies as well as the development of skills in social, artistic, and academic areas. They are ambivalent at best about wanting to stand out from the pack and yet be a part of the group. Young people at this point in their lives deal with:

- foreseeable and avoidable stress, for example, avoiding certain environments or people;
- unforeseeable and unavoidable stress, for example, an unexpected accident or death; and
- foreseeable but unavoidable stress, for example, a major examination (Elkind, 1998).

Therefore, a major characteristic of adolescents and youth is that, as a group, they have much anxiety as well as anticipation.

In working with this population, community counselors must stay on track in offering both preventive and treatment services that are multifaceted and that pay attention to the environment in which this population lives. On the preventive side, services can be offered by community counselors to the leaders and directors of community-based organizations, such as recreational centers or clubs. These would include the YMCA/YWCA, Boys and Girls Clubs, scout groups, and Big Brothers/Big Sisters. Community counselors may also visit educational institutions where early adolescents spend much of their time and serve as consultants to school counselors and other school personnel (e.g., teachers or principals) who work directly with these young people. As an illustration, consultant services might focus on topics related to helping teenagers with issues of assertiveness, adolescent depression, or issues of anxiety that appear to be associated with concerns of possible embarrassment.

Offering direct services that cater to the needs of this population is challenging because of the developmental differences among children and adolescents. However, having adolescents and youth role-play as well as talk about their concerns can be helpful. Individual counseling, while needed, is usually not enough. Some theories of counseling, however, such as Adlerian theory, are particularly appropriate to use with this population (Sweeney, 1998). Thus, making use of group work, family counseling, peer facilitators, and providing assessment services are important. Neighborhood visits to areas where adolescents and youth live or hang out may also provide insight into their needs. Community visits may help the community counselor form alliances with other public agencies (e.g., the health department or social services) that can take care of special needs counselors are not equipped or trained to deal with, such as medical concerns, legal assistance, or educational deficits.

Overall, the counselor who provides leadership in a community setting is one who develops services for children and adolescents based on the needs of this population at a particular moment in time. Because environments and children and adolescents change, following up on these services, and creating new ones when needed, is crucial to the mental health and well-being of all. Thus, looking for opportunities as well as modifying more established programs is a crucial component of the leadership process.

## Agencies and Services for Adults and the Aging

Another point in the developmental continuum highlights challenges for community counselors in providing prevention and direct treatment for adults and the aging, because the needs manifested in this population are so diverse. Counseling issues for adults include topics as different as career development, singlehood, marriage and family lifestyles, substance abuse, midlife transitions, and coping with chronic and persistent mental health issues. Community counselors, no matter how skilled and dedicated, cannot deal with all of these concerns adequately. Therefore, they must develop networks that are both preventive and treatment oriented in order to provide services needed.

Some community counselors specialize as generalists who know how to work initially with many client concerns and then make appropriate referrals. These counselors are often employed in Employee Assistance Programs (EAPs) established by companies as either internal or external (contracted) programs. In these positions they work in a variety of ways by assessing client needs from physical to mental health, as well as assisting clients by providing brief counseling in a variety of areas or making appropriate referrals. EAPs appear to be particularly good settings for community counselors who embrace the "both/and" philosophy and practice this specialty.

Other community counselors prefer to concentrate on one or more areas of adult concerns. These counselors, even though they are focused, must be knowledgable and skilled in prevention and direct service skills. Areas that employ a number of community counselors are career counseling centers, mental health centers, prisons, crisis control centers, substance abuse facilities, and domestic violence programs. It is not possible in this chapter to cover the specific duties of counselors in each of these settings, so substance abuse facilities will serve as an example.

In substance abuse facilities, community counselors are challenged to provide care for both the clients and their families. Counseling is provided in various levels of care, predominantly intensive outpatient services. Community substance abuse counselors must be masters of a variety of counseling skills, especially those involving group counseling and confrontation when the client denies or minimizes what he or she is doing and its impact on others. Counselors who work in substance abuse must also be skilled in helping families deal with issues that they have inadequately addressed, including individual and collective needs and responsibilities. The task is multifaceted in nature and environmentally focused. The physical and psychological well-being of all involved is a matter for treatment. In most cases of adult substance use problems the dysfunctional and enabling behaviors have been going on for years. Thus, the intensity surrounding and within sessions may be significant, because even those who have suffered as a result of the behaviors may be hesitant or resistant to change from a pattern they have known to one that is new. Behavioral, cognitive, insight-oriented, existential, and structural/strategic family counseling approaches may be quite powerful with this population.

In addition to working directly with the client and his or her family, community counselors also use preventive and ongoing services, including the use of bibliotherapy, 12-step groups, and remedial services. Alcoholics Anonymous, Al-Anon, and other 12-step programs are frequent referral places for clients and their families once initial treatment has occurred. These organizations and others like them help the addicted client and his or her family develop and practice recovery skills to reduce relapses that trigger the addictive cycle.

Considerable leadership is demonstrated as the counselor makes available both direct and indirect services to the client and the family. Such services might encompass alternatives to a traditional medical or disease model orientation that have demonstrated promise for those with substance-related problems. These include motivational enhancement therapy or motivational interviewing (Miller & Rollnick, 2002), which has gained appeal in its emphasis on gentle persuasion (rather than confrontive tactics aimed at "breaking down" one's "denial" or "resistance"), empathic and reflective statements, and cultivating the client's intrinsic motivation for change. Brief interventions, community reinforcement, and social skills training are additional approaches that have demonstrated positive outcomes in well-controlled clinical trials (Miller, Andrews, Wilbourne, & Bennett, 1998) and therefore deserve further consideration by those in leadership positions in substance abuse treatment facilities.

Of course, the community counselor can also provide educational programs for the community and for professionals in the community around issues of substance use. This may entail working as a member of a multidisciplinary treatment team, providing expertise in the area of substance abuse, and offering in-service programming for staff at the county jail or municipal court, for instance, on screening for problematic substance use and implications for sentencing. Knowing how to identify appropriate services and how to access the services is a leadership skill that clinicians may develop as they learn from working with more experienced colleagues. Advocacy work through professional counseling organizations targeting legislative changes pertaining to substance use issues, for example, is another area in which a community counselor provides leadership.

The aging, those 65 years and over, are a growing population in the United States and one in need of multiple services that community counselors can provide (Myers & Schwiebert, 1996). Often a way to promote the health and well-being of members of this population is to modify the attitudes and behaviors of people within the systems in which they live

(Colangelo & Pulvino, 1980). Such a task may begin in working with older clients themselves in educational and advocacy groups where they learn to be themselves instead of acting according to predetermined age-prescribed roles. Preventive services for older adults can also include the promotion of social interaction, the facilitation of self-expression, and the recall of past events. For instance, at a seniors gathering, music may be played that inspires movement and memory that are beneficial to all involved (Gladding, 1998).

Treatment of older adults is mostly individual and group-oriented. Individual work with the aging is complicated by physiological and psychological factors that occur in aging, for example, slower physical and mental responses. However, older adults have much to talk about and sometimes resolve. They also have a sense of perspective that is refreshing and insightful. Thus, investing in individual work with them is well worth the effort and is an important service community counselors, especially those in nursing homes, can provide.

Likewise, group work with seniors is an excellent way to help them interact and resolve present or lingering problems. Among the most popular groups for the treatment of the aging are:

- reminiscing groups that assist members in becoming more fully integrated by reviewing and accepting aspects of their lives,
- psychotherapy groups that focus on particular problems for the aged, such as loss,
- remotivational therapy groups that help older clients become more invested in the present and the future, and
- member-specific groups that assist older adults dealing with particular transitional concerns, such as dealing with in-laws.

In deciding what services to offer adults and the aging, the counselor can be a leader in developing programs that are either underdeveloped or nonexistent. This type of leadership is exercised by conducting needs assessments that create awareness and then by working with others to turn awareness into proposals for services. Counselors who are leaders go one step further: They form coalitions and provide energy and vision for others so that services become realities in a step-by-step or systematic way.

## DEVELOPING ONESELF AS A PRACTITIONER AND LEADER

Although community counseling is an exciting and evolving field in counseling, it should be stressed that the particular work conducted by community counselors is not for everyone. Persons who strive toward being professionals in the field must do so with certain awareness and considerations. Development as a person and a clinician and the growth of the profession are among the most important concerns for the community counselor.

## Development as a Person

The skills necessary to be a community counselor are those that can be taught to most individuals who are bright, articulate, sensitive, and motivated. These qualities are often listed as essential for anyone who aspires to be a counselor. Yet, in addition to these basic attributes, a community counselor must be someone who is willing to develop himself or herself as a person. Such development means investing time in experiences that enrich oneself as an individual and a contributing member of society.

Counselors who engage in a number of activities, from bird watching to reading to bowling, demonstrate healthier personal development. They know when to let go of their clinical responsibilities and how to enjoy themselves. They take time away from work to be with family and friends. They take mental health breaks of a few minutes to a few days when needed in order to avoid burnout and toxicity. In other words, they maintain their own emotional and physical health before they try to help others retain or regain theirs.

## Development as a Professional

In addition to taking care of themselves personally, community counselors continuously develop themselves as professionals. This type of development is costly in financial resources and time. Yet, community counselors are aware that learning is something that does not stop. Thus, they take the time and effort to invest in continuing education courses on topics that are of most concern to them, such as ethics, substance abuse, or wellness.

Community counselors who are growing as professionals also become involved in associations that promote the counseling profession and the work of counselors. They attend and participate in state, regional, and national conventions such as those sponsored by the American Counseling Association and its affiliates. This participation may involve becoming a committee chair or involvement in a special interest network. Community counselors often become members of Chi Sigma Iota (CSI, the counseling academic and professional honor society international). Through CSI they may learn leadership skills by attending workshops the association offers on the national and sometimes college or university levels. Likewise, community counselors are inclined to become certified counselors with the National Board for Certified Counselors and may simultaneously or as an alternative seek licensure as a counselor in their state.

Community counselors also form local clusters of counselors in order to be supportive of and learn from one another. This may include establishing a peer supervision network that meets monthly and operates according to well-defined guidelines of confidentiality, serving on the county mental health board's quality assurance team, maintaining ongoing and productive relationships with the graduate counseling program at the local college or university (by serving as a site supervisor for internship students, for example), and attending open house and fundraising events hosted by a sister agency in town. In such clusters, leadership skills can be developed by observing others, taking on new responsibilities in regard to the cluster organization, inviting outside speakers or experts to share with the group what they have learned over the years, and advocating for direct services and supervisory positions that include community counselors.

By virtue of their broad and diverse training (e.g., specific coursework in group work, psychological assessment, career development, and multicultural counseling), community counselors can provide valued service as members, and possibly leaders, of multidisciplinary treatment teams (Bemak, 1998; Seligman & Ceo, 1996), meeting within a particular agency or periodic meetings involving staff from local agencies. Such involvement offers opportunities to learn from professionals trained in other disciplines and specialty areas; it also allows community counselors opportunities to establish their distinct professional reputations, informing others of their capabilities and the special contributions they can make on such a team. The time and effort it takes to be active in this way is an investment by community counselors in themselves, their colleagues, their communities, and their profession.

## Development of the Profession

Finally, community counselors realize that an essential part of their lives and interests as well as incomes is tied to the counseling profession as a whole. Thus, through their networks locally, regionally, and nationally, they advocate for counseling as a profession and the clients it serves because they realize that what they and other counselors do contributes to the betterment of individuals, groups, and society. Parity around insurance reimbursement and services to disenfranchised groups are two areas of particular importance within advocacy.

In the process of advocacy, community counselors become aware that they may face skepticism from others about what they are proposing and why. They may also come to realize that winning others over to their viewpoints is harder than it may first appear to be. However, as they continue with advocacy efforts, community counselors learn how to work with legislators and government bodies around laws and regulations governing their practice (Remley, 1992) and they come to realize that they can influence regulatory procedures. Illustrations of this might be found in the gains made by counselor licensure in various states and the employment opportunities realized by counselors in human services–type settings.

## SUMMARY

Community counseling developed in the late 1970s as an idea that contained a philosophy espoused by Lewis and Lewis (1977). This philosophy holds that counselors should be helping professionals ready and able to work in a variety of settings with an emphasis on both prevention and remediation. As such, community counselors should focus their attention on the environment in which they and their clients live as well as be able to respond to clients in multifaceted ways. Whereas the philosophy of Lewis and Lewis was not always stressed or heeded, from 1977 on, community counseling became a counseling entity. It was recognized as an alternative to school counseling and focused on the work of counselors in agencies other than those that were primarily educational. In addition, outside of school counseling, community counseling has become the most frequent of the CACREP accreditations.

Today, community counselors work in a variety of settings with diverse populations. They are involved with children, adolescents, adults, and the aging. They work in not-for-profit and for-profit agencies. They conduct individual, group, and family counseling and try to better the communities they live and work in through direct and indirect means. As persons, community counselors take care of their health and well-being. Likewise, they invest in the profession of counseling as participants, leaders of associations, and advocates.

Community counseling is an intentional specialty, and those who become involved as community counselors need to realize both its focus and mission. The Lewises started in motion a process that continues to evolve and that holds much promise for the betterment of individuals, groups, families, and society.

## REFERENCES

Bemak, F. (1998). Interdisciplinary collaboration for social change: Redefining the counseling profession. In C. C. Lee & G. R. Walz (Eds.), Social action: A mandate for counselors (pp. 279–292). Alexandria, VA: American Counseling Association.

Carter, B., & McGoldrick, M. (1999). Overview: The expanded family life cycle. In B. Carter & M. McGoldrick (Eds.), *The expanded family life cycle* (3rd ed.; pp. 1–26). Boston: Allyn & Bacon.

Colangelo, N., & Pulvino, C. J. (1980). Some basic concerns in counseling the elderly. *Counseling and Values, 24*, 68–73.

Corey, G., Corey, M. S., & Callanan, P. (1998). *Issues and ethics in the helping professions* (5th ed.). Pacific Grove, CA: Brooks/Cole.

Elkind, D. (1998). *All grown up and no place to go: Teenagers in crisis.* New York: Perseus Press.

Erikson, E. H. (1968). *Identity: youth and crisis.* New York: Norton.

Gladding, S. T. (1997). *Community and agency counseling.* Upper Saddle River, NJ: Prentice-Hall.

Gladding, S. T. (1998). *Counseling as an art: The creative arts in counseling.* Alexandria, VA: American Counseling Association.

Landreth, G. L. (Ed.). (2001). *Innovations in play therapy: Issues, process, and special populations.* New York: Brunner-Routledge.

Lewis, J., & Lewis, M. (1977). *Community counseling: A human services approach.* New York: Wiley.

Lewis, J., & Lewis, M. (1989). *Community counseling.* Pacific Grove, CA: Brooks/Cole.

*Merriam Webster's Collegiate Dictionary.* (1993). Springfield, MA: Merriam-Webster, Inc.

Miller, W. R., Andrews, N. R., Wilbourne, P., & Bennett, M. E. (1998). A wealth of alternatives: Effective treatments for alcohol problems. In W. R. Miller & N. Heather (Eds.), *Treating addictive behaviors* (2nd ed.; pp. 203–216). New York: Plenum.

Miller, W. R., & Rollnick, S. (2002). *Motivational interviewing: Preparing people for change* (2nd ed.). New York: Guilford.

Myers, J. E., & Schwiebert, V. L. (1996). *Competencies for gerontological counseling.* Alexandria, VA: American Counseling Association.

Remley, T. P., Jr. (1992, Spring). You and the law. *American Counselor, 1,* 33.

Seligman, L., & Ceo, M. N. (1996). Multidisciplinary mental health treatment teams. In W. J. Weikel & A. J. Palmo (Eds.), *Foundations of mental health counseling* (2nd ed.; pp. 163–182). Springfield, IL: Charles C. Thomas.

Sweeney, T. J. (1998). *Adlerian counseling: A practitioner's approach.* Philadelphia: Taylor & Francis.

# CHAPTER 5

# Tapping the Potential: Leadership Possibilities for Master's Degree Students

Jane A. Cox

*The fact that there are many kinds of leaders has implications for leadership education. Most of those seeking to develop young potential leaders have in mind one ideal model that is inevitably constricting. We should give young people a sense of the many kinds of leaders and styles of leadership, and encourage them to move toward those models that are right for them.*
(Gardner, 1990, p. 5)

Master's degree students in counselor education programs are a diverse group. They enter counselor education with a variety of personal perspectives, educational backgrounds, and work experiences. Consider the differing circumstances of Rosa, David, and LaTonya, a cohort of students who just completed their first semester in a counselor education program:

Rosa is 25 years old and has been a special education teacher for 2 years. In working with children with special needs, Rosa discovered that many of these children had personal and family problems that appeared to affect their learning. Though Rosa was motivated to help her students with these issues, she knew she was unprepared to do so. This realization motivated Rosa to pursue a master's degree in counselor education, specializing in school counseling. Rosa's school agreed to grant her a leave of absence in order to pursue her degree full-time. After one semester in a counselor education program, Rosa's faculty are impressed with her activities both within and outside the classroom: Rosa participated frequently in her classes, organized a study group for students in her theories of counseling class, and attended several "brown bag" lunches sponsored by the counseling honor society.

Since receiving his undergraduate degree in business, David has worked for 15 years in various jobs related to sales. Although David enjoyed his career for many years, in recent years he began to find his job unsatisfying. Outside of work, David enjoyed working with the youth group at his church, particularly the one-on-one conversations with the kids. David wondered if he could find a new career that would be consistent with some of the work he was already doing with the youth group. He investigated various graduate programs and decided to "try out" a few courses in a counselor education program. Due to his family responsibilities, David decided to continue to work full-time, while taking two introductory counselor education courses. When first beginning his classes, David felt rather uncomfortable since he had not been a student for many years. He also felt that he couldn't "compete" with the students who had undergraduate degrees in the helping professions, and those who had been working in more "helping"-related fields. As a result, David rarely participated in his classes, although he performed well on exams and written assignments. By the end of the first semester, when asked, David's instructors couldn't remember much about him.

LaTonya is just beginning a community counseling program. She completed her undergraduate degree in psychology 6 years ago, and since that time has worked in the Department of Family Services (DFS) as a caseworker. LaTonya's hard work and initiative on the job were rewarded, and she was quickly promoted to a supervisory position. LaTonya felt "burned out," however, and decided she needed a career change. In her work with DFS, LaTonya consulted with counseling agencies and she now believes she would enjoy working in an adult outpatient setting. She decided to attend a community counseling program as a full-time student, and she works part-time for DFS in order to support her family financially. In her classes, LaTonya feels competent contributing to class discussions due to her work experiences and background in psychology. Because of her family obligations, however, LaTonya is reluctant to take on any responsibilities beyond the requirements of her courses. LaTonya's instructors believe she has great leadership potential, but they are disappointed that she did not accept their invitation to become part of a student committee in the department.

Although the backgrounds of each of these students are quite different, it is not unusual to find students in counselor education programs with characteristics and histories similar to Rosa, David, and LaTonya. Many other students with unique talents and circumstances are also part of counselor education programs. With such a diverse group of students, discovering leadership abilities and providing appropriate leadership opportunities can be a daunting task for counselor educators. Yet, all three of the students described above undoubtedly have some unrecognized, untapped, or underutilized leadership abilities.

In his book *On Leadership*, Gardner (1990) noted that some people have such obvious abilities that their talents emerge naturally without much encouragement. For most, however, "the maturing of any complex talent requires a happy combination of motivation, character and opportunity. *Most human talent remains undeveloped*" (p. 158). One of the tasks for counselor educators is to provide opportunities for master's degree students to discover and develop their leadership skills. Students then have the challenge of deciding which opportunities to explore, which ones fit best with their "happy combination of motivation [and] character" (p. 158).

Therefore, it may be helpful to consider the types of leadership opportunities that counselor education programs often provide for master's degree students. This chapter focuses on such opportunities, including possible activities within counselor education curricula as well as experiences outside of the curriculum. By focusing on these opportunities, it is hoped that master's degree students in counselor education will become aware of and take advantage of those leadership opportunities that fit best with their unique combinations of talents. The importance of master's degree students learning about leadership and the relevance of this learning for the profession of counseling will be considered first.

## THE NEED FOR EFFECTIVE LEADERS

As with all other professions, counseling needs effective and dedicated leaders. Master's degree students graduating from counselor education programs are the future leaders in the counseling profession. Upon graduation, they may assume positions as counselors in mental health agencies, schools, community colleges, correctional institutions, and many other settings where mental health services are needed. Some will eventually assume supervisory and administrative positions, and some will decide to return to school to pursue doctoral degrees.

Regardless of the paths master's degree graduates follow, skilled leaders are needed on all of these journeys. Leaders are needed to advance the counseling profession through activities such as client advocacy and program evaluation and development. Leaders are also needed in the political arena to address such issues as counselor licensure and reimbursement for services. Graduates' contributions in these areas can potentially expand services to clients and ultimately improve the practice of counseling.

Recognizing this need for leaders in the counseling profession, what characteristics do effective leaders possess? Several leaders in the counseling profession (Rose A. Cooper, Joan T. England, and the late Nicholas A. Vacc) addressed this question in an issue of Chi Sigma Iota's (CSI, Counseling Academic and Professional Honor Society International) newsletter, *Exemplar* (Chang, 1997). Cooper described a "good" leader as one who develops a unique vision and voice, becomes a catalyst for uniting the talents of others and for building community, uses language to motivate and inspire others, and becomes aware of his or her own strengths as well as ways to express them. England remarked on the need for leaders to possess a strong sense of purpose and high ethical standards, commitment to service, high energy, a desire to advocate for and empower others, capacity for reflection rather than reactivity, and respect for and recognition of the contributions of others. Vacc noted that good leaders are adept at building teams, motivating people, taking appropriate risks, and obtaining and analyzing information.

Although no one person can possess all of these leadership qualities and skills, can some of these skills be learned or are they inherent abilities? This debate between innate and learned leadership has not been resolved. Yet, many believe that those who are committed to becoming effective leaders can successfully develop their unique skills as they take responsibility for this development (Chang, 1998). The remainder of this chapter discusses opportunities for master's degree students in counselor education as they face the challenges of taking responsibility for their development as leaders.

## LEADERSHIP OPPORTUNITIES WITHIN THE CURRICULUM

Students can discover their strengths, areas of expertise, and leadership potential by taking advantage of opportunities provided through counselor education curricula. As the opening scenarios to this chapter illustrate, students enter master's degree counselor education programs with various personalities and histories. For some, the initial experience with leadership development may be learning to take responsibility for their own education; they may need to learn to take responsibility for getting the most from their counselor education program and for developing their unique strengths through their experiences as students. As Rose A. Cooper was quoted as saying,

> To become a leader one must become the maker of one's own life. . . . In becoming a leader the need for self-invention and self-expression is critical and crucial. To be authentic is literally to be one's own author, to discover one's own native energies and desires, and then to find one's own way of acting on them. (Chang, 1997, p. 7)

Reflecting on Cooper's words, perhaps students can nurture their own leadership abilities by becoming the "authors" of their own learning. One way for students to accomplish this is by taking full advantage of their curricular experiences. For example, group projects in classes may provide opportunities for students to gain awareness of their abilities and beliefs and to exercise their leadership abilities. One such group project in an introductory counseling course might require groups of students to work as a team to research current issues in the profession (e.g., licensure, ethics). They would then present their groups' findings to the class. A student participating in this group project might practice leadership skills by taking the lead on researching material to present, facilitating team members' discussions, or presenting the material to the class. Such group projects allow students to experiment with team building, negotiation skills, and organization and management skills. They allow students to experiment with being a leader as well as a team member. When students are afforded these exploratory projects, they may then choose how involved to be in such projects; those who devote the energy to such projects and risk active involvement seize opportunities to discover and exercise their leadership skills.

In addition to gleaning the most from their classroom experiences, students might also provide leadership within the curriculum by initiating experiences that would augment those of the classroom. For example, students might organize study groups, help each other with tips on how to use the library, or assist each other with technology applications. They might share information with one another about their extracurricular reading or about an upcoming workshop or conference. Students might share information about upcoming university or community activities and organize groups to attend these activities. For example, students in a community counseling course might organize a visit to a county mental health board meeting to gain information about current issues facing local agencies. By facilitating such experiences, students help themselves and their peers broaden their understanding of the needs and resources within their communities.

Of all the requirements of a counselor education curriculum, internship is perhaps the time in a student's program with the most opportunity to practice leadership skills. Internship is a capstone experience for master's degree students, and by the time students start internship, they have completed all or most of their academic course experiences. Therefore, internship is a time to apply what they have learned, including what they have learned about their leadership abilities.

Students focus on getting to know their internship sites and beginning their work with clients at the start of their internship. One leadership skill that can be honed at this time is learning the importance of context, that is, the circumstances and atmosphere of the work in which they engage. To learn about context, interns can develop a plan for learning about their agency and the clientele it serves. This plan might include learning the organizational chart of the agency, the role of the board of directors, the funding streams, the services provided, and the nature of the communities in which their clients live. Such activities are another opportunity for students to "author" their work, as they take initiative to learn about the context of their work.

Once interns have spent significant time at their sites and are comfortable with the site and its procedures, they can assume more leadership roles. For example, experienced interns often help with the training of new interns. They may also organize a site visit for their university instructor. If internship sites are willing, interns can present current information from the counseling field to staff members. Experienced interns with strong leadership skills might also offer to sit on committees within their organization.

Apart from their experiences at internship sites, interns can also practice leadership skills by working with master's degree students who are just beginning their program. For example, in programs that provide such opportunities, interns might work with students in a beginning interviewing skills course. This work could entail providing written and verbal feedback on practice tapes or facilitating a small group of students as they practice their interviewing skills. One of the challenges of this experience is the need for supervision; although the interns have more experience than the students in the skills course, interns still have limited experience with providing feedback to beginning students. Therefore, faculty members would have to provide supervision and feedback to both the interns and the beginning students. Such experiences would give students at the end of their master's program (interns) leadership experience as they work with beginning students. Also, many counseling graduates will become supervisors in the field a few years after graduation, and these leadership experiences would give them a taste of the supervisory activities in which they will eventually engage (Ullery & Cox, 1999). Additionally, interns would have "the opportunity . . . to become familiar with a variety of professional activities other than direct service" (Council for Accreditation of Counseling and Related Educational Programs, 1994, p. 55).

Clearly, there is a wide variety of leadership experiences from which students can choose. And there are countless other strategies that students could use within a curriculum to enrich their leadership experiences. By offering a variety of leadership opportunities, counselor education programs observe Gardner's (1990) warning not to "constrict" potential leaders. A wide variety of strategies is offered in hopes that students will select those that nourish their unique leadership styles.

## GOING "ABOVE AND BEYOND": EXTRACURRICULAR LEADERSHIP ACTIVITIES

Unlike curricular experiences, extracurricular experiences are usually "optional." Therefore, student motivation, faculty encouragement, and adequate opportunity combine as the driving forces behind students' involvement in such activities. Examples of possible extracurricular experiences include: participation in mentorship programs; presentations to campus and community organizations; experience with regional, state, and national counseling organizations; participation in volunteer activities; involvement in advocacy issues; and work as a graduate assistant. For many students, the most readily accessible leadership opportunities come from involvement with CSI, the counseling honor society.

CSI has addressed leadership in counseling perhaps more than any other counseling-related organization. As the "international honor society for counselors-in-training, counselor educators, and professional counselors," part of CSI's mission is to promote and recognize leadership in the counseling profession (CSI, n.d.). This is accomplished at both the local chapter level and through CSI's international headquarters. Local chapters sponsor counseling-related speakers and workshops, participate in community service activities, provide networking and social events for members, induct new members into the honor society, and provide many other services to members and their communities.

CSI international headquarters provides leadership training for interested members. One way this has been accomplished is through leadership workshops during "CSI Day" at the American Counseling Association's annual conference. CSI also has fellowship and internship programs for students, which nurture potential leaders in the counseling profession. Additionally, CSI promotes leadership by recognizing the accomplishments of its members through its awards program. Readers can find more information about CSI online at http://www.csi-net.org.

"Student-to-student" mentoring programs offer another leadership opportunity for master's degree students. These programs pair beginning master's degree students with experienced students (mentors) in an effort to help beginning students transition into their graduate program. For example, one such program was implemented by Purdue University's Counseling and Personnel Services section (Bowman, Bowman, & Delucia, 1990). Mentors' responsibilities included "making introductions, providing advice and informal information, . . . providing emotional support, and helping the new student deal with personal concerns" (p. 60). In addition to helping with new students' adjustment and allowing experienced students to serve as leaders, a program evaluation indicated that mentored students were more involved in their graduate program; student leaders reported that their student mentors had positively influenced their level of activity.

Students can also develop their leadership skills by sharing information with others through presentations. Students who are inexperienced presenters may wish to begin by looking for opportunities to practice their presentation skills on campus. Presentations are often needed in residence halls on topics such as stress management, relationship issues, and self-esteem. Other on-campus possibilities for presentations include honor societies, campus wellness centers, and sororities or fraternities. Community agencies and organizations (e.g., schools, church groups, etc.) might also be served by students willing to share their ideas and information with others.

Another outlet for student presentations are local, regional, state, and national counseling organizations. In order to provide a positive leadership experience, it is helpful for students to involve a faculty member in planning such presentations. Students who desire such faculty assistance should first discern which faculty member might have the greatest interest in their presentation topic. They can then think through how to present their request for involvement to the faculty member. A student could write a brief outline detailing a tentative plan for the presentation. The student can then schedule an appointment with the faculty member to review the outline and discuss possible collaboration on the presentation. Such a student, one who is proactive and well organized, will be successful in enlisting the assistance of faculty members.

In addition to presentations, there are other ways students can become involved in counseling organizations, such as participation in committee work or helping plan a conference. Through such participation, students can gain experience as team members, observing leaders at work, and expanding their ideas about the leadership skills they hope to develop.

Students can also gain experience and practice leadership skills through volunteering. Women's centers, hospice organizations, crisis hot lines, and other community organizations need volunteers to provide services to clients. Students can serve community agencies by helping with organizational needs, such as collecting data for a needs assessment or planning a fund-raising event. Such activities provide students with exposure to varying leadership styles and organizational issues, such as communication, planning, and management. When selecting volunteer activities, care should be taken to ensure they are manageable ones for master's degree students, ones in which students can experience success and build confidence as emerging leaders.

Advocacy activities are closely related to these community service activities and present another opportunity for master's degree students to experience leadership in the profession. Committed people are needed to advocate for the rights of those needing mental health services, for underrepresented populations, and for the profession of counseling itself. Students can contact their state and federal legislators to advocate for legislation that will further the counseling profession and meet the needs of people counselors serve. They can also inform their peers about current issues, pending legislation, and means of contacting legislators. Because advocacy is a procedure used by professional counselors, students would want to involve a faculty member in their plans to advocate on behalf of individuals, groups, or relevant issues.

Finally, students may also develop their leadership skills by securing a graduate assistantship in the counselor education department or in another department on campus. This part-time work exposes students to the leadership efforts of faculty and staff and creates opportunities for students to further develop their own leadership skills. Although the assignments of graduate assistants vary, they may include assisting faculty in research endeavors by conducting library research or entering statistical data. Graduate assistants may also help with administrative tasks, such as publication of a newsletter, preparation for an accreditation review, or communication with organizations on campus and in the community.

Graduate assistants may also recognize their leadership qualities through teaching. For example, some counselor education programs offer undergraduate courses in small group development or career selection. Graduate assistants assigned to teach or coteach such courses might help in developing a syllabus, in delivering class lectures, and in structuring student activities. This would allow them to explore planning, presenting, communicating, organizing, and implementing, all vital skills for effective leadership.

Because many of these activities will be new experiences for graduate assistants, close faculty involvement and supervision are needed. This involvement will provide graduate assistants with helpful feedback, allowing them to further hone their leadership skills.

Master's degree students in counselor education have a wide range of possible extracurricular activities from which to choose, and certainly opportunities exist in addition to those listed earlier. Although probably no student has the time or energy to pursue all these opportunities, the variety of possibilities allows students to select activities that are consistent with their goals and schedules.

## ENCOURAGING DIVERSITY IN LEADERSHIP

There is little in the literature that addresses leadership development among those often underrepresented in leadership positions, particularly women and people of color. In order to increase the number of potential "nontraditional" leaders, Young (1986, p. 109) suggested members of diverse populations be identified as potential leaders. These potential leaders should first be encouraged to focus on their individual leadership development through increased self-awareness and personal growth. They might address this by exploring their values, interests, strengths, goals, and other aspects of their personalities and belief systems. Young suggested that potential leaders should then be encouraged to develop leadership within their "affilial" groups. Finally, leadership should be developed within diverse settings.

Although Young's (1986) model targeted women and people of color, she viewed this model as helpful for all promising leaders. All students should experience opportunities for leadership self-awareness, be taught about basic leadership principles, and be provided "training opportunities for them to learn skills and behaviors for leadership roles and services on diverse levels (e.g., personal, family, campus organizations, careers, community organizations, and public service)" (Young, p. 109).

Young's (1986) suggestions are respectful of differences among students and allow for the possibility of unique pathways to leadership development tailored to individual students. This is consistent with the quote that opens this chapter; as Gardner (1990) noted, there are many types of leaders, and counselor educators who hope to nurture future leaders must help them "move toward those models that are right for them" (p. 5). By doing so, counselor educators honor and affirm the valuable contributions that a variety of students and leaders can make.

How might master's degree students put into action some of Young's (1986) ideas? Students first must be open to cultural learning, and perhaps the simplest way is by learning from those around them. For example, students in practicum and internship might learn from their clients through listening about a variety of cultures, religions, sexual orientations, and so on. When working with clients, they have the privilege of hearing about how cultures influence their clients' lives, the strengths that their clients possess because of their culture, and the challenges they have confronted.

In addition to clients, students also learn about culture from one another. A student leader may organize a discussion group that includes counseling students from diverse cultures. The campus community provides a ripe opportunity to explore culture because of the diversity that often exists among national and international students who enter counseling programs. A student leader also can facilitate or cofacilitate a support group centered in a particular culture that is offered on campus or in the community, such as support groups for gay or lesbian individuals, individuals with disabilities, or minority youth. Student leaders can participate in international groups on campus as well.

Because students have the responsibility as counselors and leaders to learn about and integrate cultural differences in the counseling profession, they can take classes that explore cultural diversity. These classes may be offered in their counseling programs; if not, students may need to seek out cultural classes in other departments on campus. Literature in and out of courses (e.g., journal articles, autobiographies, novels, etc.) can be another avenue for exploring one's own and others' cultures and experiences (White, 2001). Students may read about people and groups with whom they identify to further their own self-growth and understanding. They may also choose to read about those with whom they have little experience or knowledge to gain new appreciation for others. A student leader may also wish to organize a reading group with fellow students where they can discuss cultural understandings discovered in reading as well as cultural implications to the counseling profession discovered while reflecting.

Another means of gaining awareness of and appreciation for diversity is for students to attend campus and community events. Again, such events might be related to a student's identity or may be a means of learning about others the student perceives as "different" than herself or himself. Campuses often abound with such opportunities; a student may wish to invite classmates to attend an international festival, a lecture by a gay-rights advocate, or a poetry reading by a Latino author. Such experiences help participants broaden their appreciation for the contribution of diversity in our communities.

These examples of ways students can develop cultural awareness and sensitivity imply that students are open to cultural learning, they actively engage in cultural experiences, and they integrate cultural sensitivity into their leadership styles. They intentionally spend time with people for whom they hope to develop greater understanding and appreciation. When they realize they have little knowledge about other people, they commit to gaining greater awareness and knowledge when they are unsure of what to say or do. In whatever ways students choose to be involved in cultural diversity, being involved means confronting their discomfort in working with those they view as different from themselves. By doing so, student leaders reap the rewards of broadening their worlds, becoming more competent counselors, and implementing effective leadership.

Because students in the counseling profession will encounter diversity, students may choose to expand their cultural knowledge and experience as suggested here. Students are cautioned, however, not to make assumptions or generalizations that all cultural experiences are the same for persons of a similar culture. They are encouraged to seek information about cultures from several sources of information as described in this section. In an effort to gain appreciation for their own culture or another's culture, they may ask questions throughout their process. Will I try to make my voice be heard louder than that of others? Will I focus my attention on one group, one cause, one voice, or will I encourage the expression of many voices and perspectives? Am I supportive of cultural pluralism which encourages persons of diverse identities to retain their identities? Do I affirm and appreciate, rather than merely tolerate, diversity?

## LEADERSHIP IN ACTION

As noted, leadership development can take many paths. To further illustrate this, consider the experiences of Carlos and Fran. Both are nearing the end of their master's programs in counselor education.

For the past 2 years, Carlos has been a full-time student and graduate assistant in his department, which afforded him many opportunities to develop his leadership skills. He began his assistantship at the time when his program was undergoing a review by the Council for Accreditation of Counseling and Related Educational Programs (CACREP), and many of his assistantship responsibilities revolved around working with faculty on preparation for this review. Carlos' other graduate assistant responsibilities included (a) organizing the departmental newsletter, (b) helping applicants to the master's program with the application process and with their questions about campus, and (c) assisting faculty in their research endeavors. In addition, as part of his internship, Carlos worked with beginning students, giving them feedback on their interviewing skills. Carlos also served as the charter president for the CSI chapter on his campus. As the CSI chapter president, Carlos focused on community service by engaging chapter members in activities such as helping the local hospital with depression screenings. When reflecting upon his master's program, Carlos stated that his experiences in leadership helped him realize that he could pursue his dream to become a faculty member in a counselor education program, something he had previously thought about but lacked the confidence to seriously pursue.

For the past 4 years, Fran has been a part-time student in a master's counselor education program. During this time she has worked full-time as a high school mathematics teacher. Fran lived an hour from the university and therefore found it difficult to attend extracurricular events. Yet Fran hoped to apply what she was learning in her courses to the "real world" and spoke with her faculty about ways she could serve others with the knowledge she was gaining in her classes. Because her passion was working with adolescents, and because one of her greatest worries about young people was potential violence, Fran decided to organize a peer mediation program at her high school. Fran had read about the effectiveness of peer mediation in her "Consultation in the Schools" class and had done further research on her own to identify the most effective programs. With help from her high school's administration and university faculty, Fran got the program off the ground by first obtaining training for herself and other interested teachers. By the time she graduated with her master's degree, Fran was training her second group of students to be peer mediators. She hopes to continue such program development when she becomes a school counselor, to further meet the needs of students.

Although Carlos and Fran had very different leadership experiences during their master's programs, they had at least one thing in common:

they pursued experiences consistent with their strengths and hopes and had faculty who recognized and nurtured their strengths. As Nicholas Vacc was quoted as saying, "in many ways I believe what people really need to do to improve their leadership is pay attention to who they already are and use what has shaped them as a person while being mindful of their skills of communication, management, and planning" (Chang, 1997, p. 12).

Revisiting the experiences of Carlos and Fran, one added consideration is that they were both in "master's only" departments (that is, there was no doctoral program available). Would their experiences have been different if their departments had offered doctoral programs in counselor education? If a doctoral program was present, would the faculty's investment in nurturing Carlos's and Fran's leadership potential have been as strong, and would these students have been offered as many leadership opportunities? Certainly, the answers to these questions depend on the faculty and the programs themselves. Yet departments with both master's and doctoral programs face the challenge of providing leadership opportunities to students at quite different points in their careers. Care must be taken to not overlook the abilities of master's degree students by focusing too strongly on doctoral students' potential. Similarly, master's degree students in departments containing doctoral programs face the challenge of not deferring leadership possibilities to doctoral students. Rather, if they wish to explore their talents as leaders, master's degree students must risk "trying out" leadership roles, even if they fear there are others better suited for the job.

## FINAL THOUGHTS

Counselors and leaders have many characteristics in common, perhaps the most striking of which are their dedication to service and their commitment to reviving and sustaining hope. Effective counselors and leaders are devoted to serving others; as Thomas J. Sweeney said, "a good leader is someone who begins with a desire to be of service" (Chang, 1998, p. 9). There are many leadership styles and many ways of providing service; a rich diversity in leadership will address the vast array of client needs, as well as needs within the profession.

What is the ultimate purpose of the service that counselors and leaders provide? Counselors work with people who may have lost hope in some aspect of their lives, and perhaps a counselor's most important purpose is to help clients discover and reclaim hope. Similarly, "The first and last task of a leader is to keep hope alive" (Gardner, 1968, p. 134). As students, and ultimately as counselors, master's degree students in counselor education have the great privilege of serving others and "keeping hope alive," within both their communities and the counseling profession.

## REFERENCES

Bowman, R. L., Bowman, V. E., & Delucia, J. L. (1990). Mentoring in a graduate counseling program: Students helping students. *Counselor Education and Supervision, 30,* 58–65.

Chang, C. (1997, Fall). Academy of leaders for excellence address: "What is a good leader?" *Exemplar, 12,* 6–7, 12.

Chang, C. (1998, Spring). Academy of leaders for excellence address: "Can anyone be a good leader?" *Exemplar, 13,* 8–9.

Chi Sigma Iota. (n.d.). *What is Chi Sigma Iota?* Retrieved July 15, 2000 from the World Wide Web: http://www.csi-net.org/htmls/whatis.htm

Council for Accreditation of Counseling and Related Educational Programs. (1994). *CACREP accreditation standards and procedures manual.* Alexandria, VA: Author.

Gardner, J. W. (1968). *No easy victories.* New York: Harper and Row.

Gardner, J. W. (1990). *On leadership.* New York: Free Press.

Ullery, E. K., & Cox, J. A. (1999, October). *Master's level supervision training: A working academic model.* Content session presented at the meeting of the Association for Counselor Education and Supervision, New Orleans, LA.

White, L. (2001). *Introduction to marriage and family counseling.* Unpublished syllabus, Southern Illinois University Carbondale, IL.

Young, J. L. (1986). Developing nontraditional leaders. *Journal of Multicultural Counseling and Development, 14,* 108–115.

# CHAPTER 6

# The Doctorate in Counselor Education: Implications for Leadership

Susan Jones Sears and Thomas E. Davis

Individuals who attain a doctorate in counselor education have achieved the highest level of formal preparation in counseling (Zimpfer & DeTrude, 1990). The primary focus of this terminal degree is to prepare graduates to advance knowledge and understanding of the counseling profession. The Preamble of the Council for Accreditation of Counseling and Related Educational Programs (CACREP) Doctoral Standards describes what is expected of counselor education programs. It reads:

> Doctoral degree programs in Counselor Education and Supervision are intended to prepare students to work as counselor educators, supervisors, and advanced practitioners in academic and clinical settings. Doctoral programs accept as a primary obligation extending the knowledge base of the counseling profession in a climate of scholarly inquiry. Doctoral programs prepare students to generate new knowledge for the counseling profession through research that results in dissertations that are appropriate to the field of counselor education or supervision. This extension of knowledge should take into account the societal changes of the 21st century and prepare graduates to be leaders and advocates for change. (CACREP, 2001, p. 48)

Considering the expectations described in the CACREP Preamble, it is reasonable to assume that those who graduate from doctoral programs in counselor education have been prepared to be leaders in their profession. Given that, in what areas or domains of the counseling profession are doctoral graduates expected to lead? In addition, how do counselor education programs create or nourish these leaders? Do they offer courses or experiences designed to study leadership concepts and theories and to build leadership skills? Are counselor education programs doing enough to prepare future leaders?

## LEADERSHIP IN COUNSELING

Assuming the 2001 CACREP Standards represent the content and skills that are and should be taught in doctoral-level counselor education programs, it would seem that most doctoral graduates are prepared to lead in four general domains: professional counseling, research, teaching/supervising, and writing and publishing. We briefly describe how doctoral programs attempt to prepare their students in each of these domains so they will be equipped to advance the profession. Then, we propose that counseling programs should be preparing their doctoral graduates to become a different type of leader: one who commits to and advocates for the counseling profession. To support that contention, we describe a university course that attempts to challenge doctoral students to think of themselves as leaders, particularly in their profession.

### Preparing Leaders in Professional Counseling

One of the expectations of doctoral degree programs in counselor education is that they will prepare students to work as advanced practitioners in academic and clinical settings (CACREP, 2001). In other words, one of the primary goals of counselor education programs is to prepare individuals who can counsel effectively in agency, school, or private practice settings (Sexton, 2000). That part of counselor preparation, which has as its goal to improve students' counseling skills, is referred to as clinical training. The clinical training that occurs in both master's- and doctoral-level programs includes coursework directly related to the counseling process, such as clinical skills instruction in structured classrooms or during field experiences (i.e., practicum and internship; Whiston & Coker, 2000). Clearly, clinical training is critically important to counselor education as well as to the counseling profession in general. The credibility of the counseling profession depends upon a public perception that counselors are competent to provide counseling services. If counseling is to continue to be a viable profession, counselor education programs must prepare competent professional counselors.

To prepare students to be more effective counselors, doctoral programs frequently require them to engage in additional study of counseling theories and techniques and to participate in advanced practica or internships. Thus, through further study and advanced field experiences, doctoral students can update and increase their knowledge about human behavior and theories of change. Indeed, Swickert (1997) reported that all 10 of the doctoral graduates she interviewed who are now in private practice stated they had chosen a counselor education doctoral program as continuing education. However, it is important to remember that more may not result in better. For example, Christensen and Jacobson (1994) reported that professionally prepared clinicians did not perform better than those without training. Thus, the clinical training provided in doctoral programs (as well as master's programs) must integrate available research into the training curricula (Sexton, 2000; Whiston & Coker, 2000). Whiston and Coker proposed that clinical training needs to be reconstructed to focus on instruction related to (a) establishing effective therapeutic relationships, (b) increasing counselor skillfulness, and (c) training in counselor–client matching.

Sexton (2000), in a discussion of the Whiston and Coker (2000) article, also stated that clinical training must be restructured and he advocates for an evidence-based approach to clinical training that integrates research findings while promoting scientific thinking. We also endorse the need for restructured clinical training and propose that one way doctoral preparation programs can demonstrate their leadership in the profession is to review and revise their clinical training. Doctoral-level graduates must know how to provide effective counseling by utilizing evidence-based intervention programs (Sexton, 2000). As Sexton pointed out, professional counseling cannot continue to ignore evidence-based practice.

## Preparing Leaders in Research

A common view of research is that it is an organized scientific effort that seeks to advance knowledge. Research is a process for proving or rejecting theoretical assumptions and claims or practices and helps establish truth (Gibson & Mitchell, 1995). Clearly, leadership in counseling includes conducting research to expand knowledge about counseling and related counseling practices such as assessment and supervision. Counselors must be able to offer defensible evidence that what they do makes a difference in service to their clients. Conducting research can help counselors provide that evidence.

To prepare doctoral students to be leaders in research, counselor education programs require their students to gain knowledge through courses in qualitative and quantitative methods of analysis. Today's students learn research design and various methods of statistical analysis to enable them to engage in independent research. Innovations such as interuniversity collaborative research teams have worked in some settings. For example, professors at Loyola University (Chicago) and Michigan State University developed a collaborative research team to enhance research training for students (O'Brien, 1995) because they felt that an interuniversity team could expose students to a wider variety of research approaches.

In addition to gaining knowledge through coursework or research teams, doctoral students must apply their knowledge by conducting research, under their advisors' supervision, and completing a dissertation. In completing their dissertation, most students learn how to generate and test hypotheses, analyze data, present findings, and draw conclusions. Thus, the coursework (knowledge) and its application (completing research leading to a dissertation) are methods used to assure doctoral graduates' competence and future leadership in research.

## Preparing Leaders in Teaching/Supervising

Teaching and supervising others are important ways to advance the counseling profession. The contribution made by those doctoral graduates who teach either part-time or full-time in colleges and universities is significant. Doctoral graduates who teach advance the profession by stimulating the development and learning of both master's- and doctoral-level practitioners by passing on the knowledge and skills of the profession in a systematic and orderly manner.

Every profession needs master practitioners who can direct less experienced colleagues as well as preservice trainees. Functioning within apprenticeships and internships, doctoral-level supervisors promote the transfer of learning from classrooms to other settings where the profession is practiced (Bradley, 1989). Supervisors who work in universities, schools, and agencies are key in providing continued professional development of their colleagues as well as encouraging professional role identity.

To prepare doctoral students to lead in the area of teaching, counselor education doctoral programs provide opportunities for them to serve as graduate teaching associates or as teaching assistants in master's-level classes. Some doctoral students assume all teaching responsibilities for undergraduate classes in career exploration, study skills, or human relations. Others assist their advisors in teaching courses or delivering workshops. Innovative programs have even established doctoral-level teaching internships at other universities, where doctoral students can try out their teaching in a setting similar to the one in which they may eventually work. A few colleges offer courses focusing on how to teach graduate and undergraduate students. These courses are designed to help those with no pedagogical training to acquire skills in curriculum development, instructional strategies, and evaluation so they will be better prepared to teach when called upon to do so. Finally, one of the ways that doctoral advisors mentor their students is by observing their in-class instruction and giving them suggestions for improving their skills.

Effective supervision is another way to increase the knowledge and improve the skills of others. Many graduate programs offer coursework in supervision theory and practice to help their doctoral students gain the needed knowledge base to provide adequate supervision. In addition, counselor educators provide opportunities for their doctoral students to gain valuable experience by involving them in the supervision of master's degree trainees. Doctoral internships often have supervisors who are able to be models of effective supervision.

## Preparing Leaders in Writing and Publishing

Displaying leadership in writing and publishing is expected of doctoral-level graduates. Writing about innovations in the profession and/or publishing research findings informs others, gives direction to counseling interventions, and ensures a scientific foundation for the future of a discipline (Glassi, 1989). Some would argue that counselor education graduates fall far short in this domain. Zimpfer (1993) found that only 26% of counselor education and 25% of counseling psychology graduates have published in professional publications. A random sample of doctoral students in CACREP- and American Psychological Association–approved counseling programs reported low self-efficacy ratings in writing and in research (Poidevant, Loesch, & Wittmer, 1991).

What can counselor education programs do to better prepare doctoral graduates to write and publish in their professional journals? Smaby and Crews (1998) suggested that novice authors have to overcome doubts about their (a) ability to write successfully and (b) uncertainty about the worth of their ideas. They also need to target, conceptualize, organize, and manage their writing. Choosing a journal that matches their expertise will assist them in keeping a focus to their writing (Smaby & Crews 1998). To help students manage and organize their writing, some counselor education programs have weekly or bimonthly seminars focusing on writing and publishing, while others encourage their students to use courses taught outside their departments that teach students how to develop their writing skills. Another common practice is for advisors to encourage their doctoral students to collaborate with them and other faculty members on publications. It does appear that leadership development in this area uses more informal methods such as mentoring rather than more formal ones such as coursework. Perhaps this informal approach sends a message to students that writing and publication is less important than the other domains. Doctoral graduates who plan to work in academic settings must be motivated to publish during their early years if they are to survive and advance (Smaby & Crews 1998). Leadership development in writing and publishing, therefore, needs to improve in most doctoral programs.

## Advocating for the Profession

Although leaders can advance their profession through research, writing and publishing, and teaching and supervising, we propose that counseling also needs leaders who can advocate for their profession. For example, pioneers in counseling accreditation are examples of leaders who realized that some standardization of training in the profession was necessary if counseling was to gain the stature it needed to be considered one of the primary helping professions. They recognized that public trust of our profession is based on a perception that counselors are competent, and specialized education helps ensure that competence (Blocher, 1987). Similarly, those who fought for counselor licensure, state by state, also saw the importance of codifying clear and public standards and principles governing the counseling professional's behavior vis-a-vis clients. They realized that protecting the public welfare enhanced the profession.

Finally, individuals who have served as officers in the major national counseling associations brought with them some commitment to advocating for and advancing the profession. Perhaps they wanted to increase the stature of their specialty, such as school counseling, marriage and family counseling, or group counseling, or raise the status of the entire profession. Whatever their motivation, these leaders often possessed a vision of a changed future.

Accreditation standards and counselor licensure have both made enormous impacts on our profession. Without the leaders who had the vision and skills to make these two dreams into realities, counseling might not be a viable profession today. In our opinion, we believe such leaders are important to the continued success of counseling, and developing and nourishing these kinds of leaders can be seen as an important responsibility of doctoral-level counselor education programs.

Does the doctorate in counselor education include knowledge and experiences designed to develop individuals who are committed to advocate for their profession? Unlike the domains of research and teaching/supervising, courses or experiences designed to help doctoral-level students learn advocacy skills to advance the counseling profession do not appear to exist, or at least are not reported in the literature. Many college and university programs appear to encourage their students to join state and national counseling associations and to present at professional conferences. Occasionally, students may serve on state association committees and, even more rarely, on national association committees. Are these experiences sufficient for developing leaders who can advance the counseling profession? We do not think so.

Very little is reported in the primary counseling journals related to the leadership skills necessary to advocate for the profession. A survey attempting to identify the goals of counselor education programs, however, found that nearly 20% of the programs surveyed placed no emphasis on preparing their doctoral graduates for a general leadership role (Zimpfer, Cox, West, Bubenzer, & Brooks, 1997). Even in the informal curriculum, defined as including mentoring, modeling, and collaboration with faculty, the nurturing of leadership in advocacy ranked lower in importance than developing leaders in research, teaching, and supervision. If this survey is indicative of current practice, perhaps counselor education programs do not view the preparation of advocates for the profession as their job, or maybe they believe students pick up an advocacy orientation on their own (Zimpfer et al., 1997).

We believe that doctoral-level counselor education programs need to be intentional about developing and fostering leadership knowledge and skills related to advocacy for the profession. It seems clear that professional associations look to those with doctoral degrees to become their future leaders. For example, since its establishment in 1985, Chi Sigma Iota (CSI), the counseling academic and professional honor society, has had 17 presidents, and all have held doctorates (CSI, n.d.). We were not able to identify similar information about the educational level of past and current presidents of the American Counseling Association, but we speculate that many also had attained doctoral degrees before becoming leaders in counseling.

For whatever reason, there is little or no evidence to suggest that the leadership domain defined as "advocacy for the profession" is being taught in most counselor education programs or that experiences are being designed to help students practice becoming leaders in advocating for the counseling profession. At this point we will offer a discussion of a peda-gogical framework for a course in leadership with an emphasis on develop-ing leaders who can advocate for the profession. A sample syllabus for this doctoral-level course can be found in Appendix A.

## PREPARING LEADERS WHO CAN ADVOCATE FOR THE PROFESSION

Leaders are not typically developed through their participation in a series of academic courses. However, leadership theories and concepts and op-portunities to practice leadership skills can provide doctoral-level counsel-ing students with new perspectives and skills. We have offered leadership courses at the doctoral level at our respective institutions, and students have greeted the course with enthusiasm. A description and discussion of the course is included in the final section of this chapter.

### Purpose of a Leadership Course

We designed a course that focused on leadership principles and concepts as well as on the experiences that may contribute to developing leaders (see syllabus in Appendix A). Theories of leadership development were ex-amined and discussed. These theories were not exclusive to the counseling profession but are relevant to almost any profession. Helping students learn how to become leaders in their profession and their communities and how to apply leadership principles to the preparation of professional coun-selors were important goals of the course.

### Course Content

The leadership course was divided into three phases. The first four class sessions were described as "Leadership: The Big Picture." Doctoral stu-dents learned about and discussed general principles of leadership. This was accomplished through the study of theorists such as Bennis and Gold-smith (1997), Burns (1978), and Gardner (1995). Students were exposed, through their reading, to the lives and contributions of leaders such as Mahatma Gandhi, Martin Luther King, Jr., Robert Maynard Hutchins, and Eleanor Roosevelt. Exploring the leadership qualities and skills of influen-

tial individuals outside the counseling profession allowed students to reflect upon the relationship between individuals' personal characteristics
and their leadership styles. Course readings, by focusing on individuals
with very different leadership styles, allowed students to reflect upon the
complexity of leadership as a concept and a process.

The next three class sessions, "Leadership: The Person," required students to consider how general leadership principles applied to their own
lives. They engaged in self-reflection and self-assessment of their own leadership potential. Thus, students moved from a focus on those who were generally accepted as influential leaders to a focus on themselves. Topics and
class activities included the creation and communication of a personal vision, reinventing oneself through leadership development, and reflection on
the personal qualities that allow individuals to generate and sustain trust.
Participation and intense discussion characterized these sessions.

The third and last phase of the 10-week course addressed "Leadership
in Professional Counseling." Doctoral students explored leadership practices by interviewing a leader within the counseling profession. To accomplish this, students collaborated in the design of a protocol to guide their
interviews. Their interview questions were based on the leadership theories and concepts addressed in the course and solicited the views of current
leaders regarding leadership and its importance to the profession.

## Assignments

Students' assignments promoted reading, critical thinking, reflection, and
inquiry. First, students were required to write a paper that focused on some
aspect of leadership in the counseling profession. The goal of this assignment was to increase students' knowledge and encourage their critical
thinking about how leadership theories and principles can be applied to
counseling. Preparing the paper also helped them think about the kinds of
questions they wanted to include in their interview protocol.

Second, students were expected to conduct an interview with a counselor who has held or currently holds a leadership position in the profession. Students first communicated with the counseling leader by telephone
or electronic mail and then arranged a follow-up telephone interview. They
conducted the interviews using the protocol the class developed. This
interview allowed students to gain yet another perspective on leadership
from a recognized leader in the counseling profession. Students reported
that this assignment was informative and exciting and created within them
a strong feeling of professional identity. The leaders who were interviewed
also described the experience as positive.

Third, each student was required to lead some of the in-class activities from *Learning to Lead* (Bennis & Goldsmith, 1997), a workbook used throughout the course. We explained that we wanted students to assume a leadership role with their peers. We gave students feedback using a scoring rubric that focused on presentation skills, as well as skills in leading others through structured activities.

The application or third phase of the course, "Leadership in Professional Counseling," gives counselor educators the flexibility to substitute any number of assignments to fit their needs. For example, an earlier version of this same leadership course taught at The Ohio State University required doctoral students to design a day-long workshop focusing on leadership in school counseling. The students, working as a team, designed and delivered the workshop to practicing school counselors in local school districts after conducting a needs assessment to determine what school counselors wanted to learn about leadership. The free workshop provided a valuable professional development opportunity for school counselors while giving the doctoral students experience in leading a workshop.

## Course Evaluation

As instructors, we were surprised how enthusiastically students participated in the assignments and the in-class activities. Even though the study of leadership represented a relatively new set of concepts to many students, they were eager to express their views about the leaders they were studying. Students typically finished the readings quickly because, as they reported, they found them interesting. They evaluated the course positively and describe how the course influenced them with these comments:

- "This course has changed my thinking about leadership."
- "I believe I can be a leader. I never thought I could be before."
- "The interviews made me proud to be a counselor."
- "I could not believe I had to take this course and now I cannot imagine not taking it!"
- "Thinking about leadership from so many different perspectives has made it seem so much more important to me."

The course afforded us the opportunity to address leadership concepts and practices in a way that stimulated students' thinking. Although no follow-up has been conducted, we suspect that students' views about leadership and their potential to see themselves as leaders are broader than before the experience.

## SUMMARY

The doctorate in counselor education prepares both current and future leaders in professional counseling, research, teaching/supervising, and writing and publication. In our opinion, it is reasonable to expect that doctoral programs will create leaders in these domains. However, we do not believe this is sufficient. We propose that counselor educators consider the importance of developing leaders with skills to advocate for the counseling profession. Those leaders who advocate for counseling contribute to the continued growth and stature of the profession in important ways. In this chapter we described a course focusing on leadership as one method of increasing the leadership knowledge and skills of doctoral students in counselor education.

## REFERENCES

Bennis, W., & Goldsmith, J. (1997). *Learning to lead*. Reading, MA: Addison-Wesley.

Blocher, D. H., (1987). *The professional counselor*. New York: Macmillan.

Bradley, L. (1989). *Counselor supervision: Principles, process, and practice*. Muncie, IN: Accelerated Development.

Burns, J. M. (1978). *Leadership*. New York: Harper & Row.

Chi Sigma Iota. (n.d.). *Historical perspectives*. Retrieved November 4, 2001, from http://www.csi-net.org/htmls/history.htm.

Christensen, A., & Jacobson, N. S. (1994). Who (or what) can do psychotherapy: The status and challenge of nonprofessional therapies. *Psychological Science, 5*, 8–14.

Council for Accreditation of Counseling and Related Educational Programs. (2001). *The 2001 Standards*. Alexandria, VA: Author.

Gardner, H. (1995). *Leading minds: An anatomy of leadership*. New York: Basic Books.

Gibson, R. L., & Mitchell, M. H. (1995). *Introduction to counseling and guidance*. Englewood Cliffs, NJ: Prentice-Hall.

Glassi, J. P. (1989). Maintaining the viability of counseling psychology: The role of research training. *Counseling Psychology Quarterly, 2*, 465–474.

O'Brien, K. M. (1995). Enhancing research training for counseling students: Interuniversity collaborative research teams. *Counselor Education and Supervision, 34*, 187–198.

Poidevant, J. M., Loesch, L. C., & Wittmer, J. (1991). Vocational aspirations and perceived self-efficacy of doctoral students in the counseling professions. *Counselor Education and Supervision, 30*, 289–300.

Sexton, T. L. (2000). Reconstructing clinical training: In pursuit of evidence-based clinical training. *Counselor Education and Supervision, 39*, 218–227.

Smaby, M. H., & Crews, J. (1998). Publishing in scholarly journals: Part 1—Is it an attitude or technique? It's an attitude. *Counselor Education and Supervision, 37*, 218–223.

Swickert, M. L. (1997). Perceptions regarding the professional identity of counselor education doctoral graduates in private practice: A qualitative study.
*Counselor Education and Supervision, 36,* 332–340.

Whiston, S. C., & Coker, J. K. (2000). Reconstructing clinical training: Implications from research. *Counselor Education and Supervision, 39,* 228–253.

Zimpfer, D. (1993). A comparison of doctoral graduates in counselor education and
counseling psychology. *Counselor Education and Supervision, 32,* 227–240.

Zimpfer, D., Cox, J. A., West, J. D., Bubenzer, D. L., & Brooks, D. K. (1997). An
examination of counselor preparation doctoral program goals. *Counselor Education and Supervision, 36,* 4, 318–331.

Zimpfer, D., & DeTrude, J. (1990). Follow-up of doctoral graduates in counseling.
*Journal of Counseling & Development, 69,* 51–56.

## APPENDIX A: COURSE SYLLABUS FOR "LEADERSHIP IN COUNSELING"

*Course Title*: Leadership in Counseling

*Course Description*: This course focuses on leadership principles and theories and their application. Particular attention is paid to the application of
these principles and theories to the development of professional counselors
so they can learn to become leaders in their profession and in their communities. Doctoral students will be encouraged to develop their own leadership
capacities as they read about and interact with leaders in various disciplines.

*Course Objectives*: As a result of this course, participants will be able to:

1. Describe at least two major theories of leadership development.
2. Discuss and evaluate the applicability of leadership theories to the
   counseling profession.
3. Apply leadership development concepts and processes to their own
   lives.
4. Review the literature in leadership development that is relevant to
   the counseling profession.
5. Demonstrate leadership in simulated leadership situations related to
   the counseling profession.
6. Learn how leadership concepts and principles can be used to advocate for the counseling profession.

*Texts*:

Bennis, W., & Goldsmith, J. (1997). *Learning to lead.* Reading, MA: Addison-Wesley.

Gardner, H. (1995). *Leading minds*. New York: Basic Books.

Other readings as assigned.

*Topical Outline/Assignments:*

Leadership, The Big Picture

Session
#1:   Introduction to Leadership Principles.

#2:   A Cognitive Approach to Leadership.
      Read chapters 1–3 in Gardner's *Leading Minds*.
      Also read chapter discussing Margaret Mead as a leader. Discussion
      will focus on Gardner's criteria for leadership and how Mead exem-
      plifies those attributes. (Student Facilitators.)

#3:   Read chapters on Robert Hutchins, Alfred Sloan, Martin Luther
      King. Discussion will focus on Gardner's criteria for leadership and
      how subjects exemplify those attributes. (In-class activities led by
      Student Facilitators.)

#4:   Read chapters on Jean Monnet and Mahatma Gandhi as well as Chap-
      ter 15 in *Leading Minds*. Discussion will focus on Gardner's criteria
      for leadership and how subjects exemplify those attributes. Papers on
      "Leadership in Counseling" are due this week.

Leadership, the Person

#5:   The Reinvention of Self: Chapter 2 in *Learning to Lead*.
      The Leadership Crisis: Chapter 3 in *Learning to Lead*.
      Complete leadership development activities in class led by Student
      Facilitators.
      Students will develop protocol for Counseling Leader Interviews.

#6:   Knowing Yourself and Creating and Communicating a Vision.
      Read chapters 4 & 5 in *Learning to Lead*. Complete development of
      the "Counseling Leader Interview" protocol. Students choose coun-
      seling leaders to contact for interview—see end of syllabus.

#7:   Trust and Leadership: Realizing Intention Through Action.
      Read chapters 6 & 7 in *Learning to Lead*. In-class activities led by
      Student Facilitators.

Leadership in Professional Counseling

#8:  Class Presentations of Interviews of Leaders in Counseling. Students will be expected to prepare a 30-minute presentation based on their interviews. A one-page summary of the interviews is to be made available to other students.

#9:  Class Presentations: Interviews of Counseling Leaders.

#10: Class Presentations: Interviews of Counseling Leaders.

*Evaluation*

Evaluation will be based on the following:

1. Student participation in all simulated activities. This will include completion of chapter activities offered in *Learning to Lead*. Students are to come to class prepared to discuss their ideas. (10%)
2. Facilitation of In-Class Activities Focusing on Leaders. (10%)
3. Write a term paper on a specific topic related to leadership development and professional counseling. The intent will be to publish the collection as a monograph for use by practicing counselors and counselors in training. The class will develop and agree upon topics important to the project. (40%)
4. Students will conduct an interview with a current counseling leader. Class participants will develop a questioning protocol to be used as the framework for all informational interviews. Students will submit a written summary of the interview. (40%)

*List of possible counseling leaders to be interviewed:*

- ACA president or ACA president-elect,
- ASCA president or ASCA president-elect,
- ACES president or ACES president-elect,
- AMHCA president or AMHCA president-elect,
- AAMCD president or AAMCD president-elect.

Others may be appropriate, please contact instructor for permission.

# Part II

# Noted Leaders and Their Legacies

# CHAPTER 7

# Michael Kent Altekruse

Melanie E. Rawlins and Michael C. Altekruse

*I want to better the counseling profession through accreditation,*
*licensure, and credentialing.*

Michael Kent Altekruse has dedicated his life to promoting the field of counselor education to a level of respectability and prominence. His ability to bring people together and listen to various viewpoints has been useful in developing standards for the profession. Perhaps it was no coincidence that Mike's own life journey was also born from a need to develop direction from disorder.

Mike was born in Fort Wayne, Indiana, in 1939 to Carol and Lloyd Altekruse. His life began in the midst of marital discord. These marital problems culminated in Mike being abandoned by his mother at age one and his parents' subsequent divorce. Lloyd asked his own parents, Robert and Mabel, for help in raising Mike. Soon thereafter Lloyd enlisted in the Merchant Marines and served in the Pacific Theater during World War II. He asked his parents to care for Mike until he returned. Mabel was initially reluctant to take him, because she already had the responsibility to care for Robert, who had Lou Gehrig's disease. Nevertheless, she did care for him even after his father returned from the war. Mike's relationship with his grandmother was special. He describes her as the "major influence in my life."

Mabel instilled in young Michael the values of unselfishness and benevolence that contributed to his ultimate success in counseling. Mike's early years were marked by the death of his grandfather, Robert, when Mike was 5 years old and the death of his father, Lloyd, when Mike was just 16. Despite the loss of his mother, grandfather, and father, Mike continued to demonstrate the resilience his grandmother modeled, as well as her philosophy of self-determination and self-reliance.

A first-generation college student, Mike was a source of pride for his grandmother. After graduating from high school, he accepted an academic scholarship to attend Heidelberg College in Ohio. He subsequently earned a Bachelor of Science in Education degree from Indiana University in Bloomington, Indiana.

Mike married Ruth Dill in 1961. The couple have three children: Barbi, who is training to be a school counselor; Michelle, who is a corporate divisional merchandising manager for Women's Accessories for the May Company; and Michael, a counseling psychologist who works at the University of Wisconsin Oshkosh Counseling Center. Mike and Ruth also have seven grandchildren: Jared, Krista, Andrew, Alex, Natalie, Jordan, and Megan. As a father and grandfather, Mike continues to demonstrate the love, compassion, and unyielding resolve that Mabel instilled in him.

Mike first became enamored with teaching as a way of helping others. He taught at the Indiana University junior high school and coached swimming and considered getting a master's degree in history. However, Mike was influenced by the school counselor, Don Barr, and a professor in the Department of Counseling and Educational Psychology, Jack Cody, to join the National Defense Education Act (NDEA) Institute at Indiana University. Mike returned to the Indiana University junior and senior high schools as a school counselor and coach and was encouraged by his advisor, Jim Brown, to pursue his doctorate. With the help of mentors from the program at Indiana University and his wife, Ruth, Mike earned his Ed.D. degree in counselor education at the age of 27.

## CAREER PATH AND MAJOR ACCOMPLISHMENTS

Mike's exemplary leadership and contributions to the profession of counseling span nearly 35 years. He has provided significant leadership to universities. He began his career as assistant professor of counselor education and as a counselor and clinical coordinator for the Clinical Center at

Southern Illinois University at Carbondale (SIU-C). Eventually, he served as coordinator of the Counselor Education Program at SIU-C for over 11 years, and it became one of the most respected counselor education programs in the country. Mike believes that counselor educators should continue to counsel as well as conduct research; therefore, he counseled in private practice in addition to his university work.

Mike eventually left SIU-C to develop a doctoral program and, later, to become chairperson of the Department of Counseling at the University of Nevada at Las Vegas (UN-LV). Enjoying success at this position, he was recruited to serve as Chairperson of the Department of Counseling, Development, and Higher Education at the University of North Texas (UNT), where he is currently located. Under his leadership, the UNT counseling program recently received the Robert Frank Outstanding Program Award, presented by the Association for Counselor Education and Supervision (ACES). The program is annually rated in the top 5% of counselor education programs by *U.S. News and World Report*.

Mike has provided leadership to the counseling profession through sustained and remarkable scholarly efforts since 1967. He has published over 40 articles, 10 books and monographs, and 4 book chapters and has given more than 150 professional presentations. The article "Duty to Warn" (Costa & Altekruse, 1994) is frequently referenced. In addition, his "Accreditation in Counselor Education" (Altekruse & Wittmer, 1991) article is one of the most historically accurate accreditation accounts. Mike's *Mental Health Counseling in the 90's: A Research Report for Training and Practice* (Altekruse & Sexton, 1995), which describes mental health counseling, is often used as a textbook. The research on group supervision versus individual supervision (Ray & Altekruse, 2000) has had a tremendous impact on training master's-level counselor trainees. In 1993, Mike and his colleagues identified a critical need for school counselors and counselor educators for the following decade (Maples, Altekruse, & Testa, 1993). Mike was one of the first to define the difference between the professions of counselor education and counseling psychology (Altekruse, 1991). A 1992 article examining the effects of the American Personnel and Guidance Association (now the American Counseling Association, ACA) presidency has been enthusiastically received by ACA past presidents and others (Bradley & Altekruse, 1992).

Mike was among the first counselor educators to engage in Web-based scholarly activities. He developed several Web-based courses for the University of North Texas on topics as diverse as supervision, ethics, professional issues, and career development. Mike received a 1999–2000

Teaching with Technology Grant from the University of North Texas and contributed to the ACA's cybercounseling book (Altekruse & Brew, 2000). Another accomplishment has been securing nearly $500,000 through 12 grants during the past 25 years.

Mike has provided exceptional and sustained leadership in the counseling profession in virtually every possible capacity. His pioneering accreditation work is a major contribution to the counseling profession. He was a founding member of the ACES Accreditation Committee, which rewrote the standards first written in 1961. He was the first Secretary-Treasurer of the Council for Accreditation of Counseling and Related Educational Programs (CACREP) and was also Chairperson of the ACES Standards Review Committee that was instrumental in revisions of the 1988 and 1994 CACREP standards. He served as the first on-site team trainer and developed the *ACES Accreditation Training Manual* (Altekruse & Karmos, 1979). He has served as chairperson of more accreditation on-site teams than any other person and has consulted with over 30 programs for CACREP. Recently, he was awarded a small grant from CACREP to study the effectiveness of accreditation. Through a series of doctoral dissertation studies, differences were found after comparing graduates of CACREP-accredited and non-CACREP-accredited programs on employment patterns, faculty involvement, quality of students, and professional involvement of students and faculty.

In addition to his accreditation activities, Mike has served as president of ACES and president of the North Central ACES, the Illinois Counselor Educators and Supervisors (ICES) association, and the Illinois Counseling Association (ICA). He has served on governing boards, chaired numerous committees, and served as *ICA Journal* editor and as an editorial board member in national, regional, state, and local professional counseling organizations. Among the awards and special honors Mike has received are the C. A. Michelman Award, which recognizes the highest contribution to counseling in Illinois; a 1988 ACES Presidential Award for launching the first ACES Convention in St. Louis; and the ACES Graduate Student Committee Mentor Award in 1989 and 1992. In 1992, his son, Michael C. Altekruse, was selected to present the award to him. He was recognized again in 1992 with an ACES Presidential Award for rewriting and reorganizing the doctoral standards to follow the same format as the master's-level standards in the 1994 *CACREP Accreditation Standards and Procedures Manual*. This work involved traveling to all ACES regions over a span of 2 years in order for counselor education programs to have input in revising the standards. Currently, Mike is chairperson of the ACA Professionalization Committee. He is leading a movement toward the portability of counselor license from state to state.

Some leaders are comfortable "taking charge" while others prefer to "lead by example." In Mike's case he sees advantages in doing both. He has taken charge as ACES President and as the Department Chairperson at both UN-LV and UNT. In each of these capacities, he has found ways to collaborate with his colleagues and find solutions to problems. Mike is not afraid to make the decisions that promote progress for the profession and his department. In his work with CACREP, he has shown a consistent desire to improve the counseling profession and maintain high standards. He also is able to create a vision that brings others on as partners in a project by listening to multiple viewpoints. As projects and positions become clear, he will lead by example by following through on the standards and tasks he helped to create. In the midst of his challenging leadership style, Mike uses optimism, compassion, and his knowledge of people to move others forward. He is not afraid to handle the inevitable conflicts that leadership brings, and he considers ways to bring everyone on board to work as a team.

Mike exemplifies the expectation to think for oneself in his roles as an educator, mentor, leader, counselor, and parent. He has the knack for getting people to perform to their potential or to make necessary changes without giving advice or steering them toward his way of thinking. In addition, he earns respect by demonstrating loyalty to those around him. Although his own life may have been challenged by loss, he takes it upon himself to provide a beacon for others overcoming similar situations.

## AUTHOR'S MEMORIES

Mike has been my (Melanie Rawlins') mentor, colleague, role model, consultant, and friend since 1978, and he continues to have my deepest respect. Having known Mike in this variety of professional roles, I have had numerous opportunities to follow and admire his professional skills, contributions, and accomplishments. His relentless energy, dedication, and exceptional and sustained efforts devoted to our profession have been inspirational and are rare.

During my first year as a counselor educator, I met Mike at the ICA Convention (then Illinois Personnel and Guidance Association). At that point he became a role model for me as a leader in ICA. He has also been of assistance as I considered other responsibilities: presenting at professional conferences, managing a private practice, preparing scholarly manuscripts, and serving in administrative roles. In all of these areas I have telephoned Mike, met with him at conventions, and e-mailed him to consult. Mike always takes time to help. Most recently, a member of my faculty and I visited the counseling clinics in his department. Not only did Mike meet us at the airport, arrange meetings, and take us to the clinics, but he also invited us to stay in his home. Few people extend themselves to spend the quality time that Mike does helping peers, students, and colleagues. With the level of his responsibilities and the depth and breadth of his professional involvement and contributions, I am amazed at how he does what he does! Mike gives unsparingly as he shares his knowledge, competence, expertise, caring, and leadership.

Through the years I have attended Mike's professional presentations, because I knew I would learn new, cutting edge information. When I look at his vita and see the extensive compilation of presentations and publications, I realize the extent to which Mike creates "the wave of the future," helps set the agenda for professional counseling issues, and extends the horizons of the profession. He has been a model for me and other counselor educators for involving graduate students and colleagues in presentations and publications and mentoring them effectively to share knowledge, experience, research, and expertise.

Mike encouraged, inspired, and reinforced my participation in professional organizations. I had the opportunity to observe his leadership style when he was president of ICA and ICES, and chaired committees. I witnessed Mike's impact on the ICA Governing Council for the six years I served on the Council with him. As a backbone member, he helped keep the Governing Council on track to meet membership needs. When Mike left Illinois, there was a void in the organization. He influenced my decision to run for offices, and I am now president of ICA as well as past-president of ICES.

As a mentor, Mike has significantly impacted my life, inspiring and gently encouraging me to find and open new doors to personal and professional growth. Most recently, he validated my move into administration; his belief in me has been empowering. One example of Mike's helpfulness was to point me toward an administrator workshop that proved useful as I began my administrative position.

I consider Mike a "broker of people." His sense of personalities and institutional or departmental qualities enables him to predict a "good match." Mike has the rare ability to see where and how people can give their best effort, and then he helps them succeed and realize their full potential. With his finger on the pulse of what is going on in our field, Mike is an exemplary networking model from whom all can learn.

I am just one person who benefits from and greatly values the opportunity to work with and learn from Michael K. Altekruse. When I consider the countless others he has mentored, I know Mike has contributed to strengthening, expanding, and enhancing the counseling profession. The values of unselfishness and benevolence learned as a child underlie Mike's career path. He is the epitome of the core counseling conditions: empathy, acceptance, and genuineness. Mike's legacy is his example as one who "walks the talk."

## REFERENCES

Altekruse, M. K. (1991). President's message: The doctorate in counselor education and counseling psychology. *Counselor Education and Supervision, 30,* 178–182.

Altekruse, M. K. (1994). A cooperative clinic as a mental health center. In J. E. Myers (Ed.), *Developing and directing counselor education laboratories* (pp. 165–181). Alexandria, VA: American Counseling Association.

Altekruse, M. K., & Brew, L. (2000). Using the web for distance learning. In J. Bloom & G. Walz (Eds.), *Cybercounseling* (pp. 165–181). Alexandria, VA: American Counseling Association.

Altekruse, M. K., & Karmos, J. (1979). *ACES accreditation training manual.* Falls Church, VA: American Personnel and Guidance Association.

Altekruse, M. K., & Sexton, T. (1995). *Mental health counseling in the 90's: A research report for training and practice.* Orlando, FL: The National Commission for Mental Health Counseling Training, Inc.

Altekruse, M. K., & Wittmer, J. (1991). Accreditation in counselor education. In F. O. Bradley (Ed.), *Credentialing in counseling* (pp. 53–62). Alexandria, VA: American Association for Counseling and Development.

Bradley, R., & Altekruse, M. K. (1992). Effects of APGA presidency. *Journal of Counseling & Development, 70,* 502–504.

*CACREP accreditation standards and procedures manual.* (1994). Alexandria, VA: Council for Accreditation of Counseling and Related Educational Programs.

Costa, L., & Altekruse, M. K. (1994). Duty to warn. *Journal of Counseling & Development, 72,* 346–350.

Maples, M. F., Altekruse, M. K., & Testa, A. (1993). Counselor education 2000: Extinction or distinction? *Counselor Education and Supervision, 33,* 47–52.

Ray, D., & Altekruse, M. K. (2000). Effectiveness of group supervision versus combined group and individual supervision with master-level counselor trainees. *Counselor Education and Supervision, 40,* 19–30.

# CHAPTER 8

# Roger F. Aubrey

William C. Briddick and Richard L. Hayes

*A constructive, gentle critic.*

It is one thing to understand oneself and know what you want to be. It is quite another thing to have the courage to be who you really want to be. This is the message of hope reflected in the life of Roger F. Aubrey. Whether as a teacher, colleague, author, supervisor, professional leader, father, husband, mentor, or friend, those who knew him understand this message well. It conveys a form of hope that we can all achieve because hope resides in the meaning we give to our lives. As the American philosopher John Dewey (one of Roger's favorites) argued: "The self reveals its nature in what it chooses" (Dewey, 1980, p. 150). Having mentored others in their efforts to actually become who they wanted to be, Roger challenged everyone with whom he came in contact to seize the opportunity and to do it in their own way.

## EARLY YEARS AND EDUCATION

When Roger was hospitalized with an infection shortly after his birth in Moline, Illinois, on November 1, 1929, the nurses took to him immediately and called him their little "buddy boy." His father later named him "Roger" after baseball player Rogers Hornsby, and "Frederick" after his grandfather. A parent's wishes aside, "buddy" became "Bud" and the name stuck, at least until it seemed too undignified for the academic colleagues he would join at the University of Chicago years later.

According to Sheeley (1977), Roger received his A.B. degree in Psychology and Philosophy from the University of Miami in 1954 and began teaching the same year in Florida as an elementary school teacher at Ronsom School in Miami. From 1955 to 1956 he worked as the manager of a Miami sporting goods store. Later, before landing another teaching job near his hometown of Rock Island, Illinois, Roger worked as a hotel clerk from 1957 to 1959 (Sheeley, 1977). His teaching career resumed in the Quad Cities area of Illinois in 1959, particularly the United Township High School of East Moline, Illinois, where he worked as a social studies teacher from 1959 to 1962. In 1961 he met Dixie Cook, whom he would soon marry and with whom he would eventually have three sons: Josh, David, and Chris. By 1963 Roger set up shop as an elementary school principal and counselor in the community of Riverdale, Illinois, while pursuing the M.A. degree in Counseling and Educational Psychology at the University of Chicago, from where he graduated in 1964. Roger worked as a research director, counselor, and practicum supervisor at the University of Chicago Lab School from 1965 to 1967 and became its director of guidance in 1967. In 1966 he attended his first national conference of the American Personnel and Guidance Association (APGA; now the American Counseling Association, ACA).

## LEADERSHIP FOR AN EMERGING PROFESSION

It was at Chicago that Roger was introduced to the works of the developmental theorists who would shape his views on education, notably the works of John Dewey, Jean Piaget, Lev Vygotsky, and Jane Loevinger. In addition, he spoke often of the great influence his teachers at Chicago had on his own development as a person and as a scholar. Bruno Bettelheim and Lawrence Kohlberg would profoundly shape Roger's commitment to promote human development through helping others to master the life tasks of their social environment. Chris Kehas, later president of the Association for Counselor Education and Supervision (ACES), had newly arrived from Harvard and became Roger's mentor. It was Kehas who introduced Roger to former Harvard colleagues David Tiedeman, Ralph Mosher, and Norman Sprinthall. It was to their notion of deliberate psychological education as a means for promoting personal and social development (Mosher & Sprinthall, 1970) that Roger turned his attention when fashioning school guidance programs and then counselor education curriculum.

In 1969, Roger accepted a position as director of guidance and health education in the school system of Brookline, Massachusetts, where he would remain from 1969 to 1977. He spent the summers of 1968 and 1969 as a graduate instructor at Wisconsin State University and joined North Atlantic ACES. He was soon invited to join the ACES Commission on the 1970s, authoring one of several statements regarding how counselors should respond to the future (Sheeley, 1977). In 1970 he was called as an expert witness for the Special U.S. Senate Subcommittee on Alcoholism and Narcotics, and in 1972, he served as an expert witness for the President's Committee on Health Education. From 1972 to 1973, Roger served as a member of the Advisory Group for the National Drug Abuse Training Center in Washington, DC, and from 1972 to 1975 he served as a member of the ACES Executive Council. He also chaired the Budget and Finance Committee (1972–1974) for ACES and served as an ACES representative on the APGA Board of Directors (1973–1974) and as a senator in APGA (1974–1975).

In 1972, Roger was elected president of ACES and was one of the first counselor supervisors to ever hold that position. During his presidency (1973–1974), the preparation standards that were the original work of Robert O. Stripling were accepted. In addition, while leading ACES, Roger entered doctoral study at Boston University to complete the academic preparation he had begun at Chicago.

I (Richard Hayes) first met Roger Aubrey at a party in the spring of 1973. We were both the guests of Ralph Mosher, who would become our major professor as we each entered the doctoral program at Boston University the next year. I had just finished my master's degree and was feeling quite self-assured and "experienced" at the ripe old age of 28. Roger, then 44, had already had two careers and was starting yet another. I don't remember much that was said that evening between us, but I remember so well how much I liked this man, how interested he was in what I had to say, and how supported I felt by his interest. Typical of Roger, it was only later that I learned from others of his significant position in the profession I was just entering: of his recent election as ACES President and of his national recognition as an expert on career and vocational development, evidenced by a long list of publications and service on professional committees.

It was not to be the last talk that we would have or the last party that we would attend together. In many ways it was like no other evening I have had with most "academics" (before or since), and in many ways it was like nearly every evening I ever had with Roger over a period of nearly a quarter century. My professional life with him was an intellectual *tour de force* and a recurring opportunity to attempt an answer to the question posed by one of his favorite philosophers, Buckminster Fuller (1969): "How big can we think?" Roger was a visionary for a profession recurrently lost in its own search for identity.

By 1973, Kohlberg had come to Harvard and Mosher had moved across the river from Harvard to Boston University. Together, they would fashion a national model for infusing a developmental perspective into counselor preparation and practice, and collaborate in testing a democratic model of moral education in the public schools. With Mosher's encouragement, Roger completed a definitive dissertation on school guidance entitled *An Examination of Selected Constraints on the Practice of School Guidance and Counseling* and received his Ed.D. degree in Counseling Psychology from Boston University in 1975.

That was a pivotal year for him professionally as he ended one set of responsibilities and assumed yet another. Roger ended his term as a member of the editorial board of *Focus on Guidance*, on which he had served since 1969, and completed a 3-year term as a member of the editorial board for *The School Counselor*. In turn, he joined the editorial board of the *Personnel and Guidance Journal*, where he remained until 1981. The year also marked the beginning of a 5-year term spent as a member of the Secondary School Research Committee for the Education Testing Service in Princeton, New Jersey. While on that committee, Roger served as secretary from 1978 to 1980 and as a member, writer, and consultant to the Guidance Counselor Committee for Revising and Rewriting the National Teacher Examination with the Education Testing Service from 1977 to 1978.

## MENTORING FOR EMERGING PROFESSIONALS

During his time at Brookline, Roger came under the mentorship of Brookline's Pupil Personnel Director, Frances McKenzie, who had hired Roger on the spot at a convention in Chicago. "Mac" had a profound personal effect on refining Roger's style as an empowering leader. In turn, Roger surrounded himself with a talented group of seasoned professionals. Jim Muro, another ACES president, and Peg Carroll, editor of *The School*

*Counselor* and the first female president of the Association for Specialists in Group Work, were his constant companions at annual conferences and on professional committees.

Mike and Judy Lewis relied on Roger's keen intellect and vision to develop a model for community counseling. Judy became one of the leading authors in the field and the ACA's 49th president. Among the school counselors Roger supervised at Brookline were Patricia Arredondo, who went on to coauthor the national standards for multicultural counseling; Bree and Richard Hayes, who each later became president of the Association for Specialists in Group Work; Louise R. Thompson, who became the first female president of ACES in 1980; and Diana Paolitto, who coauthored a bestselling text on applying Kohlberg's moral development theory to educational practice (Hersh, Paolitto, & Reimer, 1979).

Roger's article "Historical Development of Guidance and Counseling and Implications for the Future" (Aubrey, 1977), published in the *Personnel and Guidance Journal*, became a cornerstone for the historical study of the profession. The same year Roger accepted an academic position as coordinator of the Human Development Counseling Program at George Peabody College for Teachers in Nashville, Tennessee, and in 1979 Roger became a member of the Board of Directors for APGA, serving until 1981.

Roger spent over 12 years working, as time permitted, as either an adjunct or visiting professor before his move to Peabody. During his years in Chicago, he taught at the University of Chicago and at Wisconsin State University in Superior, Wisconsin. Upon his arrival in Boston, Roger taught at the University of Maine, Northeastern University, Fairfield University, and Boston University. By 1977, Roger had already acquired a reputation for being what one journal editor would term "one of the best and most prolific writers our field has produced" (Aubrey, 1977, p. 28). From his position at Peabody, Roger embarked on a 20-year journey as a constructive, gentle critic of the counseling profession, asking important soul-searching questions of the profession through his writings. He mentored a new generation of professionals in Loretta Bradley, who became ACA's 47th president and coauthor of a leading text on counseling women, *Counseling Women Over the Life Span* (Lewis, Hayes, & Bradley, 1992), and Michael D'Andrea and Judy Daniels, who have distinguished themselves as tireless advocates for the rights of underrepresented groups within the counseling profession.

His work with professional journals in the field of counseling continued as Roger became a member of the Publications Committee for ACES from 1981 to 1982 and a member of the editorial board for *The Vocational Guidance Quarterly* from 1982 to 1984. From 1984 to 1989 Roger served as a member of the editorial board for the *Journal of Counseling and Human Service Professionals*. He served as chairperson of the Publications Committee of the National Career Development Association from 1985 to 1989. Starting in 1985, Roger began a one-year term as a member of the Committee on Technology for the American Association of Counseling and Development (AACD; now ACA).

## A LASTING CONTRIBUTION

Roger contributed over 90 publications to the professional literature during his career. His writings tended to focus on school guidance and counseling, developmental and social issues, and historical trends in the counseling profession. He was recognized with the Writer of the Year Award from the American School Counselor Association in 1974.

Like so many who came to know him, I (Chris Briddick) first met Roger F. Aubrey in the literature. As an undergraduate I came upon Roger's name as a citation in a textbook. Later, a journal article introduced me to one of the profession's truly big thinkers. Shortly thereafter, I unknowingly signed up for a course at a college near my home taught by Terry Cooper, one of Roger's former students. It would be Terry who would soon accompany me to my departmental interview with Peabody's Human Development Counseling Program at Vanderbilt University. Terry Cooper and I arrived late for my first meeting with Roger. After friends dropped us off at the wrong location we were forced to hitch a ride across Nashville, in the back of a pick-up truck full of hay. As we pulled up to the restaurant, Roger and another Peabody faculty member, Peggy Whiting, sat gazing at us from the front window of the restaurant. Roger never let me forget that my arrival at a rather prestigious institution had been via a bale of hay. Most of all, he never let me forget the significance of my roots as a son of the working class and the importance of my strong ties to a rural, union family, and community.

Roger's own identification with growing up "a river rat" in the Midwest during the Depression tempered his enthusiasm for the merits of what he called a service approach to counseling. He was a persistent advocate for a systems approach that supported a set of integrated programs. He was frequently called upon as an expert witness or to serve as a member of professional advisory boards. Roger consulted with publishers to shape the literature and worked with businesses, community agencies, and educational institutions, including state departments of education, public and private schools, and numerous universities, to shape a comprehensive response to the enduring problem of preparing the next generation of Americans for meaningful participation in the workforce. He truly believed that the skills acquired by counselors could be valuable outside the confines of the counseling session and the counselor–client relationship. Roger's vision was that of a system of counseling that encompassed the various perspectives and roles of the practice from developmental educator to self-reflective practitioner to collaborative consultant.

In an interview (Briddick, 1997) shortly before his death, Roger was still advocating for reform in counselor education and practice:

> I think the profession needs to continue to explore and search for a system that can tie together and integrate the diverse elements within our profession. We're far from arriving at that, and I must say I think in years gone by that was much more of a desirable goal for the leading figures of our profession than it is today. We've got a lot of people pursuing self-interest groups, which is fine and dandy, but somehow, someone has got to think of a way to tie together the entire profession and what we're all about. (p. 15)

The challenge Roger set for all counselors was also the challenge he set for himself, that is, the task of "giving away" his own knowledge and skills. He taught others to publish (i.e., the politics of journals, the nuts and bolts of writing, etc.). He also introduced them to the "powerful" people and ideas shaping the profession and he took an active interest in their careers, opening doors as yet unseen with an invisible hand that made things happen as if they had actually earned these things by their own diligence. In so many ways he made others feel important and yet never tolerated those moments when they might think that they actually were, and he would caution, "We're none of us that important that we can't be replaced by someone who can do it better."

Roger's life was one made up of complex conversation. Conversations and exchanges that Roger and I (Chris Briddick) had ranged through topics from union labor to the advancement of high technology. We talked about the integration of developmental theory into counseling practice as well as where the best places were to camp and fish near my home in southern Illinois. During our last meeting in late 1996, I asked him to fill in the gaps with regard to the counseling profession and what had happened in the twenty years since his historic article. After two hours, I left with two completed cassette tapes, a head full of ideas, and a stack of reading materials Roger thought would be of interest to me.

Roger delighted in even the simplest discoveries. "Have you heard Willie's latest song?" he'd ask. (Only Roger could make a lesson on developmental theory from a Beth Nielsen Chapman lyric about "going through the stages; going through the changes)."[1] Always the teacher, Roger would shoot pool (in which he took greater pride than in any article he ever wrote) and discuss whether Lawrence Kohlberg's theory supports a seventh stage, argue the case that Emmylou Harris has the "sweetest voice in country music," and rave about his latest discovery in frozen, microwaveable foods ("Wait 'til you see these great little sausage biscuits I found!").

Hospitalized for liver disease in 1996 and again in 1997, Roger made some necessary adjustments. "I think I stayed a little too long at the party," he explained. But the recovery was to be temporary; the damage to his health was too great. Enduring months of heroic medical efforts to "restore" his health, Roger died at home in Nashville on June 20, 1997.

## FINAL REFLECTIONS

Roger Aubrey left this world a richer place for having been here. His writings continue to inspire new generations of counselors, and his vision for the profession remains a beacon by which to steer a course to a better world. In today's parlance, he was an empowering and visionary leader who could see beyond the ordinary in articulating a clear and inspiring vision and encourage attainment of the extraordinary. Roger had a unique way of being able to break his vision down into activities and pursuits that seemed within our reach. Although his writings and teaching advanced his vision, Roger also realized the importance of working behind the scenes. He was adept at identifying the leader in others and then encouraging the realization of others' leadership through a set of ennobling tasks that made even small successes worth the effort.

Roger was not afraid to challenge those around him, whether through an exchange of ideas or by handing them something thought provoking he

---

[1] Song lyrics from "Nothing I Can Do About It Now," Words and Music by Beth Nielsen Chapman © 1989 WB Music Corporation and Macy Place Music, All Rights Administered by WB Music Corporation. Lyrics Reprinted by Permission of Warner Brothers Publications, All Rights Reserved.

had just read. Roger's interactions with us were driven by an unselfish, humanistic philosophy of helping others. He was widely read and he continually scanned the horizons of literature and looked back at the roads the profession had traveled, evaluating the significance of our profession's progress toward an altruistic destination. He sought out the writings of great thinkers and visionaries outside the field of counseling for parallel reference and intellectual contrast. Unlike others who might waver, Roger's vision remained largely intact through his last commentary on the profession shortly before his death. Within that broad and encompassing vision, however, was the hope that one idea or notion would propel the profession forward in its "search for a system."

Roger surrounded himself with very bright, energetic, and caring people and maintained an honest interest in their lives and a deep appreciation for their work. He was perhaps too humble to consider himself a facilitator or networker for leaders and emerging leaders, but nonetheless he brought together established professionals and talented rising professionals in an effort to gently nurture the next generation of the profession. He could move beyond asking the hard questions to the harder work of remaining faithful to the vision, negotiating new relationships, and letting everyone share in the success. Although aspects of his vision never reached fruition, Roger's tireless hope remains as perhaps his greatest gift to us.

Described as "prolific" by some and as a "visionary" by others, Roger was above all remarkably human, a decent man. His bigger-than-life presence in the field of counseling was balanced by a rather simple philosophy of life: Love your family, love your friends, and love your work. His kind, gentle questions to a profession in search of itself still echo with resounding clarity today. He supported us, he challenged us, he frustrated us, and he loved us. But if his life has taught us anything, it is how to make a difference in the lives of others. "I will always be with you," wrote his favorite songwriter Willie Nelson, "for I am the forest and you are the trees."[2] Because we have all been his student at some time, Roger will continue to teach us for the rest of our lives. Let us thank him for that. We still have so much to learn.

[2]Song Lyrics from "I Am the Forest," Words and Music by Willie Nelson ©1983 Full Nelson Music, Inc/EMI Longitude Music, Lyrics Reprinted by Permission of EMI Longitude Music, All Rights Controlled and Administered by EMI Longitude Music.

## ACKNOWLEDGMENTS

The authors would like to thank several key individuals who helped make our contribution possible. Roger's sister, Joni Kahn of San Diego, California, his son David Aubrey of Statesboro, Georgia; Sherrie Lane and Richard Percy of Naples, Florida; and Chris Kehas of Manchester, New Hampshire all lent their resourcefulness to our efforts. Finally, a special thank you to Willie Nelson, who e-mailed us from his bus on the road somewhere out there to provide a much-needed reference for one of his lyrics.

## REFERENCES

Aubrey, R. F. (1975). *An examination of selected constraints on the practice of school guidance and counseling.* Unpublished doctoral dissertation, Boston University.

Aubrey, R. F. (1977). Historical development of guidance and counseling and implications for the future. *Personnel and Guidance Journal, 55,* 288–295.

Briddick, W. C. (1997). Twenty years since and beyond: An interview with Roger Aubrey. *Journal of Counseling & Development, 76* (1), 10–15.

Dewey, J. (1980). *Theory of the moral life: "Part II of Dewey and Tufts' Ethics from the revised edition of 1932."* New York: Irvington Publishers. (Original work published 1908)

Fuller, R. B. (1969). *Operating manual for spaceship earth.* New York: Harper.

Hersh, R. H., Paolitto, D. P., & Reimer, J. (1979). *Promoting moral growth: From Piaget to Kohlberg.* New York: Longman.

Lewis, J. A., Hayes, B. A., & Bradley, L. J. (Eds.). (1992). *Counseling women, over the life span.* Denver, Colorado: Love Publishing Company.

Mosher, R. L., & Sprinthall, N. (1970). Psychological education: A means to promote personal development during adolescence. *American Psychologist, 25,* 911–924.

Sheeley, V. L. (1977). *Presidential Review: ACES leaders create ties, 1940–1977* [Brochure]. Washington, DC: Association for Counselor Education and Supervision.

# CHAPTER 9

# Loretta Bradley

Gerald Parr, Judith A. Lewis, and Aretha Marbley

*Advocacy: A voice for counselors, clients, and communities*

Loretta grew up in Ashland, Kentucky, a town with a population of about 50,000. Hers was a typical family of that era in that her father worked outside the home and her mother was a homemaker. In childhood, she had several role models in her mother, grandmother, and aunt, each of whom valued independence. A family norm was encouragement to be the best one could be in whatever one chose to do. Loretta's father, although not always as vocal as her mother, supported her ideas and encouraged her achievements. Loretta never heard the phrase, "Don't try this, for it may be too difficult." Instead, she was led to believe that with determination and hard work, almost anything could be accomplished. Loretta's husband, Charles Bradley, was a neighbor and classmate during Loretta's youth. They now have two children, a first-born son who is in his third year of medical residency in surgery and a second son who has an MBA degree and is in investment banking.

Throughout junior and senior high school, Loretta was active in both academic and social activities. She received several awards and was elected to several positions of leadership. Her years in junior and senior high could be characterized as being pretty "normal." Loretta attended the

University of Kentucky, where she majored in biology and minored in English and psychology as an undergraduate. She graduated with a Bachelor of Science degree and received teacher certification in the biological sciences. In college, she served on several committees where she assumed leadership roles. Loretta graduated from the University of Kentucky with a Master of Arts degree, majoring in Counseling and Guidance with minors in Psychology and Rehabilitation Counseling. She attended Purdue University and studied under Bruce Shertzer for her Doctor of Philosophy degree. Her dissertation focused on the personality correlates of effective and ineffective counselors. In graduate school, her major professor, Bruce Shertzer, encouraged her to join professional organizations, and she joined three: the Association for Counselor Education and Supervision (ACES), the American Counseling Association (ACA), and the National Career Development Association (NCDA). On campus, she spent a lot of her time as an organizer. She remembers that she and several other graduate women organized some activities focused on women's issues. While at Purdue, one of her friends nominated her for president of the West Indiana Personnel and Guidance Association. At that point, running for a leadership position was the furthest thing from her mind, but she agreed to run. Even she was surprised when she won! This milestone marked the beginning of Loretta's leadership in professional organizations. The following year, she was elected treasurer of the Indiana Personnel and Guidance Association (IPGA), and the next year she was elected vice president of IPGA. She was later nominated for president of IPGA, but she moved to another state and therefore withdrew her name from the ballot.

## CAREER PATH

Loretta taught high school biology in Lexington, Kentucky, followed by a joint appointment as a teacher and a counselor for 1 year in Wichita, Kansas. She was a full-time counselor for 2 years in Winchester, Kentucky.

Loretta has held several positions in higher education. She was director of Student Services at Purdue University for five years, a position that she began while completing her doctoral studies at Purdue. She was a lecturer at Indiana University, Villanova University, and Cambridge University. She served as an assistant dean at Temple University for one year. She was an associate professor in the Department of Human Resources/Counseling at Vanderbilt University for 9 years. Since 1987, Loretta has been at Texas Tech University, where she holds the rank of full professor. She has been coordinator of the Counselor Education Program and chairperson of the Division of Educational Psychology and Leadership.

Loretta was president of ACA from 1998 to 1999 and president of ACES from 1995 to 1996. She is currently the treasurer of ACA. Her work with ACA has also included serving as chairperson of the Executive Committee, chairperson of the Financial Affairs Committee, member of the Governing Council, chairperson of the Nominations and Elections Committee, co-chairperson of the Professional Practice Network, member of the Strategic Planning Committee, member of the Bylaws Committee, member of the Insurance Trust Board, and member of the Budget and Financial Affairs Committee.

Loretta has received many awards. They include being invited as a participant to several important conferences: the White House Mental Health Conference (chaired by Tipper Gore), Secretary of Education Riley's Press Conference on School Violence, and the Salzburg Institute Conference on Aging in a Global Society. At Texas Tech University, Loretta has received the President's Excellence in Teaching Award and was a nominee for the Barney E. Rushing Jr. Research Award, the Leadership Texas Award, and the Presidential Achievement Award. While at Vanderbilt, she received the Peabody Innovative Teaching Grant for innovative ideas in teaching. She has received many awards from ACA. These include the ACES Publication Award for a book on supervision, the ACA Research Award, a Southern ACES Research Award, and an ACA Foundation Grant Award.

Loretta has been a prolific scholar, authoring or coauthoring over 60 refereed articles, books, or book chapters. The focus of her work spans the areas of supervision, multicultural aspects of counseling, advocacy, and integrative counseling interventions. Many of her publications have been coauthored with doctoral students, including Aretha Marbley, who addresses her role as a mentor to junior faculty later in this chapter. The following sections provide the reflections of three colleagues who have worked closely with Loretta over the years.

## REFLECTIONS OF A CURRENT COLLEAGUE

My (Jerry Parr) first impression upon meeting Loretta some 13 years ago was that she was a polished and experienced counselor educator. Initially, I wondered if it would not be a painful adjustment for her to leave the lush, wooded landscape of the Southeast for the somewhat flat, desolate plains of West Texas. Surprisingly, though Loretta occasionally mentioned sadness over leaving friends, colleagues, and family (especially her mother) behind by moving to West Texas, I never heard Loretta complain about Lubbock. Likewise, she did not seek to denigrate our regional university as inferior to her previous affiliation with a top-tiered university. Thus, over time, I came to appreciate Loretta as someone who is adaptive and positive.

Within a few short years, our Program and the College called upon Loretta to fill leadership positions. She served as coordinator of the Counselor Education Program for 6 years. Her greatest challenge was responding to the Texas State Coordinating Board of Higher Education's decision to place our Program under review. With our Program's fate in jeopardy, Loretta led a charge to defend the viability and value of our doctoral program. She wrote a comprehensive report for the Board, oversaw a site visit by an external reviewer, and negotiated a favorable outcome for us. I learned to value another dimension of her leadership: tenacity and determination.

Loretta's next appointment was as chairperson of the Educational Psychology and Leadership Division in our College. In short, she was my immediate supervisor, the person who wrote my annual report and decided my merit raises. What stands out to me from this relationship is her ability to nurture, support, and encourage a person's best efforts and intentions. Thus, I see her leadership as anchored in humanness.

Our roles changed as Loretta stepped down from the chairperson's position to serve as ACA president, and I became her immediate supervisor. On her last annual report, I noted that she is the quintessential professor, excelling in scholarship, service to the profession, excellent teaching, and conscientious citizenship to the College and University. I suspect we will be exchanging roles again in the near future, and I will again find inspiration from her leadership as my supervisor.

## REFLECTIONS OF A LONG-TIME COLLEAGUE

When Loretta Bradley served as president of ACA, her presidential theme was "Advocacy: A Voice for Our Clients and Communities." I (Judy Lewis) was very happy that Loretta gave me the opportunity to work with her on implementing that theme by generating theme papers and conference programs related to advocacy. Many people have told me how deeply they appreciated Loretta's support for the counselor's advocacy role. The fact that she championed this cause in such a public and effective way has had a major effect on our profession.

Many ACA members have voiced their respect for Loretta's work on advocacy, but only those who know her well realize that advocacy is not just her professional interest, it is an integral part of her life! Loretta and I have been close friends and collaborators for 20 years. We first worked together as colleagues in the same counselor education department. She probably isn't aware of the first time I really noticed her as a formidable person, a "woman of substance," someone I wanted as a friend. A student in our program had been mistreated by a person in one of the offices of the university (I think it was financial aid). I couldn't help but overhear Loretta's conversation with that financial aid officer. Needless to say, the problem was quickly resolved in the student's favor. Wow! I was bowled over! I had known that Loretta was a good researcher and a talented professor, but I hadn't observed until that time the power of her ability to advocate on behalf of vulnerable people. Over the years, I have seen her go to bat for individuals, particularly students, again and again. She is both fearless and effective, not on her own behalf but on behalf of others. She is the very model of a counselor/advocate.

When I was elected president of ACA, my first act was to ask Loretta to serve as treasurer. This was another situation in which Loretta's combination of attributes made her unique. I knew that Loretta's knowledge of financial affairs alone would make her a great treasurer. Her personal attributes, however, were even more important to me. The ideal association treasurer is ethical, trustworthy, and willing to stand up for what's right. And that's Loretta in a nutshell.

I've always been proud to be Loretta's friend and I've followed in her footsteps several times. She was ACES president; then, a year or two later, I became a division president. She was ACA president and I followed her 2 years later. Her son got married; my son got married. (She's a grandmother now, so I guess my son will be giving me some news pretty soon.) I've learned a great deal from her. The behaviors she models so well have had great impact on how I carry on in my roles. I think I'm just one of many who can say this about Loretta Bradley.

## REFLECTIONS OF A MENTORED COLLEAGUE

My (Aretha Marbley) mentorship with Loretta began in 1995 when I took a doctoral-level course in supervision. Her supervision textbook, *Counselor Supervision: Principles, Process, and Practice* (1989), was the assigned textbook for that course. Although the book at that time was dated, the instructor commented that it "was the best out there." (I might note that following her ACA presidency, a new edition of the book was published.) In the spring of 1997, I gained respect for and knowledge of this great woman after reading her ACA Presidential Candidate Biography. I was most impressed with her high integrity, sense of fairness, grassroots approach to leadership, and commitment to advocacy, inclusiveness, and diversity. As an ACA member, I felt very proud to cast my vote for Loretta J. Bradley.

As fate would have it, in January 1997 our mentoring relationship was formalized. We met in person for the first time at the National Holmes Partnership Meeting in St. Louis, Missouri, and she became the active force in recruiting me to Texas Tech University. I arrived at Tech in the fall of 1997, and that was the semester that Loretta and another senior faculty decided to pilot a mentorship program at our university.

During the following year, at the 1998 ACA National Convention in Indiana (the year Loretta was ACA president-elect), I was pleased to overhear many ACA members from several of the divisions discussing their hope, excitement, and confidence in Loretta Bradley as president. I was also pleased that so many people knew her and had such confidence in her ability to restore ACA to financial solvency and unite all of its divisions stronger than ever. I believe her to be "the best out there." The legacy of her presidency proved that my confidence and hope in her were not misplaced. Loretta contributed greatly to the success of my third-year tenure-track faculty review. As an African-American female, I appreciated Loretta providing me with professional contacts and resources and encouraging me to become more actively involved in our professional organization. More concretely, Loretta took the initiative in organizing, coleading, and involving me in our College of Education Mentorship program. I feel honored and proud to call her my mentor and my friend; after all, "she is one of the best out there!"

## REFERENCES

Bradley, L. (1989). *Counselor supervision: Principles, process and practice*. New York: Taylor & Francis.

# CHAPTER 10

# David Kendrick Brooks, Jr.

Earl J. Ginter

*"To work arduously, to love deeply, and to live fully."*[1]

David K. Brooks, Jr., was born on March 20, 1944 in Jackson, Mississippi, to David and Maggie during a period of great turmoil in the United States as well as throughout much of a world embroiled in war. In contrast to the conflicted outer world of the late 1940s and early 1950s, David's own familial world, which included a sister, Beverly, was characterized as supportive and nurturing. David remembered his father and mother as parents who "encouraged me in everything I have undertaken. From them I learned to believe in myself because they believed in me" (Brooks, 1984, p. ix).

---

[1]Bette Brooks provided the slogan appearing at the beginning of this chapter. When requested by the author to provide a personal slogan that captured how David would have wanted to be remembered, Bette sent an e-mail on July 26, 2001 that stated, "I do not know when I have been handed so simple yet difficult an assignment! After talking with several people, I keep coming back to a phrase from the foreword of a book about gifted girls—the phrase epitomizes David, his life, and his work—the essence of who he was." The phrase was taken from Kerr, B. A. (1994). *Smart girls two: A new psychology of girls, women and giftedness*. Dayton, OH: Ohio Psychology Press. (Quote located on page xvii.)

This belief in David's ability to accomplish meaningful goals was not a distorted parental perspective; David and Maggie's belief reflected an accurate assessment that was later mirrored in the opinions held by many professionals concerning David's leadership ability.

The typical reaction to meeting David for the first time was that one had encountered a consummate professional who possessed an eloquent command of the spoken word, a quick wit, an extensive knowledge of professional issues, an achievement-oriented drive, and most importantly, a person who advocated for counseling. To be a leader in one's profession requires that others *believe* in your ability to direct, guide, and command attention. David's leadership qualities made it easy to believe in him.

Simply stated, David was a natural leader whose leadership efforts directly contributed to the development of counseling's current status. Inclusion of David in this text, as one of only 23 examples of leadership in the counseling profession, reflects highly on David's accomplishments, especially in light of his truncated career due to an early death in June 1997, a span of only 13 years after earning his Ph.D.

At the time of David's death he had been married to Elizabeth (Bette) Walston Brooks for 26 years and they had four daughters: Laurel Elizabeth, Caroline Rebecca, Amanda Dell, and Beverly Elaine. Today, Bette serves as director of the Office of Professional Development and Partnerships at Kent State University's College of Education. She is currently working on her dissertation in curriculum and instruction that pertains to "teaching as a calling." Laurel and Caroline have graduated with honors from Wellesley College and from The University of the South, respectively. Amanda and Beverly are members of the class of 2004 at Roosevelt High School in Kent, Ohio.

One reason David was an exceptional leader was that he had a profound understanding of the difference a counselor could make in a child's life. While teaching social studies at Goldsboro High School in North Carolina, David decided to pursue an M.A.Ed. degree in counseling at East Carolina University in Greenville, North Carolina, under the direction of Frank G. Fuller. Graduation was followed by 6 years of "testing" in the Greensboro public school system what he had learned in his master's degree program. During this period David's interests expanded to areas of counseling beyond his program of study and school setting. Entering The University of Georgia in 1978, David was to spend the next 6 years actively involved in both completing the doctoral requirements and building upon various professional activities and commitments he started before arriving in Georgia. By 1984 David had earned his Ph.D. degree in Counseling and Student Personnel Services, and he had worked on a number of important professional projects with many of the current and future leaders of the counseling profession—individuals such as Don C. Locke, Bill Weikel, Rick Wilmarth, Steven Ender, Lawrence Gerstein, John Dagley, Roger Winston, Jerold Bozarth, and George M. Gazda. David wrote about the influence these individuals had on his personal and professional development (Brooks, 1984), but it is important to recognize that the influence referred to by David was actually a mutual influence. One could not encounter David without being positively affected.

## APPOINTMENTS, PROFESSIONAL DEVELOPMENT, AND MAJOR ACCOMPLISHMENTS

Starting in 1971, David's career path entailed working as a school counselor at Dudley Senior High School in Greensboro, North Carolina; an associate program specialist in the Office of Adult Counseling at The University of Georgia; an assistant professor of counselor education at Syracuse University; and an associate professor of Counseling and Human Development Services and coordinator of the master's degree programs in school counseling and community counseling at Kent State University. David's devotion to graduate teaching was complemented by his leadership efforts via service on university committees and professional counseling organizations. David served on numerous university committees at the program, departmental, college, and university level. Of particular note was David's interest in serving on committees that were studying the potential use of computers and related technologies in instructional settings. Unlike some counselor educators who were uncomfortable with what they perceived as the needless encroachment of computers into counseling, David saw computer technology not as an obstacle but as an opportunity to open new vistas in counselor education. In addition to these committee involvements, David was devoted to working with doctoral students, especially in relation to internships and mentoring. By the time of David's death, he had taught 25 different graduate courses, the content of which spanned the full range of concerns found in school counseling, community counseling, and counseling in general.

Beyond the boundaries of David's own university environment, many professionals across the nation best remember David for his unfailing commitment to professional organizations and his advocacy concerning the role counseling should play in the mental health arena. He played a significant leadership role in 13 of the 18 professional organizations to which he belonged. David served as either a member or chairperson of many committees that focused on an array of issues such as licensure, public policy and legislation, third-party reimbursements, bylaws, governance restructuring, convention programs, nominations and elections, human resources, health counseling, supervision, professional recognition, testing, professional standards and ethics, and the role and function of the counselor. He also served as an evaluator of professional enhancement grants for the Counseling and Human Development Foundation (CHDF), and he filled many leadership positions (i.e., secretary-treasurer, executive committee, board of directors, and standards revision committee) for the Council for Accreditation of Counseling and Related Educational Programs (CACREP).

David's unique set of leadership skills was recognized by members of various organizations on several occasions when the membership elected David to serve as a president of the organization. David was president of the North Carolina Counseling Association (1976–1977), the Ohio Association for Counselor Education and Supervision (1994–1995), the North Central Association for Counselor Education and Supervision (1996–1997), and the American Mental Health Counselors Association (1986–1987). In addition to the role of president, he filled many other types of leadership roles in professional counseling associations. For example, he served on the Governing Council for the American Counseling Association (ACA), as Secretary and then Treasurer of the American Mental Health Counselors Association (AMHCA), and on the Executive Council for the Association for Counselor Education and Supervision (ACES). These are just a few of the "leadership labels" that can be applied to David. Finally, David's leadership ability was not only manifested at the university and professional organization level; it also spilled over into his scholarship.

While David was devoting enormous amounts of time and energy to teaching and professional service, he was still able to find time and energy to author or coauthor 11 articles for refereed journals, 2 books, 9 chapters in edited books, and 5 reports/training manuals. He also made over 100 presentations at national, regional, state, or local professional conferences. A complete sense of the true significance of David's body of scholarship can only be obtained by reading his writings in full. In doing so, it becomes abundantly clear that frequently the various leadership roles he held served as the impetus for a particular work. A publication that exemplifies the melding of leadership efforts and the actual written content of a work is an article David coauthored with Lawrence (Larry) H. Gerstein and published in the *Journal of Counseling & Development* in 1990, titled "Counselor Credentialing and Interprofessional Collaboration."

David's leadership contributions were formally honored at different points in his prolific but relatively brief professional career. He was the recipient of the Ohio Mental Health Counselors Association Researcher of the Year Award (1991–1992), AMHCA Opportunity Award (1992), nine separate AMHCA Professional Service Awards (starting in 1983), and the ACA Carl D. Perkins Government Relations Award (1989). Bette Brooks succinctly summarized David's leadership-driven contributions when she communicated (B. Brooks, personal communication, March 30, 2001) the following:

> By the time of David's death in June 1997, the impact of his work in credentialing within the field of mental health counseling could not be overestimated. Forty-one states and the District of Columbia had passed counselor licensure laws as a direct result of his leadership of the APGA [American Personnel and Guidance Association] (and later ACA) Licensure Committee. This record is remarkable; the first of these statutes was not enacted until 1976. In addition, third-party reimbursements were secured under CHAMPUS [Civilian Health and Medical Program of the Uniformed Services].
>
> David continued to research, write, and speak on the history of mental health counseling and the importance of credentialing. A developing area of interest was that of professional identity of counselors and how this moved beyond concerns of role and function. Counselor education remained a major focus of his professional activity; he remained on faculty at Kent State until his death. An interactive CD-ROM for use with his own master's-level classes was in progress.

Finally, Bette's comments indirectly reveal something about David's style of leadership. While David had the ability to clearly see that counseling's future resided in obtaining licensure, so did many others at the time. What made David unique was that he possessed talents that enabled him to lead through action: He made ideas work. Important ideas such as counselor licensure must be rooted in reality. As a leader David was able to bring ideas to fruition. He forged ideas much as an ironsmith will hammer on metal until it takes on a resilient shape. If David believed in something, he was able to discuss and argue about a needed change in such a convincing manner that even when his audience initially harbored divergent opinions he could still build bridges that allowed positive movement on a vital counseling issue. It is important to note that even though David's power to

persuade was fueled by strong beliefs about counseling's future, these beliefs were tempered with a caring attitude. In my eyes, the essence of
David's leadership style was that he was a master of networking and a
diplomat at the same time. Licensed counselors of today owe David a genuine debt of gratitude.

## PERSONAL POSTSCRIPT: DAVID'S IMPACT ON MY LIFE

I met David when I entered The University of Georgia as a doctoral student. Although we frequently talked about the important issues of the day
(e.g., licensure, third-party payments, credentialing), the discussions
tended to be of an impromptu nature and tended to occur at George
Gazda's home, where George's doctoral students met to discuss research,
dissertation topics, and other related concerns. It was after I left Georgia
that David's professional efforts had their strongest effect on my own professional work.

My early research efforts revolved around the study of performance
anxiety and loneliness, but when I returned to The University of Georgia in
1985 to assume an assistant professor position, my attention turned to the
study of and application of life-skills theory. The theoretical foundation on
which I built a line of research has been established through the collaborative efforts of David Brooks and George Gazda. Specifically, I further contributed to life-skills theory by adding to what David had uncovered via his
dissertation. David's dissertation required an atypical amount of effort and
level of persistence. David himself recognized the atypical nature of his
dissertation:

> This project has taken nearly two and one-half years. That I undertook it in
> the first place and that I completed it are nearly unrelated to each other be-
> cause these acts are so far apart in time. [After crediting George Gazda for
> bringing the project to fruition, David added the following:] Roger Winston,
> who did double duty as statistical consultant and reading committee chair,
> tried to warn me that I was biting off more than I imagined. Having failed to
> dissuade me, he helped me to keep things in perspective and to understand
> what was happening at various stages of the process. (Brooks, 1984, p. v)

Despite the difficulties David encountered, he made a major contribution to counseling theory that had important implications for future research and practice. I have discussed the details of David's work elsewhere
(i.e., Ginter, 1999). Briefly stated, however, David used a modified three-
round Delphi survey approach to distill from the body of existing develop-

mental literature a developmentally based life-skills taxonomy. David isolated 305 descriptors that could be arranged into four life-skills categories (i.e., Problem-Solving/Decision-Making Skills, Interpersonal Communication/Human Relations Skills, Physical Fitness/Health Maintenance Skills, and Identity Development/Purpose-in-Life Skills). These four categories allowed for a comprehensive counseling approach that theoretically linked interventions to the developmental issues and tasks confronting a person at any point along the age continuum.

David's findings have contributed to enhancing counseling's base of theory, which in turn has better equipped practitioners to help clients "achieve optimal functioning at the respective developmental stages" and to help clients foster "healthy development throughout the lifespan" (Brooks, 1984, dissertation abstract). Subsequent to David's landmark research, I have worked closely with George Gazda and a number of doctoral students and faculty members in Georgia (e.g., Paula Bickham, Georgia Calhoun, Cindy Darden, Brian Glaser, Ann Glauser, Tara Kadish, and Billie Picklesimer) to move David's findings to the next level, the level of life-skills assessment. As a result of these collaborative efforts, several assessment tools have been created that are at various stages of psychometric development. Assessments have been developed for different ages and groups: child, adolescent, adult, college, and adjudicated juvenile delinquent. In addition to measuring life skills, Ann Glauser and I have developed a life-skills curriculum based on Brooks and Gazda's work. This curriculum has led to a textbook (Ginter & Glauser, 2000), *Life-Skills for the University and Beyond*, which is used in a credit-bearing course offered at The University of Georgia. Approximately 600 students each year select to enroll in the classes that use this particular curriculum.

David's early work in the life-skills area has significantly influenced my understanding of what constitutes a developmental approach to counseling and, as a result, has spurred my own research efforts and application of developmental theory to clients I see in private practice and to students I teach at The University of Georgia. A true leader fulfills the role of a catalyst who guides and directs us toward a meaningful direction of purpose. David Kendrick Brooks, Jr., was a true leader.

## REFERENCES

Brooks, D. K., Jr. (1984). *A life-skills taxonomy: Defining elements of effective functioning through the use of the Delphi technique.* Unpublished doctoral dissertation, The University of Georgia, Athens, GA.

Brooks, D. K. Jr., & Gerstein, L. H. (1990). Counselor credentialing and interprofessional collaboration. *Journal of Counseling & Development, 68,* 477–484.

Ginter, E. J. (1999). David K. Brooks' contribution to the developmentally based life-skills approach. *The Journal of Mental Health Counseling, 21,* 191–202. [On page i of this issue it is noted, "This Twentieth Anniversary Issue is dedicated to the Memory of David K. Brooks."]

Ginter, E. J., & Glauser, A. S. (2000). *Life-skills for the university and beyond* (2nd ed.). Dubuque, IA: Kendall/Hunt.

# CHAPTER 11

# Mary Thomas Burke

Sylvia Nassar-McMillan

*Our inward journey is a compass for how well we can
help others do the same.*

Mary Thomas Burke was born and raised in Ireland. As a teenager, she came to the United States, where she began her training as a Sister of Mercy and her college education. She earned her Bachelor of Arts degree in social science from Belmont Abbey College in 1958. She studied mathematics at John Carroll University in preparation for high school teaching. She went on to earn her Master of Arts degree in history from Georgetown University in 1965. She earned her Doctor of Philosophy degree in counseling from the University of North Carolina at Chapel Hill in 1968.

She came from a close-knit family and has four brothers with whom she still enjoys close relationships. One still resides in Ireland, one in London, England, one in the northeastern United States, and the fourth, near her in the Greater Charlotte, North Carolina, area. Her extended family includes innumerable Sisters of Mercy, with whom she resides at the Sacred Heart Convent in Belmont, North Carolina.

When recounting childhood memories, Mary Thomas Burke speaks fondly of the influences both her mother and father provided. Her father believed that an earned education was a lifetime asset. He viewed such education as an "outline" to be filled in later in life. Her mother provided many hours tutoring in all subjects. In addition to supporting academic endeavors, she provided a role model for reaching out to those in need. That teaching was reinforced within the Irish school system, which was predominantly run by Catholic sisters. It was through that upbringing that she made the decision to become a Sister herself, because she wanted her life to count for something. Being strong willed throughout her life, Mary Thomas considers herself to have been influenced more by the church than by any specific individual.

Mary Thomas believes that spirituality is manifested by the essence of another person's being and in her own duty in helping that other person become whole. Her vows to the church include poverty, chastity, obedience, and service to the poor, sick, underserved, or uneducated. Throughout her 50 years as a Sister, she has implemented those vows in countless ways. She has worked with many diverse populations and has been drawn particularly to the elderly and the very young, because of their genuineness and spontaneity.

In her early career, as she trained to become a Sister of Mercy and attended college part-time, Mary Thomas began her professional life as a teacher. From 1952 through 1958, she served as an instructor at various elementary and junior high schools, both in North Carolina and New York. As previously mentioned, she earned her Bachelor of Arts degree from Belmont Abbey College in 1958, and went on to study mathematics at John Carroll University in preparation for high school teaching. She subsequently taught high school at two Catholic schools in Charlotte, North Carolina, from 1958 through 1960, and in 1960 became a Guidance Counselor and Director of Guidance at Our Lady of Mercy and Charlotte Catholic High School. In addition to teaching math, history, and French, she also taught typing, gave piano lessons, and advised student groups such as the student government, the cheerleaders, and the math club.

A series of turning points in her career began when Mary Thomas was asked to continue her education by pursuing a doctoral degree from Georgetown University in order to become an Academic Dean and history teacher at Sacred Heart College in Belmont, North Carolina. Although she loved her graduate work in history, she was then asked to change plans and continue her Ph.D. degree in counseling, so that she would be better trained to work with people. After completing the master's degree in history at Georgetown University in 1965, she began her counselor training at the University of North Carolina at Chapel Hill, completing her doctoral degree in 1968. Loving her new curriculum, she was well trained for her new professional responsibilities. After three years as Academic Dean at Sacred Heart, she resigned from her position and, fortuitously, was asked by the vice chancellor of the University of North Carolina (UNC) at Charlotte, Hugh McEniry, to initiate a graduate program in counseling. In 1970, while still living at the convent and continuing to wear her black habit, Mary Thomas Burke became the coordinator of the Counseling Program at UNC Charlotte.

## COMMUNITY SERVANT

At about the time she began her teaching career at UNC Charlotte, she also began a relationship with a group of B'Nai B'rith women as well as with the Junior League in the Charlotte community, and conducting professional and personal development seminars. Although not considering herself a feminist, Mary Thomas often sought opportunities to provide such groups of women with personal development programs, as well as encouragement for pursuing continuing education. Even as early as her math teaching and tutoring experiences, she recognized that girls and women often are not encouraged to meet their potential in certain areas. Partly because of the encouragement from her own family as a child, and partly due to her personal and professional successes, she had a strong faith in herself and believed that she could accomplish her goals. She sought to instill this same self-confidence in others.

Another influence from her early life, reinforced by her religious training, was to seek out those in need. Mary Thomas's role in the community was often to professionalize service to the underserved. When she saw a need for services to individuals with cancer or AIDS, or those who were homeless, battered, or drug addicted, she would begin to establish grassroots efforts for services and programs, while concurrently combating community stereotypes and prejudices. Once those were sufficiently in place, she would move on to addressing another need. For example, in the early 1970s, when drugs were becoming an issue in Charlotte, no one was providing volunteer counseling. In response to the need for services, she trained volunteers in substance abuse counseling, starting out in the basement of a local YMCA. Subsequently, she helped establish the effort as an independent entity and facility known as "Open House." Mary Thomas has the knack for getting her counseling students involved, and so includes them as interns, grant writers, and other meaningful contributors. After supporting the establishment of Open House, she proceeded to develop a shelter program for runaway youth, later named "The Relatives." As an example of her mentoring abilities, it was a grant written by a student that led to the initial funding for the shelter.

Mary Thomas Burke has been honored by numerous community groups with prestigious awards for her exemplary commitment to service. Among them are the Francis J. Beatty Humanitarian Award, presented by the Catholic Social Services in 1999, Counselor of the Year Award presented by the American Counseling Association (ACA) in 1998, the Meritorious Service Award presented by the Association of Spiritual, Ethical, and Religious Values in Counseling (ASERVIC) in 1995, and the Humanitarian Award, presented by the National Conference of Christians and Jews in 1994.

## PROFESSIONAL SERVANT

Parallel to her community service, Mary Thomas Burke has served as a leader to the profession of counseling. Her efforts have facilitated tremendous growth and change at local, state, regional, national, and international levels.

At the state level, Mary Thomas has consistently served on the Executive Council for the North Carolina Counseling Association (NCCA) for the past 30 years. She has maintained a strong presence of support for that organization, throughout its sometimes turbulent and troubled history. She has served as president and held divisional presidencies within the NCCA and has served in many other roles when needed. She also has encouraged others to develop their own leadership potential by serving as professional officers. In that capacity, she has mentored countless new professionals and leaders.

Nationally, Mary Thomas has demonstrated an exemplary record of service to the profession. To detail only a few of her service roles, she served as a Board of Directors member on the National Board for Certified Counselors (NBCC) from 1993 through 1996, as chairperson of the Board of Directors of the Council for Accreditation of Counseling and Related Educational Programs (CACREP) from 1996 through 1999, and as president of ASERVIC from 1989 through 1990. Nationally and internationally, Mary Thomas has served as a catalyst for discussions revolving around spiritual issues in counseling within a multicultural context. With her visionary leadership, she has recently spearheaded a successful endeavor to begin a doctoral program in counseling at UNC Charlotte, with a special emphasis on multicultural issues. She also recently cochaired, with Tom Elmore, an international conference for the Association for Counselor Education and Supervision (ACES) on global spiritual issues, held in her own native Ireland.

Mary Thomas's leadership style is shaped by her vision of wholeness for herself and others. In this context, she identifies needs and develops solutions to meet them. She is not above any job and can often be found working "in the trenches," all the while bringing along others with her optimism for life.

Her contributions to the literature have paralleled her other leadership accomplishments. She is one of the main contributors to the area of spirituality in counseling. Most of her publications have emerged in the past 10 years, commonly coauthored with her dear friends and colleagues, Judy Miranti and Jane Chauvin. All have revolved around spiritual issues (e.g., Burke & Miranti, 1992 a, 1992 b, 1996, 2001), including such focused topics as AIDS (e.g., Burke & Miller, 1995, 1996; Miller, Burke, Johnson, & Wilson, 2000), multicultural issues (e.g., Burke, Miranti, & Chauvin, in press), CACREP standards (e.g., Burke, Hackney, Hudson, Miranti, Watts, & Epp, 1999), and social change (e.g., Burke & Miranti, 1998), melding her many works in the teaching and service arenas.

## REFLECTIONS ON WORKING WITH MARY THOMAS

Mary Thomas Burke is truly one of the most inspirational mentors and role models I have ever had. Some of the descriptors that come to mind when I reflect on my observations of her include: visionary, holistic, nurturing of self and others, and humble. My own and others' experiences can be described in the context of these observations. In testing the strength of the lessons learned from this great teacher, I can say that I have only begun to implement a fraction of those qualities I have observed in her and that I aspire to implement in my own personal and professional life.

### Visionary

Her sense of purpose is always clear. Perhaps it is this larger picture that keeps her on track and prevents her from getting caught up in small and insignificant issues. Conversely, the largeness of her vision seems to allow her to live freely in the moment. Case in point: She does not believe in attending to e-mail, "snailmail," or telephone messages more than once; rather, she addresses each one immediately, not allowing them to clutter the bigger picture. When asked about her reflections of Mary Thomas's leadership over the years, one colleague recounted: "The year was 1971, and all nine of the faculty of the college were photographed on the campus that was largely pasture land. Dr. Mary Thomas Burke faced the camera with a smile, a twinkle, and a clear sense of purpose. Thirty years later, with a student population of 18,000, the strong sure hand of Mary Thomas Burke has guided the development of a splendid graduate program in counseling—and has helped UNC Charlotte achieve its dream of becoming a doctoral institution."

## Holistic

Mary Thomas's spirituality is contagious. Her presence is a constant reminder to take in the whole picture. She believes we must always attend to the spirit of others and ourselves, and she takes this in the context of each individual's environment. She has also taught me, through word and action, ways in which to attend to my spirituality within the context of my life. This attention will stand me in good stead for the remainder of my career and life. Several students report her influence on them:

- "Dr. Burke's presence renewed my attention to the spiritual. She inspired me to release my full human potentiality by holistically involving my mind, emotions, body, and spirit. Her positive image of fulfillment coming from service shaped my actions."
- "She opened my eyes to a possibility of G-d. I should mention that I am Jewish and she is a Catholic Nun. She also has given me confidence to work with fundamentalists of various religions and to not let religion take away individual responsibility."
- "She has shown me what being a good leader and counselor are all about. She possesses an amazing spirit, compassion, and optimism that I hope to pass along to others as a counselor and person."

Rather than stopping at facilitating the spirituality of those individuals around her, Mary Thomas has set and achieved the goal of having the profession of counseling consider spirituality, namely through the CACREP standards. She has taught me that although those around us are among the first to whom attention should be given, we must also be attentive to students and professionals throughout the counseling profession.

## Nurturing

The loving care with which Mary Thomas nurtures those around her is perhaps her most endearing human quality. In light of her vast personal and professional responsibilities and commitments, her attention to the individuals around her is striking. She taught me the importance of recognizing the positive qualities among those around me, indeed, *facilitating* such qualities among those around me. Each year, she chairs the nominations committee for the state counseling organization. This committee recognizes contributions to the counseling profession and each year, she works tirelessly to engage professionals across the state in identifying nominees and developing nomination packets to support these individuals. Said one student about Mary Thomas, "From her example I learned how important it is to give a pat on the back to those people you interact with."

She also goes out of her way, despite her busy schedule, to welcome and nurture anyone in need, whether someone new to the community or to a new leadership project. Said one colleague about her, "Mary Thomas was the first person who extended her hand to me in a gesture of friendship when I first arrived at UNC Charlotte; I think she wanted to be sure that I felt welcomed. My impression of UNC Charlotte came from her." Said another colleague who was charged with the task of developing a large-scale curricular project, "She saw to it that I was introduced to the people in Charlotte who could help me when I first started putting it all together. She left the details up to me, and encouraged and supported me at every stage of development." Said a student, "She has supported and encouraged me to take leadership positions that I probably would not have considered otherwise."

## Humble

One final characteristic that must be mentioned is her humility. Despite being so visionary, having accomplished so much, being so busy with important personal and professional responsibilities, she nevertheless takes the time to lovingly nurture those around her. Perhaps that is part of the holism mentioned earlier. One student recounts, "It is easy to forget and often easier to take for granted that every week I sit under the direction of a counselor educator who is recognized world-wide for her countless contributions and lifetime of service devoted to the area of counseling." Mary Thomas can often be seen in the trenches, working side by side with any number of individuals and organizations. Said a long-time dear friend and colleague of Mary Thomas: "My fondest memories of this awe-inspiring individual include her support, caring, and concern for all of us as the College began its journey toward the 21st Century. No task was too great or too small for 'Sister' through these many years."

## CONCLUDING REMARKS

The lessons we can learn from Mary Thomas Burke include collaboration and relationship building. We should attend to our own spiritual dimension, as well as to the spiritual dimensions of those around us, regardless of culture or religion. We must continue to nurture ourselves, and we must also renew the goal of nurturing others. Such collaboration is necessary if we are to achieve, or even mutually set, a goal of "community." Finally, we must remember that we *are* all human, regardless of our perceptions of the greatness or smallness of our own individual contributions.

## REFERENCES

Burke, M. T., Hackney, H., Hudson, P., Miranti, J., Watts, G., & Epp, L. (1999). Spirituality, religion, & CACREP curriculum standard. *Journal of Counseling & Development, 77*(3), 251–257.

Burke, M. T., & Miller, G. (1995). Counseling without illusion: Spiritual elements of counseling with AIDS clients. *Counseling and Values, 40*, 185–192.

Burke, M. T., & Miller, G. (1996). Using the spiritual perspective in counseling persons with HIV/AIDS: An integrative approach. *Counseling and Values, 40*, 185–195.

Burke, M. T., & Miranti, J. G. (Eds.). (1992a). *Ethical and spiritual values in counseling.* Alexandria, VA: American Association for Counseling and Development.

Burke, M. T., & Miranti, J. G. (1992b). Ethics and spirituality: The prevailing forces influencing the counseling profession. In M. T. Burke & J. G. Miranti (Eds.), *Ethics and spiritual values in counseling* (pp. 1–4). Alexandria, VA: American Association for Counseling and Development.

Burke, M. T., & Miranti, J. G. (1996). *Counseling: The spiritual dimension.* Alexandria, VA: American Counseling Association.

Burke, M. T., & Miranti, J. G. (1998). Spirituality as a force for social change. In C. Lee & G. Walz (Eds.), *Social action: A mandate for counselors* (pp. 161–175). Alexandria, VA: American Counseling Association. (ERIC Document Reproduction Service ED417372)

Burke, M. T., & Miranti, J. G. (2001). The spiritual and religious dimensions of counseling. In D. C. Locke, J. E. Myers, & E. L. Herr (Eds.), *The handbook of counseling* (pp. 601–612). Thousand Oaks, CA: Sage.

Burke, M. T., Miranti, J. G., & Chauvin, J. (in press). *Counseling with multicultural populations: A spiritual perspective.* Philadelphia: Taylor & Francis.

Miller, J., Burke, M. T., Johnson, P., & Wilson, T. (2000). A qualitative study of individuals living with HIV/AIDS: Life transformations in dimensions of counseling. *Research, Theory, and Practice, 28*, 4–10.

# CHAPTER 12

# Harold F. Cottingham

J. Melvin Witmer and Robert C. Reardon

*I hold myself responsible for giving counselor trainees the broadest possible opportunities for both personal and professional growth.*

Harold F. Cottingham, the only child of a modest midwestern family, was born in Charleston, Illinois, December 11, 1913. His father was a plumber by trade and his mother a full-time homemaker. Grandparents, cousins, and friends in the community were an integral part of his growing up. His early education was obtained in this college town, where he attended training school, high school, and college, all part of Eastern Illinois Teachers College. His writing interest and talent were nurtured by his mother, who encouraged him to major in journalism. News writing in high school and college and public relations work for a local radio station gave him valuable writing experience.

When interviewed about early influences (Giddan, 1979), Harold described himself as growing up in the kind of family where there was a balance between independent choices and acceptable restrictions. His mother was always supportive and backed some of his early business adventures, such as working in Chicago, selling watermelons, opening up a wholesale grocery with a friend, or taking trips to seek jobs. "My mother always gave me encouragement and yet offered me an implicit model of openness, tolerance, and patience. I guess many of my humanistic values could be due to this type of exposure" (Giddan, 1979, p. 216).

Harold met his wife and lifelong partner, Violet, in college, and they became the parents of two daughters. Violet worked for many years as a librarian at Florida State University (FSU), and the daughters also have had careers in education. Their older daughter, Rebecca C. Montague, is a high school Spanish teacher and the younger daughter, Sarah Cottingham-Page, is a high school guidance counselor. Harold Cottingham died in 1981 at the age of 67, less than one year after his retirement from FSU.

Harold Cottingham was awarded a B.Ed. degree with a major in Social Science in 1935 and an M.A. in Education with a major in Guidance and courses to qualify as a business teacher in 1940. These two degrees from Eastern Illinois Teachers College also included emphases in educational psychology and English. He received an honorary Pd.D. in 1956 from the same school. His Ed.D. degree was earned at Indiana University in 1945 with a major in Guidance, and his dissertation topic was a study of the predictive value of a paper-and-pencil mechanical test in relation to industrial arts achievement. Postdoctoral work in psychology was done at Florida State University and the University of Denver.

Harold's professional career path started with high school teaching and guidance responsibilities between 1936 and 1942. While teaching, he developed guidance programs focusing on career days, college nights, and counseling activities, with the primary emphasis on vocational and educational guidance. During the World War II years, he was an instructor in navy accounting at Indiana University. From 1945 to 1948, he was Director of Guidance and Research in the Moline Public Schools in Moline, Illinois, and he was also a part-time guidance instructor at several colleges in the region.

Harold arrived at Florida State University in 1948 as an associate professor in the Department of Psychology. He began developing a Guidance and Counseling program in the new College of Education, was the chairperson of the program from 1958 to 1968, and retired from FSU in 1980 as professor emeritus. He traveled widely across the United States as a counselor educator, teacher, consultant, and lecturer for almost 40 years. He held permanent and visiting teaching appointments at a dozen schools and colleges. His career development in guidance and counseling services and vocational guidance was greatly influenced by Robert Hoppock and Dan Feder through personal contact. Throughout his career he was motivated by the writings of Carl Rogers, E. G. Williamson, and John Darley (Giddan, 1979).

## LEADERSHIP CONTRIBUTIONS AND STYLE

Harold's leadership contributions through scholarship fall into three areas: (a) the guidance function in education, (b) counselor standards and accountability, and (c) humanistic education and the personal growth of the counselor. He was very skilled at conceptualizing information, organizing it into knowledge, identifying the principles, and describing practices for implementing the concepts. Because writing was second nature to him, he usually wrote and sketched his ideas on paper, which often led to a course handout, a publication, or an insightful comment to a colleague or student.

The first area of Harold's scholarly contributions relates to the guidance function in education. During his career, he was the author or coauthor of four books, numerous chapters, 11 book reviews, and more than 50 journal articles and special publications. His 1956 book on elementary guidance, *Guidance in the Elementary Schools*, was one of many pioneering contributions in the development of this specialty (Cottingham, 1953, 1956, 1966). The book brought together the basic concepts for elementary guidance and the practices for applying them in working with students and teachers. The practices were based upon a national survey of elementary schools that had a guidance program implemented by teachers and counselors. Later, he coauthored a similar book for the junior high level, *Guidance in the Junior High School* (Cottingham & Hopke, 1961).

A second area of scholarly contributions was professional accountability and counselor licensure. Harold was again in the forefront as author or coauthor of one book on counselor accountability (Burck, Cottingham, & Reardon, 1973) and four journal articles on counselor licensure between 1975 and 1978, which marked the beginning of counselor certification and licensure efforts in the country for nonschool personnel. His articles summarized for counselor educators, community mental health counselors, school counselors, and the American Personnel and Guidance Association (APGA) the rationale and implications of licensure (Cottingham, 1975; Cottingham & Swanson, 1976; Cottingham & Warner, 1978). Much of his knowledge came through direct involvement on licensure committees at the state, Southern Association for Counselor Education and Supervision (ACES), and national APGA levels. He was a member of the first APGA Licensure Commission and later chaired this group.

A third area of scholarly writing that extended across Harold's career is the personal growth of the student, counselor, and teacher through individual and group processes. Articles and unpublished papers between 1959 and 1981 emphasized a holistic approach—the whole person concept—for personal development. He referred to this as part of the guidance function in education, psychological education, affective education, and humanistic education (Cottingham, 1962, 1973). Even at the time of his death, Harold was writing a book with the first author with the working title, *Personalizing Learning for Both Sides of the Brain: Pathways to Personal Growth and Mental Health*. This work was later revised by the first author (Witmer, 1985) and published by Accelerated Development. The current emerging fields of wellness counseling and positive psychology might be considered aspects of the humanistic education and development movement between 1955 and 1975. His presidential address at the APGA Convention in 1966, "The Challenge of Authentic Behavior" (Cottingham, 1966), postulated authentic behavior as an important factor in greater understanding of human beings as well as a more effective utilization of one's potential, particularly in interpersonal relationships. He wrote that "the moral obligation of the counseling and guidance profession to set a high standard of personal integrity, as a matter of public image and individual influence, is very great indeed" (p. 335).

The scholarly approach Harold used in all that he did was noted very quickly by colleagues in professional organizations. He joined the National Vocational Guidance Association (NVGA) in 1938 and soon became active in committee assignments and editorial board work, and was elected its President in 1962. He received its Presidential Award for Meritorious Service in 1966. This experience and his presidency of the Florida Personnel and Guidance Association helped prepare him to become president of APGA in 1964. He had contributed to the creation of APGA in 1952 by helping to form a coalition and merge related interest groups into one national organization. Harold also brought his expertise to counselor education as president of Southern ACES from 1971 to 1972.

The language for model legislation for counselor licensure was developed by the APGA Commission on Licensure during the mid-1970s with Harold's assistance and leadership. Besides spearheading the enactment of counselor licensure laws, this small group of leaders also conceptualized ways to use counselor preparation standards and a national registry or certification board. Also, from 1979 until the time of his death, he was a member of the APGA Long Range Planning Committee.

In addition to publications and professional leadership, Harold influenced the profession of counselor education and teaching through his numerous grants, workshops, and institutional consultations. His work as a consultant took him to 16 states, 28 universities, and more than 16 school districts. Between 1960 and 1966, he directed six Summer Guidance Institutes and one Two-Year Elementary Guidance Institute, which brought school counselors from all parts of the country to FSU for advanced training in counseling. Altogether his various grants through Florida State University amounted to more than a half million dollars. Two Presidents, John F. Kennedy and Lyndon B. Johnson, invited him to the White House for meetings with educators, and he presented testimony before congressional committees on three different occasions.

Staff development, personal growth, and consultation assignments provided instruction for counselors, teachers, educational leaders, and ministers. Topics for these activities ranged from communication and human relations skills to group problem solving, interpersonal skill building, and humanistic/affective education skills. Harold pursued numerous personal and professional growth opportunities for himself. For example, in 1972, before professional counselor licensure and certification were established, he earned a Diplomate in Counseling Psychology from the American Board of Professional Psychology. He was a cofounder of the Eastwood Counseling Center in Tallahassee, where he maintained a private practice in his later years, and which is still in business. Harold's community service was through a lifelong involvement in the Presbyterian Church. His Christian faith was a part of his personal philosophy of counseling and was expressed through compassion for others and a deep sense of service.

Although Harold's leadership style was recognized for a scholarly approach to the profession and skills in conceptualizing and communicating the issues, it was his quiet dedication, gentleness, and personal qualities that earned him the respect of everyone. When in the presence of others, he was person- and group-centered, rarely calling attention to himself. No job was too small or insignificant if it benefited others or the goals of the group. When coming together for a common activity, it was always evident that Harold had done his homework. His vision of what could be and his ability to integrate an array of ideas and points of view gave clarity to the big picture and a focus on the issues at hand. Harold's leadership style was always gentle but steadfast in striving for consensus.

## MENTORING AND COLLEGIALITY

His mentoring and collegiality had a lasting impact on his students and colleagues. He seldom missed a spirited Saturday morning tennis date with colleagues and friends, and his classic 1931 black Model A Ford was immediately recognizable around the town and campus. "Dr. C," as he was often known among his doctoral students, directed approximately 100 dissertations, and the widely varying topics of these works is evidence of his student centeredness in action. He invited the first author of this chapter to apply to the doctoral program after a 1963 summer institute in school counseling. This was the beginning of a lifelong relationship in which Harold would suggest possibilities and collaborate in research, publications, and committee assignments. He recruited the second author as a beginning master's student and continued to mentor him as a beginning faculty member at FSU. A former student and past president of the American Counseling Association, Dave Capuzzi, remembers the time when "Dr. C" told him that he saw the potential for leadership in the profession, something that Dave recalls not seeing in himself at age 24. Another former student, Win Stone, now retired as Associate Dean of the Graduate College at Bowling Green State University, remembers the first meeting with his new major professor in 1969. Bearing a Ford Foundation Fellowship and a reputation as an African-American community activist, Win was told by Harold, "Win, you are a little different from the typical student we admit here, but I believe you can teach us some things and we can teach you some things." Win noted his indebtedness for the outstanding developmental mentoring experiences provided by "Dr. C." Finally, Dave Brooks, a counselor educator at Kent State University, now deceased, wrote in a tribute at the time of Harold's death that although he was never enrolled in one of Harold's classes, he considered him to be one of his teachers because of the impact of his personal and professional contributions.

In an interview published in *The School Counselor* (Giddan, 1979), Harold's reflections upon his work present us with a vision for being the kind of teacher, mentor, and leader needed for the future of our profession:

> I believe that my role as a facilitator of growth . . . must be one that permits equal emphasis on the development of skills, knowledge, and personal development. My approach to this is to model openness, use professional behaviors, and stress the mutuality of the learning task, building on the intrinsic motivation of the learner. I also attempt to exemplify helping skills, academic knowledge, and a willingness to grow personally myself. . . . In essence, I want to respond to student concerns, model helping skills, attend to affect, and constantly reassess my attempts to follow these principles. . . . These are my responsibilities, my challenges, and indeed my professional obligations. (Giddan, 1979, p. 221)

In summary, Harold was a teacher, counselor educator, mentor, colleague, leader, and friend in his commitment to personal and professional growth. His positive regard for others, empathic understanding of their frame of reference, and genuineness in interpersonal encounters were characteristics he modeled as part of a helping relationship. As a pioneer in the development of counselor education, he had a vision of what the profession could become, pursued the challenges for developing a body of knowledge, and willingly accepted the obligations in creating a professional identity for counseling.

## ACKNOWLEDGMENTS

The authors thank Janet Lenz and Gary Peterson for their helpful comments on an early draft of this paper.

## REFERENCES

Burck, H., Cottingham, H., & Reardon, R. (1973). *Counseling and accountability: Methods and critiques.* New York: Pergamon.

Cottingham, H. F. (1953). The guidance function in the elementary school. *The Personnel and Guidance Journal, 31*, 453–454.

Cottingham, H. F. (1956). *Guidance in the elementary school: Principles and practices.* Bloomington, IL: McKnight & McKnight.

Cottingham, H. F. (1962). Implementing two vital teacher functions: Guidance and instruction. *Counselor Education and Supervision, 1*, 166–168.

Cottingham, H. F. (1966). National-level projection for elementary school guidance. *The Personnel and Guidance Journal, 44*, 499–502.

Cottingham, H. F. (1966). The challenge of authentic behavior. *The Personnel and Guidance Journal, 45*, 328–336.

Cottingham, H. F. (1973). Psychological education, the guidance function, and the school counselor. *The School Counselor 20*, 340–345.

Cottingham, H. F. (1975). School counselors face the question of licensing. *The School Counselor, 22*, 255–258.

Cottingham, H. F., & Hopke, W. E. (1961). *Guidance in the junior high school.* Bloomington, IL: McKnight & McKnight.

Cottingham, H. F., & Swanson, C. D. (1976). Recent licensure developments: Implications for counselor education. *Counselor Education and Supervision, 16*, 84–97.

Cottingham, H. F., & Warner, R. W. Jr. (1978). APGA and counselor licensure: A status report. *The Personnel & Guidance Journal, 56*, 604–607.

Giddan, N. S. (1979). An interview with Harold F. Cottingham. *The School Counselor, 26*, 214–221.

Witmer, J. M. (1985). *Pathways to personal growth: Developing a sense of worth and competence.* Muncie, IN: Accelerated Development.

# CHAPTER 13

# Samuel Templeman Gladding

Donna A. Henderson

*A diplomat and synthesizer with a touch of the poetic.*

Sam Gladding sometimes introduces himself by saying, "Hi, my name is Sam and I'm a counselor." That statement cements his vocational identity but fails to recognize some of his other roles as husband, father, friend, poet, writer, teacher, mentor, leader, and sage. Most importantly, though, Sam is a person admired and enjoyed by all.

Sam Gladding was born in Decatur, Georgia in 1945. As he describes in one of his poems:

> I am the son of a fourth-grade teacher
> and a man who dabbled in business,
>     a descendant of Virginia farmers
>     and open-minded Baptists. . . . (Gladding, 1993)

Sam's family of origin consisted of his parents as well as an older brother and sister. Sam married Claire Tillson and they have three children who were born two years apart. Sam does not sacrifice family participation for his rich career involvement. He has been a Boy Scout leader, soccer coach, and Sunday school teacher for those from 3 to 93 years of age. Obviously, he manages to devote his energy to all parts of his world.

Sam's academic preparation includes the following: Bachelor of Arts with a major in History from Wake Forest University in 1967; Master of Arts in Religion from Yale University in 1970; Master of Arts in Education from the Counseling program at Wake Forest University in 1971; and Ph.D. (Child Development and Family Relations) from the University of North Carolina at Greensboro in 1977.

## CAREER DEVELOPMENT

Sam's career path provides an excellent example of exploration, transition, and establishment. He explains that as a teenager he decided to become a minister like the grandfather for whom he was named. After obtaining his undergraduate degree from Wake Forest University, Sam attended Yale University but struggled with his goal of being a minister. His exploring led him to the office of Tom Elmore, who suggested he try counseling. Sam assumed that meant enrolling in the master's degree program in counseling at Wake Forest, and so he began a course of study that year. Later, he realized that Tom might have been suggesting some career counseling. The transition, however, from becoming a minister to becoming a counselor proved to be the more fitting path for Sam's career. He had found his niche and his mentor.

Sam began his counseling career by working in a rural community mental heath center in North Carolina. He also published his first articles and poems during this time. After 5 years as a clinician, he literally crossed the street and took a position as an instructor at a community college teaching psychology. During these years he started his work toward his Ph.D. degree and served a brief stint as a lieutenant in the U.S. Army Quartermaster Corps at Fort Lee, Virginia. Simultaneously, he became actively involved in professional counseling organizations, a path that would eventually lead to his many contributions in that arena. Sam's first post-Ph.D. academic appointment was to Fairfield University in Connecticut. From there he moved to the University of Alabama at Birmingham and finally to Wake Forest University, where he became assistant to the president with a tenured appointment in the counselor education program.

Sam's contribution to the profession of counseling in scholarship is exemplary. Weinrach and Lustig (1998) tracked contributions to the *Journal of Counseling & Development* over a 15-year period. Sam fell within the top 1% of contributing authors. He continues those contributions by publishing at least one article annually. Each year since 1988, except one, Sam has written and published a book. Those books have a varied orientation, for example, family counseling, group counseling, using the creative arts in counseling, and counseling as a profession, but all emphasize unity and professionalism in the profession of counseling. The title of his "big book," *Counseling: A Comprehensive Profession* (2000), provides an example of his philosophy of both the breadth and the cohesion of the profession. Evidence of his interest in and knowledge of using creative arts in counseling can be found by surveying some of the titles of his work (Gladding, 1995, 1997, 1998). He has published 15 books, over 60 journal articles, numerous book chapters, newsletter pieces, book reviews, and professional poetry as well as serving as editor of the *Journal for Specialists in Group Work*. He recently entered a new form of media by writing and filming a video (Davis & Hanson, 2000), *Basic Counseling Skills: Nine Essentials.*

Sam has also held numerous leadership positions at the state, regional, and national levels. He has been president of the Alabama Association for Specialists in Group Work and the Alabama Association for Counselor Education and Supervision. At the regional level he has been president of the Southern Association for Counselor Education and Supervision (SACES). He has been president of the Association for Specialists in Group Work (ASGW), the Association for Counselor Education and Supervision (ACES), and Chi Sigma Iota (CSI). Sam was recently appointed to the Research and Assessment Corporation for Counseling (RACC) Board. In all of these and the other leadership positions he has held, Sam has demonstrated his commitment to the profession of counseling.

The awards Sam has received serve as evidence of the quality of his leadership. Among the honors bestowed upon him are the Professional Leadership Award from ACES, the Eminent Career Award from ASGW, the Thomas J. Sweeney Professional Leadership Award from CSI, and the Ella Stephens Barrett Leadership Award from the North Carolina Counseling Association.

When questioned about this leadership record, Sam explains that for him being a leader means being a doer, being engaged at all levels. For example, he says he began by volunteering to be on an interest network on marriage and family counseling in ACES and moved from being a member to being the network chairperson. He was then asked to coedit a

monograph for ACES on marriage and family counseling. As he continued to volunteer, he advanced, realizing that in order to gain credibility,
he had to prove that he could lead and could work as he waited his turn
on the next level. His work with ASGW and CSI followed a similar progression.

Sam describes this process as one of learning not only about people but
about groups as well. According to Sam, in order to be effective as a leader
you must discover how a system works and what your place is in that system. You must evolve and contribute as you find that position, realizing
that your place may not be out front. Another important point in becoming
involved is the recognition that sacrifices will be necessary.

Sam's leadership spans years and interests. When he speaks of the rewards, he always begins by recognizing the relationships he has built by his
involvement. He also cites the opportunities for helping something grow
and develop as a benefit of leadership. Sam includes promoting the counseling profession as another plus in his leadership experience.

When I asked Sam what pleased him about working as a leader, he
mentioned several things. He noted the pleasure in working to bring people
together and creating the harmony needed to accomplish goals. These har-
monious groups could then tackle whatever their work was and see its results. That sense of collective accomplishment leads to a spirit and pride in
what has been done as well as how it was done. Seeing his impact on others
who then emerge allows Sam to recognize how leadership spreads from his
efforts. Sam rejoices in being able to say that in the worst of times he and
his teams tried to do the best of things, which often meant taking the initiative to open discussions. Sam's ability to encourage thoughtful questions
and innovative answers paved the way to encourage the conversations. His
talent of open listening and wise synthesis allowed the deliberations to
continue. Sam has taught others, myself included, that bringing people
together begins with a leader's invitation to explore.

Sam is also a leader on campus. Since 1998 he has served as the associate provost of Wake Forest University. Before that, as previously noted, he
was assistant to the president of the University. In those positions he has
shown his gift of diplomacy, fairness, and effectiveness, often managing
extremely difficult situations to a successful conclusion. He has numerous
upper level administrative duties yet is approachable enough that many
people on campus seek his guidance. Since 1996, Sam has been the director of the counselor education program at Wake Forest University, a program that was recognized by ACES as the Robert Frank Outstanding
Program in 1999.

Leadership in counseling associations has helped Sam at the university level be able to respond productively to diverse people with differing agendas. He has learned to search for possibilities and to find a mutual meeting place to start conversations. The recognition of common ground, better defined purposes, and potential solutions are components of the attitude with which he undertakes his many responsibilities.

## REFLECTIONS ON WORKING TOGETHER

One of Sam's sons once said, "Dad, the trouble with you is that you're too optimistic." His wife, Claire, counters with a description of him as "smooth chili with a kick." A student stated, "Behind that Pillsbury Dough Boy exterior, there is one tough cookie." Recently, a colleague told me that he felt Sam was one of the most universally appreciated and liked counselors in the profession.

Up close and personal, Sam retains all those admirable traits. My work with him at Wake Forest University has made me a better person. His optimism has helped me jump many hurdles. He has never failed to encourage and support me in my professional endeavors while helping me make better choices about where to expend energy. Our days are smooth because he leads our program with a steady hand and patient demeanor. He persists in difficult as well as easy times. If he agrees to do something, it will be accomplished well and on time. I have seen his toughness emerge when we have to make hard decisions and stick to them, which is sometimes an uncomfortable experience. Sam does not avoid a challenge but faces it with compassion and strength. And the "kick" that Claire mentioned is the humor and the poetry and the songs that are so much a part of the way Sam lives. He laughs well and often, even in faculty meetings. He writes poems that celebrate as well as dissect life. He has a song lyric for almost every occasion. His creativity permeates his teaching and his decisions. He is a joy as a colleague.

Sam shares his wisdom. Once, during my early days at Wake Forest University, we were scheduled to do a presentation together. I was unprepared for the large number of people who attended because of his renown. They were expecting another one of Sam's presentations. His audiences know he will give them a great deal of information in an understandable and useful way. Whether he is in a class, seminar, workshop, conference, keynote speech, or meeting with an individual one-on-one, he speaks earnestly, with insight and discernment. He has taken our graduate students to Vienna to study Freud, Frankl, Moreno, and Adler, and our undergraduates to Calcutta to work with Mother Theresa. National borders do not impede his gifts to the counseling profession

These few words are inadequate representations of Sam's many contributions as a prolific producer of scholarly works, a respected leader of counseling groups, and an accomplished manager of university matters. And none of those accomplishments reflects the way in which he achieves the tasks. He is a prince of a person—caring, fair, good-humored, creative, and in touch with the music of life. He builds teams, exudes patience, and encourages everyone with whom he has contact. Sam insists that everything that rises must converge into a better world. He tells me that people are not going to remember who we are but they will remember the creation of a nurturing environment. Sam has survived difficulties by building or rebuilding one brick at a time and has learned that we sometimes create our own circumstances and sometimes not. We get through the events by doing something. Sam does his somethings remarkably well.

## REFERENCES

Davis, K. (Producer), & Hanson, R. (Director). (2000). *Basic counseling skills: Nine essentials* (Film). (Available from Merrill Education/Prentice-Hall, Inc., Upper Saddle River, NJ 07458)

Gladding, S. T. (1993). Beecher Road. In S.T. Gladding (2002). *Family therapy: History, theory, and practice* (3rd ed; p. 115). Upper Saddle River, NJ: Prentice-Hall.

Gladding, S. T. (1995). Creativity in counseling. *Counseling and Human Development, 28,* 1–12.

Gladding, S. T. (1997). Stories and the art of counseling. *Journal of Humanistic Education and Development, 36,* 68–73.

Gladding, S. T. (1998). *Counseling as an art: The creative arts in counseling* (2nd ed.). Alexandria, VA: American Counseling Association.

Gladding, S. T. (2000). *Counseling: A comprehensive profession* (4th ed.). Upper Saddle River, NJ: Merrill/Prentice Hall.

Weinrach, S. G., & Lustig, D. (1998). Publication patterns of the *Personnel and Guidance Journal/Journal of Counseling & Development:* 1978 to 1993. *Journal of Counseling & Development, 76* (4), 427–435.

# CHAPTER 14

# Harold L. (Dick) Hackney

Holly A. Stadler and Sherry Cormier

*Building through collaboration*

Born in January 1935 to Henry Paris Hackney and Elma Mae Lilly Hackney, Harold L. (Dick) Hackney started life as a Baptist "preacher's kid" in Hinton, West Virginia. With a much older half-brother away in the military, Dick was raised as an only child in a small town in mountainous West Virginia. He completed his schooling at a combined elementary, junior, and senior high school during the time of racial segregation. Graduating at the age of 17 in 1952, Dick had learned two contradictory views of life from his parents. He describes these views as: "there are many things in life to worry about" and "life is good and you will be well taken care of." He continues to live with these contradictions.

Leaving home to enter West Virginia University, Dick struck out on a path that would take him far from his hometown, to professional accolades, new family ties, and a prominent leadership role as a counselor educator. After graduating in 1956 with a double major in history and journalism and enough pedagogy courses to obtain a teaching position, Dick relocated to Northern Virginia. In 1961 he married Joanne Wells and their family grew to include Kirsten, born in 1964, and Jason, born in 1969. Encouraged by the school district's director of guidance, in 1959 Dick began a master's degree program with a dual concentration in School Counseling and Psychology at George Washington University, supported by a National Defense Education Act (NDEA) fellowship. In 1966 he proceeded to the University of Massachusetts to pursue a doctorate with a dual concentration in Counseling and Educational Research, completing the Ed.D. degree in 1969. Today, Dick is married to another prominent counselor educator, Janine Bernard. They live in upstate New York, where Janine is the chairperson of the Department of Counseling and Human Services and Dick is coordinator of the Doctoral Program at Syracuse University. Dick and Janine have a son, Curtis, who is 23 years old. Dick has three grandchildren.

## CAREER PATH

Dick Hackney describes his career path as comprising four "phases." The first phase encompassed a search for career direction culminating in completion of the Ed.D. degree. The second phase he terms "the formative period," which included his first academic position and 15 subsequent years on the faculty at Purdue University (where both of the present authors were his doctoral students). Dick describes phase 3 as "launching a new direction." It began with a 3-year stint in academic administration. During this time he also occupied a prominent leadership role in counseling as president of the Association for Counselor Education and Supervision (ACES). Currently, in what he would call phase 4 of his career, "a return to doctoral training," 66-year-old Dick Hackney is planting his roots in Syracuse, New York. Significant career accomplishments and important lessons for future leaders typify each of these career phases. A closer look at each phase provides insights about one counselor educator's path to leadership.

One striking conclusion to be drawn during Dick's early career years is that one doesn't necessarily need to know where he or she is going when that person starts a career journey. In fact, Dick changed his college major a number of times before settling on history and journalism. Even then, his indecision led him to take some teaching classes that opened a career avenue he eventually followed to Arlington, Virginia. There he taught history and English to junior high school students from 1956 to 1960 while listening to a colleague's career advice to pursue school guidance. While a guidance counselor, he completed the M.A. degree with the dual concentration in School Counseling and Psychology at George Washington University. In 1964 he became director of guidance, and then in 1965 he became vice principal in a junior high school in Falls Church, Virginia. Dick does not describe this period as one in which he actively pursued the positions he held. Rather, this phase of his leadership was consistent with a theme that was seen in later periods of his career. This theme is one in which others recognize his leadership potential and appoint him to leadership positions or facilitate his involvement in critical professional projects.

"One of the best decisions of my whole career" is how Dick describes his "last-minute decision" to enter the doctoral program at the University of Massachusetts in 1966. At this point in his career journey, it seems as though Dick's career indecision had subsided and he was thrilled to be learning from and conducting research with "giants," as he calls them, such as Allen Ivey, Robert Carkhuff, and Sidney Simon. These were the early days of microteaching and microcounseling and the University of Massachusetts was one of the "places to be." What we now know as counseling skills training was then studied and tested with much enthusiasm. This heady experience launched him into the second phase of his career path, the phase that he terms "the formative period."

Dick was on the faculty at Purdue University from 1969 until 1984, and he again uses the term "giants" to describe his new colleagues at Purdue during its period of prominence in counselor education. Bruce Shertzer, Shelley Stone, and Lee Issacson were each major contributors to the counseling literature, and Bruce Shertzer was soon to become president of the forerunner of the American Counseling Association (ACA), the American Personnel and Guidance Association (APGA). This phase of Dick's career was the beginning of a time of great research productivity and active mentoring of doctoral students. During this time the publication of the 1973 book *Counseling Strategies and Objectives*, with coauthor and former student Sherry (Nye) Cormier, helped to make Dick a very visible scholar in the counseling profession. Now in its 5th edition (with translations in German and Portuguese) and entitled *Counseling Strategies and Interventions* (1999), this book has been a major resource in counselor education. Hackney and Cormier have continued their publishing partnership with the book *The Professional Counselor: A Process Guide to Helping* (2001), now in its 4th edition and translated into Korean.

Leadership for Dick Hackney during this "formative" period was defined by the quality of the doctoral students a faculty member could attract and by establishing an independent publication record. A new adventure was in store for Dick Hackney and Janine Bernard in 1976 and 1977 when they traveled to Weisbaden, West Germany, for a year as visiting professors for the Ball State University European Program. An appreciation of the international aspects of counseling was to remain another theme in Dick's career. Looking back on his experiences at Purdue, Dick believes that "ego and ambition are never enough." He feels that it was later, as he discovered "a bit of humility," that his career really flourished. He mentioned that the lesson he takes from reflecting on his early experiences is that the "spiritual self is always waiting for the ego to step aside, and when it does, things really do change."

A bit of career confusion reemerged in the third phase of Dick's career path. He "launched a new direction" when he and Janine Bernard left Purdue in 1984 for a small private school in Connecticut, Fairfield University. Dissatisfied with stints in higher education administration as associate dean for the School of Graduate and Continuing Education and then as chairperson of the Human Sciences Division at Fairfield University, Dick settled into the position of chairperson of the Counselor Education Department at Fairfield University in 1995. Thoughts that his career might have "peaked out" early in this period eventually turned to a reinvestment in counselor education. This culminated in his presidency of ACES from 1991 to 1992. Furthermore, this renewal led to the publication of additional books and book chapters, including *Practice Issues for the Beginning Counselor* (2000) and "The Contemporary Counselor in a Changed World" (1990), with C. Gilbert Wrenn. It also resulted in consulting trips with Janine Bernard to Australia and Taiwan and membership on the ACA Governing Council, the ACES Executive Council, the Association for Spiritual, Ethical and Religious Values in Counseling's (ASERVIC) Executive Board, and the Board of Directors of the Center for Credentialing and Education, a corporate affiliate of the National Board for Certified Counselors. Dick was immersed in the role of a senior professor in counselor education, a role that included assuming national leadership responsibilities and helping to move the profession into the 21st century.

Since fall of 2000, Dick has been reveling in his new position as coordinator of the Counselor Education Doctoral Program at Syracuse University. For him this is a return to his first love, preparing a new generation of counselor educators. At this point in his career, Dick is not inclined to seek elected leadership in the profession, but would relish the idea of working on projects and being part of a building process.

At least two lessons for future leaders can be gleaned from the career of Dick Hackney. The first lesson is that a commitment to excellence will draw others to you for mentoring, for collegial interactions, and for involvement in leadership. A second lesson is about taking risks. Dick's journey to leadership really started when he dared to travel 200 miles and for 7 hours to leave his tiny hometown in West Virginia to attend college. Each opportunity that came his way he viewed in the context of not being "locked down" to a place or a time. We counselors would describe this journey as one of continuous movement in the direction of growth and self-actualization. Dick is not contemplating retirement, so he will continue to be a significant voice on the growing edge of the profession.

## OUR MEMORIES OF WORKING WITH DICK HACKNEY

Although I (Holly Stadler) graduated several years after Sherry, I was and continue to be among the group of grateful counselor educators that Dick spawned at Purdue University. We all knew that it was very special to be one of Dick's students and tried hard to live up to his model of excellence and professional commitment. His mentorship opened the doors to many opportunities (including leadership opportunities) for me. Dick continues to be a mentor to me to this day. Over our 30-year history together there have been interesting tensions in our relationship that we continue to manage to overcome. I have the feeling that these tensions are because we are much more alike than we acknowledge. However, because of what I sense is a healthy mutual respect, each of us has learned from the other. I had very much to learn.

I learned much from Dick about leadership. His enthusiasm for projects draws others in as partners. He listens to multiple voices, regardless of their credentials or professional status. As a leader, Dick lets his work speak for him and gives credit to others when it is due. As Sherry notes below, humility is an essential trait for one who truly seeks to lead.

Without Dick's mentorship early in my career preparation, I am certain that my professional life would not be as productive and fulfilling as it is. Indeed, if it hadn't been for the opportunity to teach a microcounseling lab under Dick's guidance, I might never have become a counselor educator, much less hold my current position as department head. Despite all of the wonderful counselor educators I have met over the years, I always seek out Dick and Janine at the annual ACES luncheon. They represent my roots in counselor education and the pride I take in being one of Dick Hackney's students.

I (Sherry Cormier) was in graduate school and entered the profession of counselor education at a time when there were very few women doctoral students or faculty. Fortunately, in my academic program at Purdue, I was surrounded by a group of wonderful and supportive male faculty, and Dick

Hackney was among this group. I received excellent mentoring from all of the faculty members. However, Dick served as my dissertation advisor and helped me conceptualize and carry out a dissertation that, due to his encouragement and guidance, would become the foundation for our first published collaborative book. The first edition of this book was published early in my own academic career and was instrumental in helping me secure both promotion and tenure at a later point.

One thing that I feel truly grateful for was Dick's active mentoring about what it takes to move up the academic ladder. From the beginning he fostered awareness in me that for a successful academic career, a body of scholarly work must also accompany good clinical practice and teaching. After I received my doctoral degree and during the course of my academic career, up to the present, Dick and I have continued to collaborate on scholarly projects. I also have had the privilege of working with Dick's life partner, Janine Bernard, on some counselor supervision projects.

I learned several things from Dick specifically about leadership. One guideline is to look beyond the place where you "lead" to consider the impact and importance of the global community. Another bit of leadership wisdom Dick passed along is about the value of humility. An arrogant person does not lead; she or he simply controls. True leaders are humble and mindful of their own limitations. They also know the strengths and contributions of those with whom they work.

There are several additional things I admire about Dick. First, he had an early and has a continuing interest in the international context of counselor education. He has helped me see beyond the myopic focus of an individual institution, state, region, or even country to the impact of globalization on counselor education.

The second thing I admire about Dick is his great wit and sense of humor and perspective. One incident occurred during my graduate training that I still actively recall on days when I tend to "fret." While I was fretting to Dick about something (which was really nothing), he replied, "If there isn't anything to worry about, I think you will find something." Today, I carry that piece of illumination about myself, as well as the confidence Dick helped to shape in me as a result of many mentoring experiences.

## REFERENCES

Hackney, H., & Nye, L. S. (1973). *Counseling strategies and objectives*. Englewood Cliffs, NJ: Prentice-Hall.

Cormier, S., & Hackney, H. (1999). *Counseling strategies and interventions* (5th ed.). Boston: Allyn & Bacon.

Hackney, H., & Cormier, S. (2001). *The professional counselor: A process guide to helping* (4th ed.). Boston: Allyn & Bacon.

Hackney, H. (2000). *Practice issues for the beginning counselor*. Boston: Allyn & Bacon.

Hackney, H., & Wrenn, G. C. (1990). The contemporary counselor in a changed world. In H. Hackney (Ed.), *Changing contexts for counselor preparation in the 1990s* (pp. 1–20). Alexandria, VA: American Association for Counseling and Development.

# CHAPTER 15

# Edwin L. Herr

Spencer G. Niles

*Leadership includes seeing potential in others and reaching out to them.*
*It's how we choose to respond to life that makes the difference.*

In discussing Edwin L. Herr's leadership and legacy, it is fitting to note the dedication from his extremely successful book, *Career Guidance and Counseling Through the Life Span: Systematic Approaches* (Herr & Cramer, 1996), which Ed dedicated to his father, stating the following: "Samuel L. Herr (August 23, 1903–September 7, 1968) weaver, laborer, mechanic, school custodian, whose respect for the dignity of work was exceeded only by his respect for the dignity of people" (p. ii). In essence, Edwin Herr continues the legacy inherited from his father. The principles embodied in this dedication guide Ed in his leadership style. Ed's career reflects the accomplishments of a person who cares deeply about people and the counseling profession.

## EARLY LIFE

Born in Carlisle, Pennsylvania, on November 23, 1933, Edwin L. Herr immersed himself in typical activities for boys in the 1930s and 1940s (e.g., baseball, music, and billiards). Entering high school, Ed enrolled in the general curriculum and planned on entering the workforce upon graduating from secondary school. Like his father, Ed hoped to make an honest living through hard work. It is not surprising, therefore, that Ed's resume includes stints as a shipping department laborer in a local shoe factory, a mail sorter for the U.S. Postal Service, a dishwasher, a laborer in heavy construction, a jackhammer operator, and a fine grade assistant foreman. Ed was even a card-carrying member of the AFL-CIO Hod Carriers Union!

In addition to these work experiences, Ed was a member of the Air National Guard, the U.S. Air Force, or the Air Force Reserve from January 1952 to December 1968 and held ranks from airman basic to captain. He also served as air crew member, personnel officer, group adjutant, staff officer to the director of civil defense for New York City, administrative officer, basic training squadron commander, and enlisted flying safety specialist.

These employment experiences are noteworthy for a number of reasons. They reflect a blue-collar history and an *esprit de corps* with groups beyond those usually inhabited by people with high levels of education and prestigious occupational titles. These employment experiences also demonstrate that Ed's history bridges experiences and backgrounds from one segment of the employment sector (i.e., blue-collar) to another (i.e., highly educated professional). But, as Ed bridges these experiences, he does so in a way that consistently honors the legacy he inherited from his father. That is, he maintains a respect for, and belief in, the dignity of all people, regardless of their educational, occupational, and socioeconomic status.

Serving as a bridge has, in fact, been a theme throughout Ed's career. His own efforts at "bridging" are reflected in his many professional accomplishments (e.g., serving as president during the year that the American Personnel and Guidance Association transitioned to the American Association for Counseling and Development) and in his dedication to helping others bridge their current situations to achieve their goals. Moreover, Ed's family and early work history provide the foundation for what would later become a second important theme in his scholarly contributions: an emphasis on issues and concerns experienced by employment-bound youth.

Although each of his work experiences was influential in important ways, it may have been his leisure activities that set the stage for his own transition from blue-collar work to a distinguished academic career. Shortly after high school graduation, Ed was working in a shoe factory and spent many of his after-work hours engaged in one of his favorite pas-times: playing pool, often for money and often successfully! Playing "money pool" one evening, a friend challenged Ed to consider pursuing a college degree. Even though he had taken academic courses while enrolled in high school, Ed had not seriously done anything related to seeking col-lege admission prior to this evening. The suggestion started him thinking seriously about the possibility of moving beyond work in the local shoe factory.

Ed decided to explore the possibility of attending the local college, Shippensburg State College (now Shippensburg University). Academic success soon followed. Ed worked his way through college and obtained his bachelor's degree in 1955 with a major in business education.

Ed's time as an officer in the armed forces coincided with his colle-giate and early postcollegiate career. His active duty tour in the Air Force exposed him to the fact that many people in late adolescence and early adulthood lacked direction and seemed to consistently make bad choices in their lives. But, it was a subsequent automobile accident that signifi-cantly shaped Ed's philosophy and reinforced for him the power of deci-sions in people's lives. Ed experienced a near-fatal automobile accident while returning from an active duty period with the Air National Guard in which he served after his stint in the Air Force. In a very heavy rain-storm, a car filled with teenagers driving in the opposite direction veered across the median strip. Ed attempted to avoid colliding with the oncom-ing car. As he veered out of the oncoming car's path, Ed's car was struck from behind and his gas tank exploded. Ed was wedged between the floor and the dashboard as his car became engulfed in flames. Fortunately, a fellow Guardsmen, who was riding with him, was able to pull Ed from the burning wreckage just prior to the car exploding. Ed suffered burns over much of his body and multiple other injuries. He was transported to a hospital near Harrisburg and physicians questioned whether he would survive his injuries. His recovery would require ten operations and five months recuperating in two hospitals.

During Ed's recovery, he encountered a physician who practiced "tough love." As Ed tried to cope with the loss of mobility, visual impair-ment, and scars he experienced as a result of his accident, his physician challenged him to consider what he would do next. The physician re-marked that although Ed's injuries were substantial, others experience more serious injuries on a daily basis ("I know your hands are burned and broken, but I work on patients who have lost their hands"). At that point,

Ed once again encountered the importance of choice in coping with life events. He understood that what matters most is not so much what happens in life, but how we respond to what happens in our lives. This insight struck a chord deep in Ed's psyche and served as the impetus for many of his later life accomplishments. (For example, Ed later developed the concept of "personal flexibility" to address the importance of being able to adapt and respond effectively to planned and unplanned life events.) This insight also guided Ed in his leadership style. As a leader, one must be able to cope effectively with unforeseen circumstances. What counts the most is how one responds to unanticipated events when they occur.

## LAUNCHING HIS CAREER

Employment as a business teacher, first in his hometown of Carlisle, then in Paterson, New Jersey, followed Ed's college graduation and active duty in the U.S. Air Force. During his work at Paterson Central High School, Ed served as a teacher-counselor and pursued his master's degree at Teachers College, Columbia University. In 1959, he received his M.A. degree in Psychological Foundations with a minor in Counseling, Student Personnel, and Administration. Also in 1959, Ed became a school counselor and, in 1960, became the director of guidance at Saddle Brook High School. In 1961, he earned a Professional Diploma in the Coordination of Guidance Services from Teachers College.

Although Ed loved his work as a school counselor and director of guidance, he was also enthralled by the learning environment at Teachers College. Columbia employed an elite faculty group within the counseling field. The professor of the first course Ed enrolled in at Teachers College was Donald E. Super. Ed was particularly taken with Donald Super's academic achievements, international background, and concern for college- and employment-bound youth. Ed recalled how Super challenged students to examine their assumptions about those lacking education and to not confuse level of education with intelligence in their work with adolescents and adults. Stimulated by the intellectual environment at Teachers College, Ed continued his educational studies and, in 1963, earned a doctoral degree in Counseling and Student Personnel Administration. He had come a long way from the shoe factory!

It was also during his time at Teachers College that Ed had the good fortune to be introduced by one of his professors to a master's degree student in elementary school counseling, Patricia Greene. One of Ed's professors had a strong hunch that Ed and Patricia, a native of Kentucky, would be a good match. The hunch turned into reality as Ed and Patricia were married and today have three grown children: Amber Leigh (36 years of age), Christopher Alan (33 years of age), and Alicia Estell (26 years of age). Each of the Herr children graduated from Penn State University and then developed successful careers in their own right. Amber works in Charlotte, North Carolina, as a physician's assistant with two degrees from Duke University Medical Center. Christopher earned an MBA from the London Business School in England and works as a very successful investment consultant and venture leasing bank officer. Alicia works as an elementary school teacher in a Montessori magnet school in the Cleveland public schools. Patricia has worked as a paraprofessional and middle school counselor for over two decades. She has provided substantial moral and professional support to her husband throughout their many years of marriage.

## LEADING WITHIN THE PROFESSION

Having the title "distinguished" defines one's accomplishments as eminent or noted. Edwin L. Herr, Distinguished Professor of Education at Penn State University, exemplifies the best of what is embodied in this title. His legacy to the profession includes accomplishments far too many to list here. Many readers will be most familiar with the obvious accomplishments: president of numerous professional organizations (e.g., American Association for Counseling and Development, National Vocational Guidance Association, Association for Counselor Education and Supervision, Chi Sigma Iota); editor of multiple journals (e.g., *Journal of Counseling & Development* and *Counselor Education and Supervision*); author of over 30 books, 15 monographs, and nearly 300 journal articles; and member of the Executive Councils for the International Round Table for the Advancement of Counselling and the International Association for Educational and Vocational Guidance; and presenter of over 300 papers at national and international conferences.

This is only a partial list of Ed's achievements. His influence reaches deep into the public school systems, where his record of service ranges from business teacher to school counselor, director of guidance, and the first director of both the Bureau of Guidance Services and the Bureau of Pupil Personnel Services for the Pennsylvania Department of Education. As the state director of guidance for Pennsylvania, Ed created separate certifications for elementary and secondary school counselors and for supervisors of guidance services, established program approval criteria for counselor education certification programs, and defined competencies for school counselors at different levels. Additionally, Ed has testified on multiple occasions before U.S. House and Senate subcommittees on behalf of the counseling profession. He has trained counselors in more than two dozen countries and served as a consultant throughout the world.

In each of these activities, Ed drew upon the extant theoretical and research literature to formulate his vision for the future of the counseling profession. Incorporating the "science" of the profession into his viewpoints helped Ed to communicate the importance of counseling to a wide range of stakeholders involved in formulating policies and practices related to the counseling profession. For example, for his testimony to the U.S. Senate, Ed composed the monograph *Why Counseling?* (1985). This monograph summarized the literature within the profession demonstrating the efficacy of numerous counseling interventions. This document helped legislators to understand the importance of having counselors serve in educational and community settings.

Thus, Ed's career is that of someone who is a leader among leaders. He has led in virtually every category in which one can lead. He has been a leading scholar, a molder of counseling programs throughout the world, a shaper of legislative policies, and a leading influence for multiple national and international professional associations. Ed is not, however, the sort to aggressively seek out leadership positions. In most instances, he has agreed to assume leadership roles because others have sought him out to do so, often as a result of reading one of his publications. Ed believes that taking on such roles is essential to the future of the profession and that such service is a way to honor the legacy of those who have preceded us in the field.

Once in a leadership role, Ed uses a leadership style that is facilitative, participatory, and inclusive. As a leader he involves others in the decision-making process. In addition to drawing upon the literature within the profession to formulate a vision for the profession, Ed is grounded in, and respectful of, the history of the counseling profession. He is mindful of the fact that, in addition to being able to understand future trends in counseling, a "vision" for leadership emerges from an understanding of past and present factors influencing the profession. Ed also believes that we need to incorporate knowledge from multiple disciplines (e.g., economics, sociology, anthropology, and psychology) to understand current trends within the profession.

As Ed leads through his scholarship, service to professional associations, and training activities, he is also aware of the fact that actions create history. He is not a reckless decision-maker. Such an approach would run the risk of not honoring the work of those who have preceded him within the profession. Although it is not a claim Ed would make, it is clear to those familiar with his work that his publications and professional service contributions in many ways become the guideposts that others rely on for gaining an understanding of the evolving nature of the counseling profession.

Ed's leadership style, dedication, and commitment to moving the field in a positive way have served our profession well. For example, Ed was the last president to serve the American Personnel and Guidance Association (APGA) and the first to serve the American Association for Counseling and Development (AACD). This transition required him to be sensitive to the views of those against the name change while also nudging the profession toward a future with a greater emphasis on counseling and development. It was also the case that as APGA-AACD president, Ed oversaw substantial changes in the association's governance structure. Managing this process required political acumen and additional sensitivity to those not eager for such changes to occur. Finally, during his time as APGA-AACD president, Ed supported efforts related to the accreditation of counselor training programs, credentialing of counselors, and state licensure of professional counselors. He clearly recognized the importance of these activities for the advancement of the profession.

In many ways (e.g., via U.S. Senate testimony; creating and supporting counselor credentials; providing early theoretical approaches to career education and to systematic approaches to career guidance; creating conceptual models of the linkage between career counseling and mental health; and authoring journal articles, book chapters, and books), Ed's leadership style also reflects the current emphasis on advocacy within the profession. Evidence of his advocacy on behalf of the profession extends beyond the boundaries of the United States. Ed has been very involved with, and facilitative of, the evolution of counseling in numerous other countries. Further, Ed has served on numerous boards of international counseling associations, helped to formulate counseling policies and practices in other countries, authored the first set of ethical guidelines for the International Association of Educational and Vocational Guidance, and helped to develop counselor training models throughout the world. Much of his recent writing has been focused on the role of policy, culture, and economics in shaping the provision of guidance and counseling in nations around the world. In 1999 and 2001, he was an invited theme speaker at two international symposia where he discussed these topics, as well as cost–benefit analyses of career counseling. Ed emphasizes the importance of being aware of, and sensitive to, global influences within the profession.

## LEGACY: A PERSONAL PERSPECTIVE

Nearly twenty years ago, when considering doctoral programs, I had come close to deciding which university to attend, but at the last minute reluctantly opted to interview at Penn State. During my visit to Penn State, I spent a substantial amount of time interviewing with Edwin Herr, who, at the time, served as head of the Division of Counseling, Educational, and School Psychology at Penn State and was president-elect of APGA. I was immediately struck by Ed's relaxed, humble, and self-effacing style. Despite his impressive professional accomplishments, Ed reflected the lessons learned throughout his life and inherited from his parents. That is, I felt that he valued me as a person and was genuinely interested in helping me develop in my career. Within the day, and as a result of my meeting with Ed, I revised my choice of doctoral programs and decided to attend Penn State. The opportunity to learn from a person of Ed's stature was just too good to turn down!

Nearly twenty years later, I continue to learn from Edwin L. Herr. Throughout this time, he has served as a mentor, advisor, and senior colleague. It was due to his mentoring during my doctoral program that I decided to pursue a faculty position upon the completion of my doctoral degree. When I expressed doubt about my potential for success as an academic, he countered with the argument that much of what I thought I lacked in potential were actually skills that I could develop with mentoring—which he graciously volunteered to provide. I published my first journal articles under his tutelage, and we continue to coauthor articles, chapters, and books.

Although I feel extremely fortunate to have been mentored by Ed Herr, I know that this experience is not unique to me. He has provided similar assistance to countless other master's degree students, doctoral students, and professionals. I have had many conversations with colleagues at national and international conferences in which the importance of Ed's mentoring has been the focal point of our discussions. These colleagues have each related an experience in which Ed's interest and support has had a major impact on their career development. Thus, his influence is felt by numerous professionals and is international in its scope.

It is my sense, however, that throughout his 40 years of leading and mentoring people within counselor education, Ed has developed a specialty. Although he works effectively with diverse people representing multiple contexts and demographics, I think he is most effective working with those in need of encouragement. Ed makes a concerted effort to help those people who may be reluctant or even fearful of considering greater possibilities. He fosters self-efficacy within those people who may wonder whether they are "good enough" or "competent enough" to succeed. He takes this approach to his work whether he is mentoring students or leading a professional organization.

It is my hunch that the suggestion offered during an evening of shooting pool over 50 years ago is never far from Ed's consciousness. Ed sees the potential in others, reaches out to them, and then stands by them for as long as it takes to help them on their way. These are in many ways the hallmarks of an exceptional leader. It is the approach he takes regardless of whether he is mentoring individuals or leading professional associations.

There are multiple themes that emerge when examining Ed's career, but two seem prominent. First, Ed serves as a bridge for others. Just as a bridge in shooting pool helps the shooter to reach places not otherwise possible, Ed helps people reach places in their careers and lives that would not be possible without his assistance. Second, Ed understands the importance of choice in life. His life experiences have taught him that it is often how we choose to respond to life events that makes all the difference in the lives we live. Ed has chosen to care about people and about the profession. His life reflects the legacy he inherited from his father and passes on to others every day.

## REFERENCES

Herr, E. L. (1985). *Why counseling?* (2nd ed.). Alexandria, VA: APGA Press.
Herr, E. L., & Cramer, S. H. (1996). *Career guidance and counseling through the life span: Systematic approaches* (5th ed.). New York: HarperCollins.

# CHAPTER 16

# George E. Hill

Thomas E. Davis and J. Melvin Witmer

*Above all I would plead in the days ahead for educational efforts
that are constantly kept focused on the primary object of
good education: the individual child.*

George E. Hill was born in Bellaire, Michigan in 1907. He was the youngest of seven children and had five sisters and one brother. Because his father was a Methodist minister, the family moved around Michigan every 3 or 4 years, which was only the beginning of what would be a somewhat nomadic life. He grew up, as he said, toughened by the snide remarks referring to him and his siblings as "PK's" ("preacher's kids"). Because of his high profile as the "son of a preacher," George was forced into constant public scrutiny. Years later, he lamented that his son and daughters were placed in the same position as "PK's" ("professor's kids"), having to always dress neatly and speak a little better than others their age.

George earned his B.A. degree at Albion College in Michigan and his M.A. and Ph.D. degrees at Northwestern University in Illinois. In 1934 he married Beatrice Kraft and they became the parents of three daughters and one son. The children have had varied careers in medical, government, social, and legal services, as well as university teaching. Several have done international work and two are now practicing law with a specialization in family and mediation services. His widow, Bea, now resides in a retirement home in Venice, Florida.

## CAREER IN COUNSELOR EDUCATION

George spent the first part of his professional life as a teacher, dean of instruction, dean of students, and director of graduate studies at educational institutions in Kansas, Iowa, Minnesota, Illinois, and Pennsylvania. During his lifetime career, he taught at 13 colleges and universities and served administrative functions in 3. He described himself as an "academic tramp" before finding his way to Ohio University.

George's identity as a counselor educator and a scholar within the newly emerging field of professional counseling took root during a most productive professional career of 24 years at Ohio University. While at Ohio University, he served as professor (1948–1964) and in 1964 was awarded the rank of Distinguished Professor of Education (1964–1972), the highest academic rank awarded by the institution to a few distinct scholars. He is only one of two people in the history of the College of Education at Ohio University to have received this university title. George distinguished himself as a teacher, researcher, and grant writer, and he distinguished himself by service to a rapidly growing university through special assignments. His reputation attracted many students, especially doctoral students who later made notable achievements in their respective fields. Although he taught in several areas such as higher education, educational research, psychology, and philosophy, his major commitment was to a graduate program in guidance, counseling, and student personnel, a program he organized in 1948 and directed until 1962.

His first graduate from the Ohio University counseling program was Charles L. Lewis, who became executive director of the American Personnel and Guidance Association (now the American Counseling Association), the largest professional counseling association in the world. The initial degree in guidance was at the bachelor's level, granted at a time before the master's degree was established as the educational entry level for the field. By 1952, the master's degree program in guidance was in place and the first graduates completed the program. George organized a doctoral program in the late 1950s. In 1962, Richard Nelson became the first Ph.D. graduate of this program, and he went on to distinguish himself in counselor education at Purdue University. By retirement in 1972,

George had advised more than 100 master's degree students and directed 14 doctoral dissertations. Through his departmental leadership, Ohio University was among the first National Defense Education Act (NDEA) Institute programs that focused upon elementary school guidance and counseling. These and other funded programs resulted in counselor training for individuals throughout the United States as well as into Asia and Europe. Today, Ohio University's NDEA Program alumni are found literally throughout the world.

## SCHOLARSHIP

George's leadership abilities were recognized very early by his colleagues and the administrators at Ohio University, with the dean in the College of Education and the university president inviting him to lead several special task forces. However, his professional reputation extended far beyond the Ohio University campus to state, regional, and national levels. He was in much demand as a keynote speaker at conferences and conventions for his ability to evoke professional challenge and stimulation while delighting audiences with his storytelling and humor.

For more than a quarter century, George's interest in guidance and counseling was expressed through his many speeches, papers, publications, discussions with students and colleagues, research studies, and school visits. He coauthored numerous monographs with colleagues and doctoral students on the development, improvement, and evaluation of school guidance and counseling. He truly helped shape the profession of counseling in general and school counseling in particular. His 1965 book *Management and Improvement of Guidance* (revised in 1974), reflects his comprehensive knowledge of the field, in both principles and practices. His efforts as a pioneer in elementary guidance and counseling culminated in his book *Guidance for Children in Elementary Schools* (Hill & Luckey, 1969). Altogether he had more than 100 publications to his credit.

To appreciate the magnitude of his work, one need only consider the first 25 years (1961–1986) of the journal of the Association for Counselor Education and Supervision (ACES). In the *Counselor Education and Supervision* (1986) silver anniversary issue, Hosie, Poret, Lauck, and Rosier (1986) list the 36 authors with five or more published articles in the first 25 years of the journal. At the top of the list, yielding the greatest number of publications, is George Hill with a total of 12. Given this fact, he may be considered one of the most prolific scholars in counselor education during the formative years of the profession.

## SERVICE AND LEADERSHIP

George was one of the organizers and the first president of the Ohio Association for Counselor Education and Supervision (OACES), chartered in 1952, the year that the American Personnel and Guidance Association (APGA) was established. Nationally, he was elected treasurer of the ACES and served in this office from 1958 to 1959. From 1959 to 1960 he served as president of the North Central ACES.

As a member of the first ACES Standards Committee, George was one of the early leaders in developing preparation standards for counselor education. As a result of his work on this committee, Ohio University in 1965 undertook one of the first comprehensive program self-assessments in counselor education and developed a self-study manual for this purpose based in part on an earlier self-study experience in the Counseling Program (Hill & Green, 1961). As chairperson of the subcommittee on Standards for the Preparation of Secondary School Counselors for ACES, his leadership provided a 1967 revision of the original 1964 standards, a prototype of the current Council for Accreditation of Counseling and Related Educational Programs (CACREP) standards. George's work contributed greatly to the establishment of not only standards of preparation but also of the self-study format used by counselor educators according to the first CACREP chairperson (T. L. Sweeney, personal correspondence, March 2001).

George Hill was the recipient of many professional awards and recognitions throughout his career. He was a member of Phi Beta Kappa, an honorary life member of the North Central Association of Colleges and Secondary Schools (NCACSS), an honorary life member of the Ohio School Counselors Association (OSCA), a Distinguished Professor of Education at Ohio University, and a recipient of the prestigious President John Baker Award from Ohio University in 1967. His contribution to counseling in the State of Ohio is recognized by the George E. Hill Meritorious Service Award given annually by the Ohio School Counselors Association. After his death in 1977, the counselor education faculty at Ohio University established the George E. Hill Distinguished Alumni Award for graduates of the program who make a significant contribution to the counseling profession. Scholarship, service, and leadership are the three areas of achievement, the three areas in which George made outstanding contributions. To date, 22 graduates have received this award for outstanding contributions to the profession.

## THE GEORGE E. HILL LEGACY

George Hill was a teacher, scholar, writer, churchman, storyteller, traveler, and distinguished professor. He pursued his vision for the profession with a passion, believed greatly in its value to our educational system, and worked diligently to establish its credibility. His knowledge, engaging personality, professional persona, commitment to the profession, and dependability for getting a job done were hallmarks of his leadership qualities. His professional creativity and leadership were significant to the early development of the counseling profession. Equally important to those who followed, Professor Hill left a legacy of responsible leadership, indefatigable commitment, and a passion for the profession of which we are a part. Ohio University faculty and students alike feel his presence in urging us to be our best both personally and professionally through leadership, scholarship, and service. Some of this legacy can be seen in the leadership roles of both faculty and graduates over the years in licensure, accreditation, standards, and advocacy for the profession and for those whom we serve.

George Hill's personality, character, and style earned him the respect of students, colleagues, and administrators. His wise counsel was sought by faculty and administrators and he was frequently asked to take difficult assignments that could be politically contentious. In a committee situation when consensus was difficult, he would remark with a smile, "Professors are persons who think otherwise." Integrity is a characteristic used by colleagues to describe him. One could depend on his word, expect him to be fair, and defend the rights of others. George showed courage to act upon his convictions, even when they were in contrast to a prevailing belief or practice. He was a true gentleman and scholar in the way he related to others.

After his retirement, his nomadic urgings led him and his wife, Bea, to move to Englewood, Florida, where he continued to pursue his hobbies of stamp collecting, gardening, and traveling, in addition to extensive reading and writing. Shortly before his death, George finished his professional memoirs in a book called *Prof* (Hill, 1977). With his typical sense of humor and tongue-in-cheek, he nostalgically takes the reader through the trials and tribulations of a college professor as he attempts to give advice and to dispel some of the common myths about the professor within the academy. His parting advice in the retirement chapter of *Prof* was:

> The best protection you can provide for satisfying and respected years in the latter part of your career, and in retirement, is to do the very best job

while you're younger. As my Dad used to say, to get the best possible job, make yourself indispensable in the job you now have. (Hill, 1977, p. 154)

## REFERENCES

Hill, G. E. (1965). *Management and improvement of guidance*. New York: Appleton-Century-Crofts.

Hill, G. E. (1974). *Management and improvement of guidance* (revised). New York: Appleton-Century-Crofts.

Hill, G. E. (1977). *Prof*. New York: Vintage Press.

Hill, G. E., & Green, D.A. (Eds.). (1961). *Appraising a counselor education program: The cooperative approach*. Athens, OH: Center for Educational Service.

Hill, G. E., & Luckey, E. B. (1969). *Guidance for children in elementary schools*. New York: Appleton-Century-Crofts.

Hosie, T. W., Poret, M., Lauck, P., & Rosier, B. (1986). Contributions to *Counselor Education and Supervision* for volumes 0–25, 1961–1986. *Counselor Education and Supervision, 25*, 284–288.

# CHAPTER 17

# Thomas Walsh Hosie

Joe Ray Underwood

*Involve everyone associated with the outcome through
cooperative decision making.*

Thomas Walsh Hosie was born in Buffalo, New York, on November 12, 1944. His Irish mother and Scotch father were the first members of their families to emigrate to the United States. They moved to New York State in the 1920s. Tom attended public schools in Buffalo, New York, through the eighth grade and then attended Cardinal Dougherty High School, from which he graduated in 1962. He then attended the University of Buffalo, which had recently merged with the New York State University system, where he majored in history and minored in secondary teacher education. After graduation he planned to further his education as a full-time student in the graduate program in school counseling. However, while seeking substitute teaching positions to fund his graduate studies, he was offered, and accepted, a teaching position at John F. Kennedy High School in Sloan, New York.

As a new teacher, Tom was asked to gain additional certifications in science. Believing his talents would be more effectively utilized elsewhere, Tom took a position in the personnel department in a large banking concern in western New York and became director of training for the bank and its branch offices. That same year, 1968, he married Denise Demmin. Although Tom gained valuable experience working in the business field, he decided to return to his original goal of becoming a counselor. He enrolled full-time in the counseling graduate program at the University of Buffalo and was given an assistantship as a supervisor of student teachers. Tom graduated in 1970 and was contracted for two successive school counseling positions, first with an inner city school system, and second in a suburban school system. He entered the doctoral program in Counselor Education at the University of Buffalo in September 1971.

The professors at Buffalo were excellent professional role models. Tom's Ph.D. degree committee and advisors were Richard R. Stevic, James C. Hansen, Stanley H. Cramer, Gilbert D. Moore, and Ronald Gentile. Tom noted that department faculty took pride in Gilbert Moore's accomplishment of being elected the 1968–1969 president of the Association for Counselor Education and Supervision (ACES). Although the department emphasized faculty scholarship, they viewed Gilbert Moore's attainment of the ACES presidency as a national honor and viewed his service to the association and profession as a major accomplishment. Perhaps Gilbert Moore had a lasting influence, because Tom later became president of the same organization.

## CAREER PATH

Tom's first faculty position in counselor education was in 1973 at Northeast Louisiana University (NLU). Department head Don W. Locke was active in state counseling organizations, the Association for Humanistic Education and Development (AHEAD), and the American Association for Counseling and Development (AACD, now the American Counseling Association). Don W. Locke encouraged his faculty to become active in the state counseling associations and to support these associations in their efforts to promote professional counseling. With Locke's encouragement, Tom pursued the position of president-elect of the Louisiana Association for Counselor Education and Supervision (LACES) and was elected in 1976. Much of Louisiana's efforts were placed on strengthening/standardizing school counselor certification. That same year, while teaching three courses a semester, Tom and a small group of interested members of the Louisiana Association for Counseling and Development (LACD) wrote Louisiana's Counselor Licensure Bill. The first year that the bill was submitted to the state legislature, Tom gave speeches and lobbied in support of its passage. The bill was approved by the Louisiana Senate, but was vetoed by a committee of the Louisiana House of Representatives.

In 1977, Tom became the only counselor educator in Louisiana to be elected president-elect of the Louisiana School Counselors Association (LSCA). That year he also was employed as the coordinator of the Counselor Education program at Louisiana State University (LSU). For several years, Tom worked to upgrade school counselor certification and to solicit school counselor support for counselor licensure (in spite of strong opposition from psychologists and social workers), which included his service as the LACD Licensure Committee Chair (1976–1980). In addition to promoting licensure, Tom was active in national counseling associations. With the support of Don W. Locke, Tom ran for and was elected to the vice-presidency of AHEAD (1978–1980).

In 1980, Ray Hosford, editor of the journal *Counselor Education and Supervision*, contracted a neurological disease and could not continue in the position. Due to Ray Hosford's unfortunate circumstances, ACES president James Muro was forced to fill this position. Knowing of Tom's editorial experience and having confidence in his capabilities, Muro asked Tom to be the interim editor. Tom had been a former editorial board member of *The Humanist Educator* during Muro's term as editor. While at NLU, Tom and two other editors initiated the *Journal of Counseling Services*. The *Journal* began as a state journal in Louisiana and Tom and his colleagues were able to take it to the national level with a reasonable subscription base. Tom also served on the editorial board of *The Personnel and Guidance Journal* and thought that he could serve as a national editor for the journal of *Counselor Education and Supervision* for at least one year. Tom enjoyed the activity to such an extent that he applied for the editorship the next year and was elected editor by the ACES Executive Council. In 1980, Tom also became the father of Sean Walsh Hosie, who is currently a junior at Mississippi State University.

Tom fostered the publication of at least two special *Counselor Education and Supervision* issues. He published more articles and pages than at any other time in the history of the journal and insisted on quality articles, as evidenced by a 22% acceptance rate for articles submitted. He also was editor of the 25th Anniversary Issue of the journal of *Counselor Education and Supervision*. Tom encouraged ACES members with valid studies and ideas to submit their manuscripts for possible publication. He assisted with editing their manuscripts and nurtured their professional development. Later, he continued to work with some of the same individuals on other ACES and ACA professional activities and projects. Tom's contribution as editor of *Counselor Education and Supervision* was so well received that he gained acknowledgment and recognition from the counseling profession that has lasted through his career. At the end of Tom's term (1981–1984), he was honored with a special ACES Editor's Award. To date, Tom is the only editor to be honored by ACES with such an award.

Never the one to seek the limelight, Tom was approached in 1984 by members and officers of LACD to run for president. Their motivation was simple: "Get Hosie to help rewrite the counselor licensure bill and make another attempt at passage." Tom won the election and work began on the licensure bill, representing a career milestone.

Tom was well known throughout the AACD membership as a leader who could harness the energy of counselors. In 1985, David Capuzzi, newly elected president-elect of AACD, asked Tom to be coordinator of the 1987 AACD Convention in New Orleans. Tom discussed a cooperative alliance with LACD members who encouraged him to run for LACD president. He proposed "that we combine our efforts to utilize the impetus of the national conference, our state volunteers, and our state organizations to pass the licensure bill." They agreed and Tom accepted the coordinator's role for the national conference.

The timing was perfect and Tom made the most of the opportunity. Working with Eloise Brown, Tom cocoordinated the 1986 Southern ACES (SACES) conference in New Orleans. Tom (personal communication, November 18, 2001) recalled these eventful years as follows:

> We were well into planning the national convention and making visits to New Orleans, so working to coordinate the SACES conference fit well into our efforts. Tom Terrell, Counseling Center Director at Southeastern Louisiana University, and I revised the licensure bill and worked with LACD to have the Association hire a lobbyist. The 1987 AACD Conference in New Orleans and the [Louisiana] licensure bill were both successful. It was a wonderful year of successes. I have had no other set of professional experiences like I had those two years [i.e., 1985–1987] . . . and no other experience to rival leading the number of people who worked together to make each event possible. I remember vividly taking the call from the lobbyist that the bill was about to pass. I rushed to the State House and went on the floor of the House to watch the bill pass. I was one of two LACD members there. There were a number of amendments to delete the power of the bill. The lobbyist brought House members to me and I suggested arguments against the amendments. No amendments were added and the bill passed.

I also remember the Awards Banquet on the last evening of the national conference. We had a New Orleans crew stage a Mardi Gras parade. Many people commented on the festivities of that evening and continue to comment about the event. People could not believe seeing the police motorcycles leading the parade and dripping oil on the rugs of the Hilton Hotel—only in New Orleans! There must have been 5,000 beads and trinkets thrown from the head table and by the audience that evening. Never before had AACD experienced such a rousing event. The volunteer group all expressed elation at staging the conference. It was a highlight for us.

The 1987 AACD Convention brought Tom into the "national counseling limelight." At the conclusion of the 1987 AACD Convention, a fellow counselor educator remarked to Tom's departmental secretary, "Tom is famous throughout the USA." This was news to the department. She replied, "Really? He sure isn't famous here!" One of Tom's most endearing qualities is his humility. Always the modest leader, Tom never seeks or acts like he is "in the limelight." He just rises to the occasion and quietly awes those of us who try to keep up with him.

After passage of the licensure bill, Tom was appointed by the Governor of Louisiana to serve as chairperson of the Licensure Board. In appreciation for his efforts in passing the bill, Tom was issued one of the first three licenses. He located the Licensure Board at LSU across the hall from the counselor education suite. He authored licensure board policies and rules adopted by the legislature. In its first year, the board licensed 450 Licensed Professional Counselors.

The Licensure Board remained at LSU for four years and operated very well. Tom later worked with Tom Terrell to revise the Licensure Act, expanding the roles of counselors and the powers of the board. In 1994, Tom was appointed again to the board, providing leadership in innovative changes (e.g., expanding the role of licensed professional counselors in the use of standardized tests, opposed by the state psychology association). Tom left Louisiana in 1996 to become department head of Counselor Education and Educational Psychology at Mississippi State University (MSU), where he continues the pursuit of excellence in professional counseling.

Tom's involvement with national associations did not end with the 1987 AACD Convention. Vernon Sheeley approached him in 1987 to be the SACES nominee for ACES president. He was elected president-elect in 1988 and served with Marianne Mitchell as president. Tom (personal communication, November 18, 2001) recalled his ACES presidency as follows:

She (Mitchell) was an excellent leader and role model. That year we were involved in holding ACES's first national conference in St. Louis. ACES was facing financial difficulties and the emphasis was on financial growth and stability. This emphasis carried over to my year as president (1989–90). The previous year I planned for the 50th anniversary celebration of the association. The celebration was held in Cincinnati. It was a wonderful opportunity to bring together many important and noted individuals in the profession. I asked Tom Sweeney and Ken Hoyt to give the keynote addresses. Paul Loans provided a comprehensive slide show of the history of the Association and Vernon Sheeley provided a booklet honoring the association and ACES presidents. Some of my goals, such as passage of the ACES Ethics Code for Supervisors, and increasing membership to 3,000 members, were attained the following year. However, I was able to institute the ACES Research Awards program.

From 1991 to 1992, Tom served on the American Counseling Association (ACA) Licensure Committee and participated in revising the "Model Licensure Bill." An explanation of model bill changes and a rationale supporting bill sections were published in the *Journal of Counseling & Development* (Glosoff, Benshoff, Hosie, & Mackey, 1995). At the conclusion of Tom's term as ACES immediate past-president, he was elected by the membership to represent ACES on the ACA Governing Council (1992–1995). Those were difficult financial times for the association. Tom emphasized the importance of ACA maintaining its subsidy to the Council for Accreditation of Counseling and Related Programs (CACREP). He worked with Don W. Locke and CACREP staff for that purpose and they were successful. Much of their time during those years was devoted to gathering financial data, revising budgets, and changing financial policies.

From 1991 to 1993, the ACA Governing Council asked Tom to chair a new coalition, the Coalition for Preparation and Practice Standards in Counseling (CPPS). The Coalition was comprised of CACREP, the Council for the Advancement of Standards in Higher Education (CAS), the Council on Rehabilitation Education (CORE), and the International Association of Counseling Services (IACS). He had chaired the ACA Professionalization Committee from 1991 to 1992 and had convened representatives of CPPS, the National Board for Certified Counselors (NBCC), and others to coalesce professional efforts. Eventually these efforts produced combined accreditation visits by CACREP and CORE and additional certification examinations by NBCC.

After serving on the ACA Governing Council, Tom was elected by the ACES Executive Council as treasurer (1995–1998). ACA experienced financial difficulties, affecting all ACA Divisions, including ACES. To alleviate financial concerns, ACA contracted with its divisions for services that previously were free or of minimal cost. This substantially increased division costs. As a consequence of this contractual arrangement, ACES became indebted to ACA for a substantial sum. Tom worked with ACA, ACES, and SACES officers to negotiate a satisfactory settlement (a delicate act of diplomacy). During his term as ACES treasurer, Tom instituted new budget practices to ensure better understanding of allocation and spending practices. ACES held two successful national conferences in Portland and New Orleans using budgets, policies, and revenue-sharing procedures with ACES regions that were developed by Tom.

During his term as ACES treasurer, Tom was appointed to represent ACA (1996–1999) on the CACREP Board. He had previously published an article (Hosie, 1995) in which he promoted the importance of a common counseling identity (rather than emphasizing specialties such as school counseling, family counseling, agency counseling, etc.). He was specifically selected to pursue this stance for ACA and he encouraged other CACREP Board members to maintain and develop accreditation standards identifying "counseling" as the primary area of graduate program emphasis. Tom was involved in the preparation of the 2001 CACREP standards in which the focus on generic "counseling" terminology is maintained, rather than variations of counseling specializations.

While serving in these positions, Tom also served on the editorial boards of the *Journal of Counseling & Development* and *Counselor Education and Supervision*. He thoroughly enjoyed reviewing manuscripts and assisting authors. The experience also kept him abreast of current ideas and emphases in the profession.

As a researcher, Tom is especially proud of some of his studies and other publications and he noted (personal communication, November 18, 2001):

> The study, "Pupil Preferences and the Premack Principle" (Hosie, Gentile, & Carroll, 1974), is the only replication of the Premack Principle (reinterpretation of the Law of Effect), and this study was an application of the principle in elementary school instruction. In addition, I view the studies by John West, James Mackey and myself (Hosie & Mackey 1995; Hosie, West, & Mackey, 1988, 1990, 1993; West, Hosie, & Mackey, 1987, 1988) as particularly important for the profession. We published most of these studies at a time when the profession was seeking information about the roles of counselors to support state licensure efforts. The studies showed that counselors were providing the same services with the same types of clients as the other licensed groups. I know that a number of state organizations of ACA and the American Mental Health Counseling Association (AMHCA) used these studies to make a case for licensure with legislators. John West, James Mackey, and I received national research awards from

AMHCA (1988), ACES (1989), and ACA (1991) for the studies. I see the studies we produced as my most significant contribution to the counseling profession.

## TOM'S UNIQUE LEADERSHIP

Thomas Walsh Hosie is living proof that nice guys can be effective. Tom is a man who empowers faculty and students to utilize their strengths and talents rather than rely on the dictates of others. He leads by example. He works diligently, yet always makes time to listen to faculty and students who seek his assistance. He chooses to spend his time efficiently by dealing immediately with important and urgent matters and by delaying reactions to matters of lesser importance. Tom also leads by working in the trenches. He was elected chair and coordinator of the Department Heads Executive Committee at MSU. If ever there was a "mission impossible," reaching consensus among department heads seems worthy of the title. Yet, Tom reaches consensus with this group on a regular basis.

Equally important to understanding Tom's leadership style is an appreciation of what he is *not* as well as what he *is*. In contrast to many leaders, Tom is *not* (a) prone to fits of rage, (b) likely to deliver boisterous/charismatic speeches, (c) "burned out," (d) offensively demanding (he respectfully requests), nor is he (e) a micromanager. Tom *is* a leader who shares responsibility.

In MSU's Department of Counselor Education and Educational Psychology, Tom delegates leadership duties for each of the department's six program areas to different faculty members who are called coordinators. He chairs timely monthly meetings with the coordinators, granting them great autonomy. He encourages without micromanaging. When he requests assistance from coordinators, they know that Tom expects them to complete their work without fear that he will supersede their efforts. Tom's leadership style is a mixture of inspiration, wisdom, respect, balance, maturity, relevancy, fairness, inclusiveness, and delegation.

Tom inspires by example. He prioritizes well and tackles tough issues "head-on." When necessary, Tom comes early and stays late to finish a project. He keeps his focus and is not distracted from his task. He remains respectful of others and does not allow deadlines to sour his disposition. I have frequently observed leaders, in moments of crisis, lose their temper and lash out at their colleagues. Tom simply does not do this. He forcefully and politely deals with relevant issues without demeaning those who enter his work space.

Tom seems to have mastered the art of judging when to pursue and when to let loose of ideas and plans in the world of counselor education. A few years ago, the department was involved in an exciting off-campus program in Puerto Rico. It had taken the faculty and adminstration many years to develop, and the faculty was very supportive of the program. However, the costs were prohibitive. After lengthy discussions with faculty and administration, Tom knew when to "let loose" and discontinue the program. He also knows when to pursue a plan. The departmental faculty had waited years for fiscal improvements to be made to their facilities. One faculty member, now retired, recalled being told that "a move to a new facility is imminent." Twenty-five years later, the move had not occurred. But, after diligent planning and negotiations, Tom made it possible for new departmental facilities this year.

## REFERENCES

Glosoff, H. L., Benshoff, J., Hosie. T. W., & Mackey, D. R. (1995). The 1994 ACA model legislation for licensed professional counselors. *Journal of Counseling & Development, 74*, 209–220.

Hosie, T. W. (1995). Counseling specialties: A case of basic preparation rather than advanced specialization. *Journal of Counseling & Development, 74*, 177–180.

Hosie, T. W., Gentile, J. R., & Carroll, J. D. (1974). Pupil preferences and the Premack principle. *American Educational Research Journal, 3*, 241–247.

Hosie, T. W., & Mackey, J. A. (1995). Employment and roles of counselors in Louisiana college counseling centers. *Louisiana Journal of Counseling, 6*, 10–17.

Hosie, T. W., West, J. D., & Mackey, J. A. (1988). Employment and roles of mental health counselors in substance-abuse centers. *Journal of Mental Health Counseling, 10*, 188–198.

Hosie, T. W., West, J. D., & Mackey, J. A. (1990). Perceptions of counselor performance in substance-abuse centers. *Journal of Mental Health Counseling, 12*, 199–207.

Hosie, T. W., West, J. D., & Mackey, J. A. (1993). Employment and roles of counselors in employee assistant programs. *Journal of Counseling & Development, 71*, 355–359.

West, J. D., Hosie, T. W., & Mackey, J. A. (1987). Employment and roles of counselors in mental health agencies. *Journal of Counseling & Development, 66*, 135–138.

West, J. D., Hosie, T. W., & Mackey, J. A. (1988). The counselor's role in mental health: An evaluation. *Counselor Education and Supervision, 27*, 233–239.

# CHAPTER 18

# Kenneth B. Hoyt

Harold B. Engen

*I believe the roots of guidance are found in human values as well as
in substantive knowledge.*

Kenneth B. Hoyt was born July 13, 1924 to Paul E. and Mary Helen Hoyt
in Cherokee, Iowa. He graduated from Wilson High School in his birth city
in 1942. College was not in his plans after high school, so Ken took a
typing test and subsequently obtained a position as a clerk-typist in the
Bureau of Internal Revenue in Washington, DC. He worked there from
June 1942 until March 1943 when he was drafted into the Army. He was
discharged from the Army in 1946, and the same year Ken married Phyllis
Howland on May 25. They are parents of three children: Roger, Andrew,
and Elinore.

Using the G. I. Bill, Ken enrolled in the University of Maryland in 1946
and graduated in 1948 with a B.S. degree in Education. He received his
M.A. degree in Counseling and Guidance at George Washington University
in the spring of 1950, and subsequently earned his Ph.D. in Educational
Psychology from the University of Minnesota in the summer of 1954.

## PROFESSIONAL DEVELOPMENT

During Ken's first semester at the University of Maryland's College of Education, he took a guidance course with Clifford Froehlich, who was to become his professional mentor. Froehlich suggested that Ken should consider becoming a high school counselor and then a counselor-trainer. In his second year at the University of Maryland, Ken was assigned to Montgomery Blair High School in Silver Spring, Maryland, for his practice teaching. He was allowed to teach a class on his own and he was paid as a full-time substitute teacher. This was his only full-time teaching experience at the high school level. In the summer of 1948, Froehlich arranged for Ken to work as a teacher/counselor at Northeast High School in Northeast, Maryland. He had three periods per day for guidance, taught a chemistry class, served as the school librarian, taught a class of 8th grade mathematics, and coached.

In 1949, while working on his master's degree, Ken became director of guidance in Westminster, Maryland. He taught one class in physics and was the counselor for about 1,500 students. In the spring of 1950 he finished his master's degree and Froehlich suggested it was time to enroll in a Ph.D. program. The University of Minnesota was selected and Ken was accepted for admission.

During his first year at the University of Minnesota, Ken served as a teaching assistant to his major advisor, Willis Dugan. At the end of that year, Dugan arranged for Ken to become a full-time instructor. His primary responsibility was teaching graduate extension courses in guidance and counseling in various parts of Minnesota and working with Minnesota high schools in developing their guidance programs. Ken stayed in this position for 3 years while working on his Ph.D. and has said he found it to be a valuable career experience.

In the fall of 1954, Ken joined the faculty of the University of Iowa as assistant professor of education in the area of counseling and guidance. As the only University of Iowa professor in this area, he had students interested in high school guidance, college student personnel work, vocational rehabilitation, and employment counseling. During the next 15 years as the division chairperson, Ken developed the Division of Counselor Education and secured outstanding faculty for each of the departments listed above. In 1969 he left Iowa to return to the University of Maryland as professor of education, and through 1984 Ken served in a variety of work settings: (a) professor of education, University of Maryland (1969–1974); (b) professor of education, University of Maryland, and director, Office of Career Education, U.S. Office of Education (1974–1976); (c) director, Office of Career Education, U.S. Department of Education (1976–1982); and (d) Member, Senior Executive Service, U.S. Department of Education, and Distinguished Visiting Scholar, Embry-Riddle Aeronautical University (1982–1984).

Ken has served as University Distinguished Professor of Education at Kansas State University since September 1984. He continues to occupy that position and he has been busy. During this time he has received seven special national honors, has been involved in 30 significant service activities, 12 major consulting activities, six monographs, seven chapters in books and printed conference proceedings, 21 special papers prepared under contract for national projects, and 45 journal articles. In addition, he has coauthored one book, *Counseling for High Skills: Responding to the Career Needs of all Students* (Hoyt & Maxey, 2001). A major proposition throughout this book is that excellence can be found in a wide variety of occupations that do not require a four-year college baccalaureate degree but do require some kind of education and training beyond high school. In Ken's career, he has written 98 journal articles, 42% of which contain "career education" in the title.

Ken's interest in professional association work began in 1956, when Clifford Froehlich, president of the American Personnel and Guidance Association (APGA), appointed him membership chairperson. Through various APGA activities, Ken became interested in the lack of involvement of individual members in the APGA's governmental policies. This is the primary reason Ken agreed to run for president and was elected for the 1966–1967 term. During his term of office, he worked toward what has become the APGA and now the American Counseling Association (ACA) Bylaws.

Ken's service to professional organizations did not end with APGA. In 1992, he became the permanent honorary president of the American Association for Career Education (AACE), as well as president of the National Career Development Association (NCDA) for the 1992–1993 term. He is a member of the American School Counselor Association (ASCA), Life Member of the Association for Counselor Education and Supervision (ACES), and is a member of eight other professional organizations. Ken was appointed the founding editor of *Counselor Education and Supervision* when ACES decided to initiate that journal.

Exclusive of state and local recognitions, Ken has been the recipient of 23 special national honors. He received the first Distinguished Service

Award from ACES in 1965, and the Arthur H. Hitchock Distinguished Professional Service Award from ACA in 1994.

When Ken came to the University of Iowa in 1954 there were few, if any, guidance programs in the Iowa schools. Drawing upon his experience in Minnesota, he provided several initiatives to get school guidance programs started. In 1957, Ken spoke to the county superintendents of Iowa, where he suggested that if they wanted to promote guidance they should hire a guidance consultant at the county level to encourage and facilitate the development of guidance programs in the schools in their counties. I was hired as one of 13 county guidance consultants and worked in two counties and started 10 school guidance programs with certified counselors. This was the age of the National Defense Education Act (NDEA), which provided funds to train counselors and start school guidance programs. Ken also directed summer NDEA Guidance Institutes to train certified counselors.

I attended meetings of the State Guidance Advisory Committee, where Ken and others created the progressive endorsement for state certification of counselors. Under the plan, an individual could be a teacher/counselor with a temporary endorsement after accumulating 15 semester hours of credit in guidance and counseling courses. The local school administration had to request the temporary endorsement and a university counselor education program had to file a plan for helping the individual complete the master's degree, which the Department of Public Instruction Guidance Section had to approve. This progressive counselor endorsement plan was another innovative approach to advocating for school guidance programs associated with the newly established NDEA Guidance Institutes.

It is not difficult to understand why Ken is an effective leader and consequently has created a legacy that has influenced the counseling profession and the work force of our country. During the early days of school guidance program development, he was a driving force in Minnesota and Iowa in creating new school guidance programs. His interpersonal skills included never talking down to individuals or groups, and his writings were readable and understandable. His writing included 11 books, 53 monographs, 32 chapters in books and printed conference proceedings, 41 special papers prepared under contract for national projects, and 97 journal articles. In addition, Ken was the first chairperson of the University of Iowa Counselor Education Program, the first director of the Office of Career Education (U.S. Department of Education), and president of three national counseling organizations, and he was engaged in 92 significant professional service activities. These contributions resulted in 23 special national honors exclusive of state and local special honors. His 55-year dedication to the career needs of all students and to career education has impacted the work force of our nation. Truly, Kenneth B. Hoyt has created a legacy by his 234 products listed above, and we will continue to see a flow of professional contributions in the future.

## MEMORIES OF WORKING WITH KEN HOYT

I first met Ken in 1961 when I was a member of the production committee of the first Iowa Guidance Handbook, *Guidance Services: Suggested Policies for Iowa Schools* (Hoyt, 1963). Ken suggested we needed a set of policies to facilitate the development of guidance in the state. He was chairperson of the writing committee, and several of us contributed rough drafts and Ken then took our material and wrote the final draft. I traveled with a group that presented the new handbook at implementation meetings in several locations around the state. At one of the meetings, I asked Ken to come in and critique my presentation on group counseling. After the presentation he said, "Well, Harold, no one knows what group counseling is and you sounded like you did, so I guess it was OK." Whenever I gave a talk, wrote an article, or developed a workshop for counselors, I would receive a memo from Ken stating how much he appreciated what I was doing. Ken continued to send me notes after he left the University of Iowa. With his help and support my career has been very fulfilling. Ken has been my mentor, much in the same way Clifford Froehlich and Willis Dugan had been for him.

## REFERENCES

Hoyt, K. B. (1963). *Guidance services: Suggested policies for Iowa schools.* Des Moines, IA: Iowa Department of Public Instruction.

Hoyt, K. B., & Maxey, J. (2001). *Counseling for high skills: Responding to career needs of all students.* Greensboro, NC: ERIC/CASS

# CHAPTER 19

# Courtland C. Lee

Barbara Herlihy and Morgan Brooks

*A gentleman and a scholar*

Courtland C. Lee was born in Philadelphia in 1949. He was the oldest of four children born to his mother, a homemaker, and his father, who worked for the U.S. Post Office. Legacies from his parents include the value of hard work, an aesthetic appreciation, and a social consciousness.

Courtland characterizes his high school years as the most challenging of all his academic experiences. He attended an all-male, all-academic, competitive high school. He remembers his first day, when the principal stood in front of the freshman class and told them that they were there to become gentlemen and scholars. Over the next 4 years, he learned two skills that would prove to be crucial to his life and career: to write and to think critically.

## EDUCATION AND CAREER PATH

After his high school graduation, Courtland enrolled at Hofstra University. His undergraduate years were a time of social upheaval. The Civil Rights Movement and the Vietnam War permeated his college experience. He marched for civil rights and protested the war, and these events were instrumental in shaping the views on access, equity, and social action that formed his core values with respect to his work in multicultural counseling.

After he graduated from college, Courtland had planned to become a high school social studies teacher. Instead, he found himself teaching elementary school in the Bedford-Stuyvesant section of Brooklyn, which at the time was one of the largest African American and Puerto Rican communities in the country as well as one of the most economically disadvantaged. His emerging leadership skills were evidenced at this early stage in his career, when he and his colleagues threw out the Board of Education's curriculum that was not meeting student needs and developed new and creative ways of teaching these extremely poor but bright and resilient children. The issues of poverty and diversity he encountered on a daily basis formed the foundation for his views on counseling clients from diverse cultural backgrounds.

Because Courtland was the only African American male teacher in the Bedford-Stuyvesant school, the other teachers would send their problematic boys to him in hopes that interacting with a male teacher would be helpful. The school's guidance counselor noticed that Courtland had a gift for connecting with these students and suggested that he might make a good counselor. She convinced him to enroll in a counseling graduate program and pursue his master's degree. He attended Hunter College of the City University of New York. There, he met Alfred Pasteur, who was the first (and only) African American professor he had in his training program and who was to become a profoundly significant mentor. Pasteur encouraged Courtland to pursue his doctoral degree and helped him obtain admission to Michigan State University, where he participated in a program funded by the National Institutes of Mental Health to prepare doctoral-level professionals to work with ethnic minority client groups in urban settings. This program helped him coalesce his experiences from the Bedford-Stuyvesant school and from working with Pasteur into a model and philosophy of mental health intervention that emphasizes both cultural responsiveness and systemic intervention.

Upon completion of his Ph.D. degree in 1979, Courtland began his career as a counselor educator at the University of North Carolina at Chapel Hill. During his years at UNC-Chapel Hill he began to develop his line of research, although his interest in studying ethnic minorities in urban areas did not really resonate with his senior colleagues. He began to achieve a national reputation for his work with African American mental health issues.

In 1987, he accepted a position as director of the Counselor Education Program at the University of Virginia, where he stayed until 2000. He considers this to be the most prolific period of his career. He published two of his most important and influential scholarly works. *Multicultural Issues in Counseling: New Approaches to Diversity* (1997), now going into its third edition, has become one of the American Counseling Association's (ACA) best-selling works. Courtland has donated the royalties from this book to the ACA Foundation to provide financial support for counseling graduate students who demonstrate a commitment to multicultural and diversity issues in their work. The second book, *Saving the Native Son: Empowerment Strategies for Young Black Males* (1996), has been a best-seller among mental health professionals and has been used by youth workers in a number of foreign countries.

The mentor who most significantly influenced Courtland's professional career path was Pasteur, whom Courtland first met when he enrolled in Pasteur's class on social systems in counseling at Hunter College. At that time, Courtland knew that the course of his professional life was set. Pasteur, one of the founding parents of the multicultural counseling movement, took Courtland under his wing and encouraged him to pursue his passion for issues related to minority (and particularly African-American) mental health. He gave Courtland the courage to question the Eurocentric ideas he had been taught and showed him that, as an African American, he had a valid alternative view of personality. As Pasteur's protégé, Courtland had opportunities to meet the "giants" of the multicultural counseling field and to attend his first professional conference, the 1975 American Personnel and Guidance Association (APGA) Convention. Working as a student volunteer at the convention, he met people whose works he had read and whose ideas about ethnic minority mental health were shaping his professional identity.

Shortly after Courtland received his doctorate at Michigan State University, Gloria Smith, his advisor, recommended him to John McFadden, the president of the Association for Non-White Concerns in Personnel and Guidance (ANWC), as an "up and comer." John McFadden offered him the position of secretary-treasurer of the organization, and his competent handling of the job brought him recognition as someone with real leadership potential. This led to Courtland's appointment as editor of the *Journal of Non-White Concerns in Personnel and Guidance*. During his 6-year term as editor, he spearheaded the journal's name change to the *Journal of Multicultural Counseling and Development* and improved its quality and content.

His editorship provided opportunities for him to become a mentor himself, assisting young scholars with their writing efforts. Additionally, after Courtland began his career as a counselor educator at UNC-Chapel Hill, he began to mentor a number of graduate students who were primarily African American. For these students he was a mentor, parent figure, confessor, and advocate, an experience that caused him to reflect on how powerful Pasteur's influence had been, as he was now passing on Pasteur's wisdom and insights to a new generation.

Courtland's years at the University of Virginia were his most active in terms of professional leadership. In 1988 and 1989, he served as president of the Association for Multicultural Counseling and Development (AMCD). This leadership position, along with the journal editorship and his own growing scholarship, provided him with opportunities to interact with leaders throughout the counseling profession. It was at this time that he began his involvement with counseling on an international level. Bob Nejedlo, who was president of the American Association for Counseling and Development (AACD) at the time, was working to hold a bilateral conference in London with the British Association for Counselling (BAC), with a theme that centered on multicultural issues. As a result of Courtland's appointment to the planning committee, he made several trips to London and developed friendships with members of the British team. He became a member of BAC, attended their training conference as ACA's official representative, and over time became actively involved in other BAC professional development activities. He presented workshops at annual training conferences, served several times as keynote speaker, and was actively involved in the division that dealt with multicultural issues. In 1999, Courtland was recognized as a Fellow of BAC, the first and only American to be awarded this honor.

In addition to his involvement with BAC, Courtland became actively involved in the professional activities of the International Roundtable for the Advancement of Counseling (IRTAC). He presented at their conferences throughout the 1990s and was the association's secretary. Beginning in 1995, he served as the association's nongovernmental representative to the United Nations, which gave him the opportunity to represent counseling internationally.

During the late 1980s and into the early 1990s, Courtland was offered a number of leadership positions within APGA/AACD/ACA that took him beyond the limits of multicultural counseling. These included: chairing the AACD Men's Committee, the ACA Media Committee, and the Association for Counselor Education and Supervision (ACES) Awards Committee; serving on the Council for the Accreditation of Counseling and Related Educational Programs' (CACREP) Board of Directors and the planning committees for two national ACES conferences; and chairing the ACA Council of Journal Editors. In addition, he served on the editorial boards of the *Journal of Counseling & Development* and *Career Development Quarterly.*

Courtland was a charter member of his chapter of Chi Sigma Iota (CSI) at the University of Virginia, and in 1994 Carol Bobby encouraged him to run for president of CSI. He served in this capacity from 1995 to 1996 and counts among the highlights his efforts in coordinating the activities for the 10th anniversary celebration and traveling around the country to speak at initiation ceremonies. He enjoyed speaking to the next generation of counselors about what was important to him with respect to leadership in counseling. For Courtland, leadership is about helping to empower people to be all that they can be and ensuring that one's efforts leave people and things better. In 1997, he was one of the inaugural members to be inducted into the CSI Academy of Leaders for Excellence.

In 1997, Courtland was elected president of ACA. He chose for his presidential theme, "Empowerment Through Social Action." This theme resulted in a book co-edited with Garry Walz, *Social Action: A Mandate for Counselors* (1998). When he assumed the presidency, ACA was in a precarious financial state and several divisions that were philosophically opposed to the mission of ACA were threatening to disaffiliate. His leadership objective was to build consensus around our core values as professional counselors regardless of our various work settings or specialties. For this reason Courtland convened the Millennium Commission, which had representatives from all ACA stakeholders, and charged it with developing a governance model that would allow stakeholders a degree of autonomy while maintaining their ties to ACA. Concurrently, the ACA Governing Council approved a policy that allowed members a certain degree of choice regarding their membership in the association and its divisions. Both of these measures helped to stave off division measures to disaffiliate. Also during his presidency, he convened a Multicultural/Diversity Summit and charged the leaders to develop a multicultural/diversity agenda for the association. From this summit came a document that charted a course for the association on issues of access and equity. Of all Courtland's accomplishments during his presidency, he is proudest of the work accomplished at this Summit.

In July 1999, Courtland's term as ACA president came to an end and he joined the ranks of the association's "elder statespersons." After having served as Dean of the College of Education at his alma mater, Hunter College, for a brief period, Courtland is now on the counseling program faculty at the University of Maryland. At this time, he looks forward to serving in a consultative role to other leaders and to contributing to the profession through his writings and presentations on multicultural issues and through his ongoing mentoring of young professionals. He plans to continue his research on indigenous models of helping in nonwestern cultures and their relationship to counseling. In addition, he plans to finish his work on a project investigating the impact of generational membership and its role in shaping counselors' views of their role and function.

## REFLECTIONS ON WORKING TOGETHER

As an endnote to this acknowledgment, we offer our personal reflections on our interactions with Courtland, from the two perspectives: a peer (Barbara) and a protégée (Morgan). In reflecting on my (Barbara's) experiences working with Courtland, my first thought is that his high school principal would be proud of him. He is, indeed, a gentleman and a scholar. Perhaps what I most appreciate about Courtland as a scholar is that, through his writings and speaking, he has challenged me to move out of my comfort zone and to rethink my vision of who I want to be and what I want to contribute as a scholar and practitioner of counseling. For example, his work on indigenous healers has caused me to redefine my concept of the helping relationship and who I am within it. Ever since I was interviewed for his "generations" project, I have found myself pondering what it means to be a member of the "early baby boomer" generation whose defining events were the assassinations of four charismatic leaders. When I view myself within the larger social context in which Courtland reminds me I am situated, I see congruence among the profession I have chosen to pursue, the city where I have chosen to live, the people with whom I have chosen to work, and the commitment I share with Courtland to mentoring the next generation of counseling professionals.

As a beginning doctoral student, I (Morgan) was honored and humbled by Courtland Lee's offer to be a mentor to me. I met him when he came to the University of New Orleans to present a workshop on Advanced Multiculturalism. His dedication to multicultural issues and his commitment to his community and giving to others opened my eyes to something that is missing in my generation. My generation has not had a defining event to rally around. We have been raised in a selfish time and we have not had a sense of community and banding together.

Courtland Lee, as a member of a generation that came together to promote causes such as peace and racial harmony, has offered me a model for the intergenerational transmission of the value of helping others. As a White female, I may not be one of Courtland's typical protégées. As I see him extend his mentoring to encompass those who are different from himself, I am encouraged that I can make a difference, as he has for so many.

## REFERENCES

Lee, C. C. (1996). *Saving the native son: Empowerment strategies for young Black males*. Greensboro, NC: ERIC Counseling and Student Services Clearinghouse.

Lee, C. C. (Ed.). (1997). *Multicultural issues in counseling: New approaches to diversity* (2nd ed.). Alexandria, VA: American Counseling Association.

Lee., C. C., & Walz, G. (Eds.). (1998). *Social action: A mandate for counselors.* Alexandria, VA: American Counseling Association and ERIC Counseling and Student Services Clearinghouse.

# CHAPTER 20

# Judith A. Lewis

Jon Carlson, John Cebuhar, and Jane Goodman

*Celebrating the human spirit*

Judy Lewis grew up in the heart of Detroit, Michigan, and still remains most comfortable in the midst of an urban throng. She is the older of two children (her brother, Bill, is 3 years her junior). Throughout her childhood, Judy's family lived in a two-family home, with her aunt, uncle, and two older cousins living downstairs. The extended family was close enough that Judy's many Adlerian friends may have asked: "Was Judy the oldest child or the third?" Fortunately, her readily apparent firstborn personality style has cleared up the question.

Judy's parents strongly encouraged her to study typing and shorthand in school. During her senior year in high school, she left school at noon every day along with other members of the retailing co-op class. Actually, she has always valued how much she learned about life at People's Outfitting Company, where she worked during high school and again during her college summer vacations. (She also continues to find her shorthand useful when taking notes at a lecture.)

Judy got accepted at the University of Michigan, where she took to academic life enthusiastically and began to surprise her family and herself. She lived in dormitory housing throughout her undergraduate years and became part of a group of close friends who still get together forty years later. Her degree was in political science (still one of her major interests), but she decided in her last year of undergraduate work to get a teaching certificate and an endorsement to teach English (her minor subject).

## CAREER DEVELOPMENT

Immediately after college graduation, Judy began her career in teaching, first in junior high school and then in high school. While teaching full-time, she earned two master's degrees from Eastern Michigan University: one in social sciences and the other in counseling. As soon as she had completed her degree in counseling, Judy embarked on her career as a high school counselor, first at Garden City High School in Michigan and then at Niles North High School in Illinois. Her doctoral work in counseling at the University of Michigan was largely completed while she worked full-time as a school counselor.

Judy was still a doctoral student when she began to publish work reflecting a lifelong theme: creating counseling models that encourage an environmental and social-justice-oriented perspective. Her earliest articles were authored or coauthored before she had completed her doctorate and included one coauthored with a high school student (Lewis & Schaffner, 1970). Judy's Ph.D. dissertation (Lewis, 1970) was written while the Vietnam War still raged. Based on data collected at Niles North High School, the dissertation focused on the characteristics of high school student anti-war activists.

Judy greeted both her new doctorate and her new son, Keith, in 1970. She and Keith followed her then-husband to Florida for one year. Her work there continued to reflect her social, political, and multicultural interests. She was part of a team of school–community relations consultants working with the Palm Beach County schools during the first year of court-ordered desegregation. While in Florida, she coedited two special issues of *The Personnel and Guidance Journal* (now, of course, the *Journal of Counseling & Development*), "Counseling and the Social Revolution" (Lewis, Lewis, & Dworkin, 1971) and "Women and Counselors" (Lewis, 1972).

Returning to Illinois, Judy obtained her first counselor education position, teaching in the master's and doctoral programs in counseling at Loyola University of Chicago. The first edition of *Community Counseling: A Human Services Approach* (Lewis & Lewis, 1977), which continued her focus on environmental as well as experiential interventions, was completed during that time. When Judy moved on to the University of San Francisco in 1975 for a position as director of community-based education, her scholarly work veered toward community-based mental health training and accessible higher education.

After four years in San Francisco, Judy left for England to teach for a year in a counseling graduate program offered under the auspices of Peabody College of Vanderbilt University. After that year, she accepted a visiting associate professorship at the home campus in Nashville, and she and the late Roger Aubrey subsequently researched and completed the article "Social Issues and the Counseling Profession in the 1980s and 1990s" (Aubrey & Lewis, 1983). Although Judy was only in Nashville for two years, she formed many lasting professional relationships. In fact, three of her recent books have coauthors who share the Vanderbilt connection: Loretta Bradley, coeditor of *Advocacy in Counseling: Counselors, Clients, and Community* (Lewis & Bradley, 2000); Michael D'Andrea, coauthor of *Community Counseling: Empowerment Strategies for a Diverse Society* (Lewis, Lewis, Daniels, & D'Andrea, 1998); and Robert Dana, coauthor of *Substance Abuse Counseling* (Lewis, Dana, & Blevins, 2001).

Judy returned to Illinois in 1982 and has been there ever since. After spending two years as director of a grant for employee assistance programming, she joined the faculty at Governors State University. She has enjoyed the university because of its diverse and interesting student body, its focus on educational innovation, and its excellent faculty. She has been a four-time recipient of the Faculty Excellence Award and has twice been named as the university's Distinguished Professor. She has also enjoyed collaborative relationships with other faculty with whom she has published extensively.

Throughout her career, Judy has been active in professional association activities. Across several American Counseling Association (ACA) divisions, she served on human rights, media, and program committees, as well as on the editorial boards of *The Personnel and Guidance Journal, The Family Journal: Counseling and Therapy for Couples and Families*, and the *Journal of Humanistic Education and Development*. In addition, Judy served as president of the International Association of Marriage and Family Counselors from 1996 to 1998 and as president of ACA from 2000 to 2001. In both of these positions, she focused on increasing the size and diversity of the pool of potential leaders and was able to maintain climates that were collaborative and inclusive.

As president of ACA, Judy led efforts to reach out to students and new professionals and to celebrate diverse cultures. Her theme, "Counseling at Its Best: Celebrating the Human Spirit," encouraged counselors to emphasize their clients' strengths and resources, to use developmental and preventive skill-building methods, to increase their multicultural competencies, and to be courageous in confronting harmful social environments. She continues to emphasize these ideas as an officer of Counselors for Social Justice.

Judy's emphasis on collaboration and inclusiveness reflects her commitment to a leadership style that has been described by Eisler (1987) in terms of *partnership* versus *dominator* cultures. Dominator cultures have hierarchical structures, make clear distinctions between superiors and subordinates, suppress differences, and resolve conflicts through competition and conquest. In contrast, partnership cultures celebrate diversity and equality and resolve conflicts through cooperation. Judy sees leadership positions as opportunities to help organizations embrace partnership models. She puts this in practice by using shared decision-making processes, modeling problem-solving methods designed to enhance creativity, and welcoming diverse voices into participation and leadership.

## WORKING WITH JUDY LEWIS

Judy takes particular joy in the relationships she has developed over the decades she has spent in the counseling profession. What follows are experiences shared by three of these people: Jon Carlson, a long-time friend and colleague; Jon Cebuhar, a student; and Jane Goodman, a current member of the ACA family of leaders.

### Reflections From a Colleague and Friend

Over the years I (Jon Carlson) have known Judy Lewis, there have been many times when the two of us looked at the same phenomena but saw different things. We have been friends, colleagues, and coauthors for many years. Judy not only saw things I did not see but was able to articulate them in a fashion that could change my vision. For example, she taught me that I had not been very gender sensitive and proceeded to invite my wife, Laura, to attend a consciousness-raising group. With Laura "enlightening me" on the practical front and Judy on the theoretical front, I have been able to raise three daughters with new eyes and ears.

Judy also taught me about multicultural relations and oppression. She did this by convincing me that hiring Mary Arnold at Governors State was a good thing. By having Mary in the next office and Judy down the hall, I learned about being a person of privilege, patriarchy, and oppression, and I learned about social justice. The amazing thing is that all of this has been done with an air of love and caring.

Judy has taught me about the importance of being inclusive. Judy and I have attended many meetings and conferences together. She is always having "dinners" and insisting that I attend. Her friends (who have also become mine) were different than my friends. They were not all White heterosexual men of European descent! Through these dinners and other contacts I learned the importance of hearing many voices rather than just the one of the privileged.

I am very thankful to have had a long life of Judy's training. Although the above are certainly not all that I have learned, they seem to be among the most important. Judy's extensive publishing record, which has given vision and voices to many who were not represented, is well known. It might not be as visible to others what a real friend and colleague she has been.

## Reflections From a Student

I (John Cebuhar) received my bachelor's degree from Governors State University (GSU) in 1986 and Judy Lewis was one of my professors. We have always stayed in touch and she has kept track of my career. When I became incapable of working because of illness, Judy managed to bring me back into the GSU family in the master's degree program. Judy has been a tremendous mentor, instructor, and friend. The quality of my life has markedly improved because of Judy's efforts. In addition, the quality of the counseling profession improved because of her efforts! Judy is one of those very special people who is bigger than life yet so down to earth that one would never know of her myriad accomplishments.

I have found Judy to be an exacting instructor and a challenging mentor. Most of all, however, she is a faithful friend. Judy's only glaring character defect is that she is incapable of accepting a compliment without brushing it off. That is sad because Judy deserves many compliments for many different reasons. Judy is a *mensch*, an old-world term that means that Judy not only measures up to the challenges of life but exceeds the measure. I think one of her greatest joys is helping others see that they too can make a difference.

## Reflections From an ACA Leader

What a treat for me (Jane Goodman) to have the opportunity to write some words about Judy Lewis. It has been my great privilege to get to know Judy personally during these past 2 years. I had known her as an acquaintance, and of course, by reputation prior to my election to follow her into the ACA presidency. But getting to know her "up close" has been one of the delights of my professional involvement.

How can I describe her to you? First, Judy is passionate in commitment to social justice, to the underdog, to the underserved, to those without representation, to those, in short, who need our advocacy. She demonstrates that commitment in so many ways. Her scholarship has often focused on advocacy. She is one of the founding members of Counselors for Social Justice, an organizational affiliate and soon to be a division of ACA. She spent time helping that group organize its activities, including a rally at the 2001 ACA World Conference in San Antonio and a day of learning about social justice for the 2002 ACA World Conference in New Orleans. She keeps ACA on its toes with regard to social justice and advocacy issues by making sure that we maintain the words of dedication to human dignity and diversity in all of our public statements, and that we follow those words with action whenever and wherever appropriate.

I have found that Judy's commitment is not confined to a macro level. On a personal level, she encourages students from diverse backgrounds to get involved professionally, paving the way when appropriate. She initiated a day of leadership training for emerging leaders to be held at the annual ACA World Conference and made sure that the leaders selected for this training represented diverse backgrounds. She supported our Hispanic colleagues through *Celebrando*, a special strand of Spanish language programs at "her" 2001 ACA World Conference in San Antonio. She nominates people for committees, recommends them for awards, and generally supports folks who otherwise might not be included in organizational leadership activities.

Finally, Judy is a loyal and generous friend. She has opened her home to me, picked me up and taken me to the train, made me dinner, and helped me throughout my year as her president-elect and in my year as president of ACA. I can't imagine how I would have fulfilled my responsibilities without her help—and gentle reminders when I forgot critical things! We are all very fortunate that she chose the profession of counseling in which to spend her energy and her talents.

## CONCLUSION

Judy's lifelong commitment to social justice, egalitarianism, and inclusion has characterized her relationships, her scholarship, and her leadership activities. Her approach to leadership encouraged many ACA members to become actively involved in the work of the association. The climate that she helped to create allowed her to write in her final presidential column (Lewis, 2001) that ACA had achieved a sense of *collective efficacy*, with members being enthusiastic about working together under the assumption that pressing problems could be solved and important tasks accomplished. As she wrote in that column, "Collective efficacy is all about saying yes to innovation, saying yes to action, and saying yes to one another."

## REFERENCES

Aubrey, R. F., & Lewis, J. A. (1983). Social issues and the counseling profession in the 1980s and 1990s. *Counseling and Human Development, 15* (10), 1–16.

Eisler, R. (1987). *The chalice and the blade.* San Francisco: Harper & Row.

Lewis, J. A. (1970). *A study of the characteristics of a group of high school student activists as compared with the characteristics of a group of peers not associated with the activist movement.* Ph.D. Dissertation: University of Michigan.

Lewis, J. A. (Ed.). (1972). *Women and counselors* [Special issue]. *The Personnel and Guidance Journal, 51* (2) (whole issue).

Lewis, J. A. (2001, June). Developing a sense of collective efficacy. *Counseling Today,* p. 5.

Lewis, J. A., & Bradley, L. J. (Eds.). (2000). *Advocacy in counseling: Counselors, clients, & community.* Greensboro, NC: ERIC/CASS.

Lewis, J. A., Dana, R. Q., & Blevins, G. A. (2001). *Substance abuse counseling* (3rd ed.). Pacific Grove, CA: Brooks/Cole.

Lewis, J. A., & Lewis, M. D. (1977). *Community counseling: A human services approach.* New York: Wiley.

Lewis, J. A., Lewis, M. D., Daniels, J., & D'Andrea, M. (1998). *Community counseling: Empowerment strategies for a diverse society* (4th ed.). Pacific Grove, CA: Brooks/Cole.

Lewis, M. D., Lewis, J. A., & Dworkin, E. P. (Eds.). (1971). *Counseling and the social revolution* [Special issue]. *The Personnel and Guidance Journal, 49* (whole issue).

Lewis, J. A., & Schaffner, M. (1970). Draft counseling in the secondary school. *The School Counselor, 18,* 89–90.

# CHAPTER 21

# Don C. Locke

Marie Faubert

*Culture is to be nurtured. Cultural diversity makes us strong.*

Don C. Locke was born in Macon, Mississippi, and grew up in Sunflower, Mississippi, the only son of Willie Raymond and Carlene Lovely Locke. He was introduced to the values that have stood by him throughout his life while he was growing up on the family farm with his parents, who encouraged him to be excellent in every way, especially to be a caring person of integrity. He married Marjorie P. Myles on June 27, 1964, and they have two adult daughters, Tonya Elizabeth and Regina Camille, both professional women. Don and Marjorie instilled in their daughters an appreciation for who they are as Lockes and as African American women. Don and his family are spirit-filled people of faith, strong and courageous, consistent in excellence and persevering.

Don graduated from Gentry High School, Indianola, Mississippi, having been elected senior class president. He earned a B.S. in history from Tennessee State University in Nashville, where he graduated with honors. He continued at Tennessee State University to obtain an M.Ed. in history education. He taught social studies at South Side High School in Fort Wayne, Indiana, for six years, having been the first African American employed in the high schools of Fort Wayne in 1964. He worked as a school counselor at Wayne High School for two years before entering Ball State University, where he earned his doctorate in guidance and counseling with a minor in psychology in 1974.

Don is an active member of the community in which he lives. He has served as a community representative on his local newspaper's editorial board, a member of the Asheville-Buncombe United Way Board, and the North Carolina United Way Board. He finds time to tutor in a local elementary school and cooks meals in a homeless shelter once a month. He is a member of Emmanuel Lutheran Church in Asheville and is a life member of both Alpha Phi Alpha Fraternity, Inc., and the National Association for the Advancement of Colored People (NAACP).

Don has consistently and conscientiously applied what he learned from his family and his education in history as the underpinnings for dedicating his life to enhancing better understanding among diverse peoples, especially the appreciation of African Americans, their experiences in the United States, and their role in building the United States. He has contributed significantly to enhancing appreciation for the consequences of racism for all.

## PROFESSIONAL LEADERSHIP

Don C. Locke has been a leader at North Carolina State University since he joined the faculty in 1975 as assistant professor. He rose through the ranks and became professor and head of the Department of Counselor Education at the campus in Raleigh. In 1993 he moved to Asheville, North Carolina, to assume the directorship of the North Carolina State University Doctoral Program in Adult and Community College Education at the Asheville Graduate Center. Don retains his appointment as professor in the Department of Counselor Education at North Carolina State University, where he sits on doctoral student committees and acts as an advisor and mentor to future counselor educators. He was appointed director of the Asheville Graduate Center in 2000.

Don has shown leadership (a) in the professional development of counseling, (b) in raising consciousness concerning the salience of multicultural issues in the counseling profession, and (c) as a teacher-mentor of his graduate students. That he has professional counselor license number 001 in North Carolina is testimony to the herculean contribution he has made to professional counseling.

Don served as President of the Association for Counselor Education and Supervision (ACES) in 2000–2001. In this capacity, he focused on diversity issues in counselor education programs. His efforts were directed toward improving the success of counselor education programs in hiring and retaining professors from diverse backgrounds and in graduating a diverse student body both competent and confident as professional counselors.

Don also served as President of Chi Sigma Iota (1999–2000), the Counseling and Academic Professional Honor Society International. In this capacity, he traveled to local chapters to enhance their success as facilitators of leaders in the counseling profession. He has been active in the American Counseling Association (ACA), the Association for Multicultural Counseling and Development (AMCD), the North Carolina Counseling Association, and other counseling organizations. In addition, Don has been active in establishing and facilitating professional development opportunities. In the latter capacities, Don has often been called upon to serve as a leader of strategic planning and multicultural diversity. His skill in this area is well known to those who have helped move organizations forward under his leadership.

He has been recognized for his professional leadership in being honored by ACA with its professional development award in 1996 and being inducted into the Chi Sigma Iota Academy of Leaders in 1997. He is a lifetime member of Phi Kappa Phi and has been included in *Who's Who Among Black Americans.*

Don has dedicated his professional life to helping people understand the significance of cultural issues in professional counseling. He has provided an important rationale for distinguishing between culture and diversity, sometimes referred to as the focused view of multiculturalism, and has developed the "Locke Paradigm" for conceptualizing issues related to cultural difference. The latter is formalized in his book *Increasing Multicultural Understanding: A Comprehensive Model* (1998). In this text, he presents "A Blueprint for Multicultural Understanding." In the introductory paragraph, he writes:

> We are living in an age of diversity. The roles of . . . counselors have been expanded to include the consideration of the cultural identities of . . . clients. . . . [C]ounselors have a responsibility to increase their awareness, knowledge, and skills so that all . . . clients are taught and counseled with approaches that recognize the influences of cultural group membership. (p. xi)

The "Locke Paradigm" investigates culture from 10 different perspectives, namely, acculturation, concept of poverty, history of oppression, language and arts, racism and prejudice, sociopolitical factors, child rearing practices, religion, family structure, and cultural values and attitudes (Locke, 1998). Don's focused view of culture allows for understanding the difference between culture and diversity. For example, gender issues, which are sociopolitical in nature and have common features across cultures, have many aspects that are culture specific. Certainly, issues of oppression for African American women are different from those for European-American women.

Another example is language. Some languages and accents are valued, and some are devalued in the culture dominant in the United States. Whether or not a language or accent is valued or devalued influences the persons speaking in those languages or accents. Don was one of the first counselor educators to address the issue of language difference in counseling. Style of language was a concern for Don early in his work as a professional counselor and later as a counselor educator.

In his book *Increasing Multicultural Understanding: A Comprehensive Model*, he writes:

> A major question within the dominant culture [in the United States] is how much the culture should tolerate those who do not speak Standard English. . . . The ability to speak Standard English . . . becomes a symbolic measure by which members of culturally diverse groups are often judged. (p. 10)

The "Locke Paradigm" investigates the above-named salient issues in the context of research, theory, and curriculum and from the point of view of the individual, family, community, culture, and world. In the world of the Internet, where communication is instantaneous, Don's contributions, as summarized in his "Locke Paradigm," serve as preface, framework, and substance for current professional conversation in counselor education. In summary, Don C. Locke has contributed extensively to theory building in the discourse on culture and diversity.

In his publications, Don facilitates inclusiveness and applies it to professional counseling. His most recent contributions have expanded his ongoing theoretical and research work into the area of cross-cultural competencies, where he has collaborated with many other authorities in the field to operationalize multicultural counseling competencies (Arredondo et al., 1996). His work has also emphasized the practical application of teaching multicultural issues in counseling both in a focused course and integrated into the total curriculum of counselor education. A recent chapter coauthored with Marie Faubert (1999) is an illustration of this work. Don has recently collaborated with Jane Myers and Edwin Herr (2001) in editing *The Handbook of Counseling,* which focuses exclusively on the counseling profession, especially its distinctiveness among other helping professions. Indeed, this book may be his greatest contribution to the profession since it extends his influence far beyond his multicultural focus.

Don's sustained contributions in research and teaching have naturally included an application of what he has learned about service to the community. He has received many research grants that have impacted his town, one of the most significant of which is *Getting on the Right Track*, a four-year grant from the BellSouth Foundation in which African American, rural, high school students were mentored and taught to appreciate their identities through rigorous academic and social experiences. The results of this research are published in the *Journal of Adolescence* (Faubert, Locke, Sprinthall, & Howland, 1996). This grant resulted in its findings being replicated successfully as far away from North Carolina State University as Houston, Texas, where it is being applied in an inner city high school that serves both African American and Latin 226American students.

A more recent research grant is *Race, Gender, and Bargaining Behaviors* (1994–1995), sponsored by the University of North Carolina at Asheville's Professional Development Fund, where he considered the intersection of race and gender in conversations that have important consequences for those engaged in them. His research project, *Talking in the Street and Talking in School* (1990–1991), was one of the first instances where professionals in counselor education took a serious look at language and its impact on student achievement in high school. An educational videotape was made as a result of this grant, sponsored by the Z. Smith Reynolds Foundation, in order that other professionals could access its findings.

## TEACHER/ADVISOR/MENTOR

Don C. Locke has been my teacher, advisor, and mentor. I met him in 1986. He was brought to my attention in a small brochure that described the Counselor Education Program at North Carolina State University, where he was at that time associate professor. I noticed that he and I had common interests in research, teaching, and service. I became part of the Counselor Education Program as a student from 1986 through 1992.

My first course in the program was his well-known course in multicultural counseling. His class was made up of a mix of African American, Native American, and European American students. His influence was already bearing fruit in terms of making the student body in the College of Education at North Carolina State University look more like the population of the State of North Carolina and of the southeastern region of the United States.

Don has challenged students' thinking, feeling, and behaving around issues of culture and race. I remember discussing the word "slave" and how denoting people with such a word was demeaning and perpetuated a deficiency model. The suggested alternative denotations were many; the one I remember is "persons held in slavery." We learned the advantage of a difference model as opposed to a deficiency model.

I tell Don that he has taught me everything I know about counseling. I know that is hyperbole, but even when I learn new things, I relate them to what he has taught me. He taught me to meet the client as a colleague in the journey of life and to have a professional conversation. He taught me how to be successful in developmental, short-term counseling. Above all, he taught me to be confident and competent in counseling in many different circumstances and with people similar to and different from me.

In 1989, I had the great privilege of becoming Don's graduate assistant as a doctoral student. In this role he became my mentor as well as my advisor. He walked me through the experience of earning a doctorate in counselor education as chair of my committee. He was there to listen when I was stressed. He was there to advise me when I strayed. He was there to facilitate the success of my research and the writing of my dissertation.

Because of Don, I attended my first ACA Conference and joined the Association for Multicultural Counseling and Development. When I joined the Texas Association for Multicultural Counseling and Development, the charter members knew of me because they had years of association with Don C. Locke. Since my graduation in 1992, Don has helped me become a successful counselor educator. In particular, he has introduced me to writing and publishing. He will always be my mentor. I will always feel comfortable asking him for advice.

In summary, I am only one of Don's students. He has a legion who remember him with great respect and appreciation, turn to him for help when they need it, and know that they have a consummate professional willing to continue to be their teacher, advisor, and mentor. It takes only a telephone call, an e-mail message, or a conversation at a conference mutually attended to continue a professional relationship that is very, very fruitful for the student and the counseling profession.

# REFERENCES

Arredondo, P., Toporek, M. S., Brown, S., Jones, J., Locke, D. C., Sanchez, J., & Stadler, H. (1996). *Operationalization of the multicultural counseling competencies.* Alexandria, VA: Association for Multicultural Counseling and Development, A Division of the American Counseling Association.

Faubert, M., Locke, D. C., Sprinthall, N. A., & Howland, W. H. (1996). Promoting cognitive and ego development of African American rural youth: A program of deliberate psychological education. *Journal of Adolescence, 19,* 533–543.

Locke, D. C. (1998). *Increasing multicultural understanding: A comprehensive model* (2nd ed). Thousand Oaks, CA: Sage.

Locke, D. C., & Faubert, M. (1999). Innovative pedagogy for critical consciousness in counselor education. In M. S. Kiselica (Ed.), *Confronting prejudice and racism during multicultural training* (pp. 43–58). Alexandria, VA: American Counseling Association.

Locke, D. C., Myers, J. E., & Herr, E. L. (Eds.). (2001). *The handbook of counseling.* Thousand Oaks, CA: Sage.

# CHAPTER 22

# John (Johnnie) McFadden

Marty Jencius, Chas Durant, and Lisa D. Hawley

*Bowls mended before broken*

John McFadden typifies the dedicated professional in the counseling profession. His life and achievements model professional scholarship that is actualized in humanitarian efforts. His scholarship includes over 80 publications (more than 35 journal articles, 18 book chapters, and 7 books) and over 140 professional presentations tied to his scholarly pursuit of transcultural counseling. His presence in the international field, including presentations in England, Germany, Spain, Brazil, France, Sweden, New Zealand, Switzerland, India, and the Netherlands, has contributed to developing perspectives on international education in the area of multicultural counseling. His major academic contribution to counseling, his second edition *Transcultural Counseling* (1999), delineates the Stylistic Model of transcultural counseling and addresses multicultural counseling by examining qualities that connect diverse cultures. This is a refreshing approach to diversity that teaches counseling students inclusion concepts. His grants and proposals have brought over $1.8 million to the University of South Carolina (USC) and have contributed to enriching the educational environment in the state.

Leadership in associations and to the university community exemplifies John McFadden's service commitment. He has provided leadership to the American Counseling Association (ACA) at a variety of levels. He has been involved at the regional level serving as the Southern Association for Counselor Education and Supervision (SACES) Multicultural Interest Network Chairperson for 7 years. On the national level, John has been co-coordinator of the ACA International Conference on Cultural Diversity, National Chairperson of the ACA Media Committee, and most prominently president of the Association for Multicultural Counseling and Development (AMCD, 1983–1984). During this time he was involved in helping the association change its name from the former Association for Non-White Concerns to the current AMCD. This name change exemplifies John's strong belief that "we all need to be at the table."

John McFadden's vita lists many major contributions to his university, including current director of the African American Professors Program and previous administrative roles such as senior vice president for Intercultural Affairs and Professional Development as well as Associate and Acting Dean of the College of Education. Over the course of more than 30 years at USC, he has been called to serve in an array of service roles at the university. His close friends know that no university service gives him more personal pride than his endowed chair as the Benjamin Elijah Mays Professor. Through the Mays Scholars Academy for Leadership Development at USC, John has provided mentoring opportunities for junior and senior high school students in the legacy of Benjamin E. Mays.

## PERSPECTIVES ON LEADERSHIP THROUGH THE YEARS

John's personal beliefs about leadership fit well with his professional pursuits of transcultural counseling. He describes leadership for him as emerging at three levels: leadership from his mentors, passing through himself, and emerging in his students. John states that he sees himself imparting some of who he is, what he believes in and what he likes, and trying to instill some of himself in others so that they will be able to be better people and better counselors and pass that on to another generation.

John McFadden attributes his development of leadership from growing up in Wilmington, North Carolina, with a mother and father and four sisters, the fourth in line with no brothers. He reports that the family had a strong connection with their church. John's mother and father divorced when he was in his early teens. His father, Jerry McFadden, worked at the local shipyard and later worked similarly in Norfolk, Virginia, and remained an influence on John's life. His mother, Emma Jane Postell McFadden, worked as an assembly person at one of the local lumber yards and later was a dietician at one of the Wilmington hospitals. She was the matriarch who kept the family together and instilled in her children good values, striving for excellence, and pursuing dreams with a warm heart.

Growing up, as he puts it, as "the little boy from Wilmington, North Carolina" (quotes of John McFadden come from an interview with Marty Jencius, June 2001), John sought the guidance of members of his community. "I found myself growing up and using a lot of people in the neighborhood: teachers, the minister, Sunday school teachers, even the midwife." He developed his natural skills of connecting with people who were of service to the community, people who encouraged him to pursue his education and make a difference with his life. From the front porch of his childhood home, John would look out over the neighborhood and wonder.

> Sitting on that front porch I'd look at the horizon across a far away area called Love Grove. I used to look out there at that skyline from the porch and watch the Atlantic Coastline train traveling back into the city. I used to notice the train a lot when I was growing up. I used to wonder where it was going, what was out there, never knowing whether I would ever get beyond the porch, beyond Love Grove, beyond the city, beyond North Carolina. I knew though that there had to be something out there. I knew that in order to go out there, I had some homework to do . . . go to school, pitch horseshoes less than my friends, go to school, play a little softball but not as much as the other guys, not hang around the corner drinking Pepsi colas, but get a part-time job.

A pivotal experience that defines John's worldview occurred to him early on in the classroom as a student. The school system he grew up in was intellectually stimulating but also segregated. Despite segregation the school allowed for him to see, to feel, and to be touched by individuals who provided leadership for him. One such teacher was Ethel Telfair:

> One of my best experiences came about when I was in the third grade with Mrs. Telfair. She was such a source of inspiration. If you asked me right now, "What happened to you, McFadden, during your lifetime that really helped you set your philosophy in perspective for who you are, what you want to do, and how you are going to impact other people?" I would have to give credit to Mrs. Telfair, my third grade teacher.

Mrs. Telfair told the students to come to school one morning with a bowl and a spoon because she was going to serve them soup on a winter school day. Dressed in his knickerbockers and long socks, clothed in a leather jacket, John was walking to school with the bowl in his brown paper bag. He was swinging his bag as he walked along to school and when the school crossing guard halted him in mid-stride, he dropped the bag on a cement sidewalk at the corner of Sixth and Campbell streets. Two things he was immediately aware of when he dropped his paper bag were that he had broken his mother's bowl and he wasn't going to enjoy any soup with his classmates that day.

> I went into the school with tears in my eyes. Mrs. Telfair was a wonderful lady. She threw her arms around my shoulders and used her thumb and forefinger to rub under my chin because that was her trademark. She asked me what was wrong and I told her. I mentioned to her that I would not be able to have any soup and she said, "Oh, yes you will," because she had brought some extra bowls. That's my story, the mended bowl. She mended my bowl right then. For third grade, fourth grade, tenth grade, twelfth grade, college, university professorship, marriage, and as I sit now, I don't have a broken bowl, it's mended, it's fixed. Is it fixed for life, yes? Does it ever crack a little bit? It gets little cracks in it but Mrs. Telfair told me how to mend it, how to fix it. So I found myself mending bowls for people, kids, students, teachers. And, man, I do that all the time and it is so rejuvenating and so fulfilling—that's what makes me tick, that's what helps me to cope and get through life.

He noted that every time he tells the story, he relives the experience; even years later it is still potent. He had a potentially discouraging experience years later with a teacher who singled him out as the worst kid in the room, or so she thought. John claimed he wasn't the worst kid, just the one who got caught for cracking up at other students' antics. At the end of the year the teacher planned to take a field trip. John was left behind from the trip because "he was too bad" in his teacher's eyes. He did get promoted to the next grade, however, and related, "I wasn't broken, because Mrs. Telfair had already fixed my bowl." He extends the charge to his adult role as an educator: "If you were to ask me about my philosophy of life, I would have to say it is about the mending of bowls."

After high school, he went to a segregated college, Winston-Salem Teachers College. Teaching wasn't his goal at the time. His goal was to be an architect. He was dissuaded by this career choice when his only Black college choice at the time for architecture was Tuskegee Institute (which was out of the question for him due to distance and resources) or North Carolina State University, which was segregated. School segregation prevented him from pursuing his dream as an architect. Even today he claims to long to be an architect and includes those design qualities in the work that he does. His Stylistic Model of counseling is one of the few counseling models to use a three-dimensional cubical model. He reconciled this loss of a career dream by saying, "I think that even if I would have designed a building by now it would have needed to be repaired or it would have been torn down, because that's what happens to buildings. But I build people. People last, eternally."

He graduated from Winston-Salem Teachers College (Winston-Salem State University) Magna Cum Laude and went to teach in the Statesville, Wilmington, and Charlotte-Mecklenburg school systems at a time when the latter school system in North Carolina was beginning to desegregate. Of that time he recalls:

> In 1966 I left Wilmington, North Carolina, for Charlotte to be a sixth grade teacher at Selwyn Elementary School for four years. I was one of the first persons to help desegregate the entire system (Charlotte-Mecklenburg). It was a marvelous experience.

John describes his experience as probably unique from what other teachers breaking the color barrier had encountered. The opposition to his being an African American teacher in a White school was minimal, which he knows may have differed from the experiences of others with desegregation. Explaining why he was not targeted for his racial heritage, he states:

> I knew who I was, I had had experience teaching, I was focused, and I was creative. I just loved working with kids. I was going to teach and educate them just like I did anybody else. Parents at that time were looking for someone who really cared and would embrace and teach their kids. They [the students] wanted to learn and that's what they got out of that. From out of that experience have come architects, surgeons, professors, and Broadway directors.

John can only recall one incident in his teaching where there was concern about his desegregation experience. While having a physical education class on the playground with his students and playing kickball, the boys were inspired to all tackle the teacher and pile on top of him. The principal of the school observed this from a distance on the hill and was certain that the students were beating Mr. McFadden. He came running to discover that the students and John were really just playing together.

John continued his studies to include an M.Ed. degree from Temple University in 1966 and a Ph.D. degree from the University of South Carolina in 1973. His dissertation was directed by Tom Sweeney, another individual recognized for leadership in this book. He sees his progression from teaching to include a process of natural advancement in his career: "I was a teacher who trained to be a school administrator; I then stumbled into a counseling communication skills class." He was encouraged by Bill Mayer, a professor from the University of South Carolina, to take additional courses in counseling. He enjoyed the process of counseling and continued with that as an educational career path. He summarizes his life of work by saying, "Teacher, school administrator, higher education associate dean, vice president and now back to teaching and scholarship."

As a counselor educator, John McFadden actualizes another belief he has about leadership in this profession:

> Counseling is a threefold charge. . . . The best people who counsel are also good to excellent teachers, because I see counseling, teaching, and leadership as intertwined. Our best counselor educators are our best teachers and our best leaders.

Although he is passionate about good leadership, John prefers to stay out of the limelight and he is not sure why the spotlight comes in his direction. "I am more of an introverted kind of a person," he says, "off to the side, out of the limelight, doing my quiet thing and I have had to come out of that because of roles and being thrust into a lot of positions." Leadership in his eyes emerges over time. He never personally defined himself as being a leader, offering that "Others seem to think that of me, more than I think of myself." The qualities that others see in John place him in leadership positions and they include "faith in me that if I get placed in a task, the job will be done, and it will be done well and in a timely fashion. This signifies a democratic, yet focused and creative leadership style."

As a leader at USC, John McFadden has achieved many firsts as an African American including a vice presidency, an endowed chair and a full professorship (the first since post-reconstruction). In recent years, USC held its rededication of the original university grounds celebrating the 200th anniversary of the university. John was asked to walk through the arched gates of the university in the rededication ceremony. Reluctant to be in the limelight, his decision to participate in the ceremonies was driven by a respect "for all those African American colleagues who at one time could not walk through these gates, those who have come before me making it possible for me to walk through these gates."

Throughout John's life and to this day, women continue to play an important role for him. His mother is still alive and they continue to have a wonderful relationship. The two immediate women in his life are his wife, Grace Jordan McFadden, USC History Professor Emeritus, and their daughter, Rashida Hannah McFadden. Of Grace, he speaks:

> Grace came in my life, she played a significant part in my life because of the tremendous respect that I have for her as a wife, partner, friend, scholar, as a person. She serves as a barometer for me in decisions that I make.

In Rashida, John sees some of his dreams as an architect and designer emerge through her professional life as a corporate communications associate with National Public Radio. He states, "Rashida keeps me balanced, sane and fatherly, a well-rounded person."

One final passion that keeps John balanced is his rose garden. John takes good care of his garden and finds it a place where he can go, work with the roses, reenergize his professional life, and meditate. He also uses the garden as a place where his design creativity comes through outside of the academic realm.

## PERSONAL REFLECTION

While working on this project, I (Marty Jencius) have been touched by John's philosophy of "mending bowls" before they are broken. As a pre-tenured assistant professor I am continually impressed with the way in which John helps me feel comfortable with my teaching ideas, scholarly inquiry, and writing. I speak to him on the phone about once a month and he always greets me with plenty of time for us to talk and share ideas. This mentoring has been extremely helpful for me and represents a model for how I try to be with my student advisees. John knows to mend bowls before they break and he truly lives that philosophy.

It was in the summer of 1977 that I (Chas Durant) received a master's degree from the University of South Carolina and several weeks later met John McFadden through my faculty advisor. John interviewed and later hired me as his administrative assistant when he was working as assistant to the Dean of the College of Education. Two years in that role and 23 years of mentoring have provided a unique perspective to share reflections on his leadership and dedication as well as be a witness to the multitude of bowls that have been enriched by his personhood. It is without doubt that my personal and professional growth is a legacy of his insight and ideals. With a nurturing and person-centered approach, he has been the embodiment of a mentor as I served in midlevel and senior administrative positions at several universities.

My (Lisa D. Hawley) personal experience with John McFadden is about transcendence. I appreciate John's ability to practice his writing and scholarship in his teaching, mentorship, and service activities. In our mentoring relationship, we were able to transcend race, gender, class, sexual orientation, and age to develop a relationship that assisted in my development as a counselor educator. I enjoyed the many conversations we had that went well beyond the scope of my classroom experiences to include politics, social justice, and historical, anthropological, and sociological references. These stimulating dialogues challenged me to think outside the box and to grow in my understanding of the role of the counselor educator in a broad framework. Two aspects of John's mentorship I have found most meaningful include his ability to promote excellence and his sense of compassion. His sense of rigor and high expectations challenged me and many other students to achieve important milestones with high quality. But ultimately, John's sense of compassion to promote a better society transcends his teaching, scholarship, and service. One of John McFadden's hopes is that his positive influences on my experiences transcend to others. Therefore, as a young counselor educator, my hope is to model these important mentorship qualities with my students and colleagues much like he would expect.

In conclusion, John McFadden's life experiences helped mold his personal leadership style. These life experiences led him to see leadership as a transgenerational process passed to him from his mentors, with a recognition that what they had given must be passed through him and on to others. Secondly, he saw leadership as something that is not chosen but that one is chosen for. John McFadden has established a reputation as a thoughtful, encouraging, and inclusive leader. He is someone who, when committed to a leadership role, works with little fanfare, as part of his own humility, to accomplish goals collectively with the membership. Finally he describes his leadership style as being democratic and participative so that everyone has a voice. Those working with John are reminded by his actions that inclusion is at the heart of his leadership style. These three concepts make up John McFadden's approaches to leadership.

## REFERENCES

McFadden, J. (1999). *Transcultural counseling* (2nd ed.). Alexandria, VA: American Counseling Association.

CHAPTER 23

# Jane E. Myers

Theodore P. Remley, Jr.

*We must be the change we wish to see.*
(M. K. Gandhi)[1]

Jane E. Myers is a native of California, born in Eureka and raised in East Oakland. Her father left a career as an electrician shortly before she was born to pursue a calling as a Nazarene minister. The family also left San Francisco to start their own business as chicken farmers. Unfortunately, they knew little about chickens and bought all males, so no eggs were forthcoming for some time and the business floundered.

The youngest of five children born within a seven-year time span, Jane recalls her childhood in rural Northern California in terms of redwood trees, apple trees, blackberries, and lots of church. With a father who was an evangelist, writer, and self-proclaimed prophet, five nights a week at the local mission was common. Jane and her sisters sang; however, as an adult, Jane will be the first to tell you she has trouble carrying a tune.

Her three older sisters provided child care while her mother returned to school to earn a bachelor's degree in two and a half years and begin working as a special education teacher. The impetus for her degree included the

[1] Retrieved from http://www.gandhiinstitute.org

realization that the only male child, Jane's older brother, was profoundly hearing impaired and severely developmentally delayed. During her childhood and adolescence, Jane often accompanied her mother to the special schools he attended. Later, when complaints of neighbors resulted in a court order for institutionalization, Jane visited him every two weeks at the state hospital and helped her mother plan parties and parent associations for the residents and their families. Jane developed important leadership skills as a result of volunteering with developmentally disabled children in schools and state hospitals.

Jane's leadership style was shaped by childhood experiences in which she developed a sensitivity to the needs of others. Her family experienced significant discrimination because of her brother's disability, her father's strong fundamentalist Christian religiosity, and the fact that her mother was Jewish.

## COLLEGE AND CAREER DECISIONS

Jane attended the University of California at Berkeley, earning her bachelor's degree in psychology in 1969. Although Berkeley was exciting in the 1960s, a desire to see the South (but not really live there) led Jane to the University of Florida at Gainesville. By the time she received her master's degree in rehabilitation counseling a year later, she had sand in her shoes (which, as any Floridian knows, means a person will come back to the state) and decided to stay in Florida. She accepted a position as a vocational rehabilitation counselor, a job she often said she simply was born to do. In reflecting on her career, Jane maintains that being a counselor is the best job she ever had (but being a counselor educator is a pretty close second).

Four years of working with a rural, general caseload allowed Jane to integrate her personal understanding of disability, based on her family dynamics, with the theory and practice of rehabilitation counseling. George Wright's classic text, *Total Rehabilitation* (1980), and the *Disability and Rehabilitation Handbook* by Goldenson, Dunham, and Dunham (1978) were frequent references that were accessed to better understand the needs of a broad range of clients. The one exception was older clients, who simply were not included in the vocational rehabilitation literature at that time. This was not surprising, as the primary criterion for working with a client in the state agency was that they have the potential for "substantial gainful activity," defined simply as the ability to work for pay. Older persons— those over 60 for sure, over 50 most likely, and over 40 in many cases—

were viewed as having low employment potential, thus low rehabilitation potential. Frustration over repeated reprimands for wasting time with older clients, whom Jane found interesting and who usually possessed great "potential," led to a change in jobs when a new and unique opportunity was presented.

The Older Americans Act, first passed in 1965 following the recommendations of the first White House Conference on Aging held in 1961, mandated services and programs for persons over 60 and the development of the first national policy on aging. Although the act was passed, funds were not authorized until the early 1970s. By 1974, Florida, then the state with the largest proportion of older persons, was ready to receive federal funds and initiate programs for older people. Jane signed on. After a two-day training session, she was given the title of "Aging Program Specialist." She was sent out to a 16-county area as a community organizer and advocate to obtain matching funds for federal dollars in order to develop grant-funded programs to provide senior centers, congregate meal programs, meals-on-wheels, transportation, health screening, and just about any other service needed by older citizens—except counseling, that is.

Feeling limited in her knowledge of how to work with older people, Jane returned to school at the University of Florida, this time in the College of Education, and earned her educational specialist degree in counselor education with an emphasis in community education and aging. School was fun, and she stayed on for doctoral studies, working full-time with the Florida Division of Adult Development and Aging, and funding her studies through supervision of master's-level interns. While working on her doctorate in counselor education, she completed the requirements for a gerontology certificate and a minor in educational leadership. She graduated in 1978, having completed her residency the same time I did, in the same institution. We did not meet until several years later, however, at an American School Counselor Association (ASCA) meeting in Arkansas. By then I knew of Jane's work (and she knew about the things I had been doing), and we hit it off right away.

Although she did not plan to leave the state agency, shortly before receiving her Ph.D. degree, Jane decided to seek a position in higher education. She began working as an assistant professor of rehabilitation counseling at Florida State University (FSU) in 1978. A year later, Larry Loesch, her former doctoral cochair, convinced her to request a leave of absence to work on a national grant on aging at the American Counseling Association (ACA) headquarters (then the American Personnel and Guidance Association [APGA]). After a busy year working with counselors and counselor educators around the country on issues related to counseling with older persons, Jane decided not to return to FSU but to seek a position where she could integrate her work in rehabilitation and aging. That position was available at Ohio University, where she worked for 6 years. During that time she developed a rehabilitation counselor training program, accredited by the Council on Rehabilitation Education (CORE), and she obtained a training grant from the Rehabilitation Services Administration to provide scholarships to students.

Larry Loesch again had a hand in Jane's career when he called to say that the University of Florida's counselor education program had an opening for a counselor educator with a specialty in gerontology. Leaving Ohio and the program she began was hard, but the sand in her shoes called Jane back to Gainesville, where she spent 4 years teaching courses on counseling for midlife and aging and enjoying being a part of the Florida faculty. In 1990, Jane accepted the position of professor in the Department of Counseling and Educational Development at the University of North Carolina at Greensboro. She is currently coordinator of the Gerontological Counseling track and the post-master's certificate program in gerontological counseling. The Gerontological Counseling track is accredited by the Council for Accreditation of Counseling and Related Educational Programs (CACREP). She teaches the master's degree core course in counseling over the life span and a doctoral seminar in advanced counseling theories.

While working as a counselor educator, Jane has written and directed five national grant projects on aging for the ACA, with funding in excess of $1,000,000. These projects developed curriculum materials to train counselors to work with older persons, provided continuing education for more than 3,200 practicing professional counselors in gerontological issues, developed a model and curriculum resources for infusion of gerontological counseling into counselor education, and provided a statement of competencies for the training of gerontological counselors. The competencies formed the basis for the National Certified Gerontological Counselor credential that was established through the National Board for Certified Counselors, as well as the national standards for counselor accreditation in gerontological counseling through CACREP.

## PROFESSIONAL LEADERSHIP

Jane has held many professional leadership positions. She was president of the American Association for Counseling and Development, now the ACA, in 1990–1991. She has been president of two ACA divisions, the Association for Measurement and Evaluation in Counseling and Development (1987–1988; now the Association for Assessment in Counseling) and the Association for Adult Development and Aging (1986–1987), for which she served as founding president. She has been an officer, member, and committee chairperson for national committees of several ACA divisions, including but not limited to the following: the Association for Adult Development and Aging, the Association for Counselor Education and Supervision, and the American Rehabilitation Counseling Association. She has served on the editorial board for several ACA journals, has guest edited several journals, including two special issues of the *Journal of Counseling & Development*, and was selected as the founding editor for the *Journal of Adult Development and Aging*, ACA's first fully electronic journal. She also served as president of Chi Sigma Iota, the international honor society in counseling, as well as Rho Chi Sigma, the rehabilitation counseling honor society, and Sigma Phi Omega, the national gerontology honor society. She has been chairperson of the Counseling and Human Development Foundation (CHDF) and of CACREP. She was also selected as chairperson of the ACA Executive Director Search Committee, a committee charged with locating a new chief executive officer to oversee ACA's $9 million budget and headquarters' staff.

When asked about her leadership style, Jane referred to her "leadership heroes," the people she has admired and whose styles have influenced her most. Her leadership "hero" when she was young was Albert Schweitzer, followed later by John F. Kennedy and Martin Luther King, Jr., and most recently John Gardner. Each of these persons evidenced a concern for others, a commitment to high ideals, and a passion for excellence. Jane described her leadership style as "inclusive." She likes to have constituents involved in planning decisions that affect them, and she likes others to take ownership for decisions. She is not afraid to tackle difficult issues, but does so in a manner that involves others in a process of gathering information, discussing alternatives and the consequences of outcomes, and a shared process of decision-making. She is a high "J" on the Myers-Briggs Type Indicator. As a consequence, she believes that leaders should do their homework, always be prepared, know as much about issues as anyone else in the organization, and, importantly, always seek consultation from multiple sources when dealing with decisions affecting the lives of others.

Any discussion of Jane's contributions to the profession would be incomplete without mention of her research and publications. She has written and/or edited more than 16 books and monographs, almost 100 refereed journal articles, and more than 50 additional publications. She coproduced seven training videotapes for gerontological counseling. Her books include *Adult Children and Aging Parents* (Myers, 1989), *Empowerment for Later Life* (Myers, 1990), and *Competencies for Gerontological Counseling* (Myers & Schwiebert, 1996). Most recently she coedited *The Handbook of Counseling* (Locke, Myers, & Herr, 2001).

After establishing the theme for her presidency of ACA as "Wellness Across the Lifespan," Jane initiated an active research agenda in the area of wellness. She is a coauthor of a model of wellness, the Wheel of Wellness (Myers, Sweeney, & Witmer, 2000), and is coauthoring a new wellness model with Tom Sweeney. A wellness assessment instrument with versions for adults, adolescents, and children, a database of more than 6,000 persons, and a large number of coauthored research projects are the legacy of the ACA theme.

In addition to her writings, Jane has lectured, consulted, and conducted research nationally and internationally. Among her numerous honors are ACA's highest award, the Gilbert and Kathleen Wrenn Humanitarian and Caring Person Award, as well as the ACA Research Award, the ACA Arthur A. Hitchcock Distinguished Professional Service Award, and the Distinguished Service Awards of both the National Rehabilitation Counseling Association and the American Rehabilitation Counseling Association. She is a Fellow of the Gerontological Society of America and the National Rehabilitation Counseling Association. She was also selected as a Charter Fellow of the Chi Sigma Iota Academy of Leaders for Excellence, and most recently was nominated for inclusion in this book.

## CONCLUSION

In 1993, Jane married Tom Sweeney. At this point in time the Myers–Sweeney duo is living on a lake in North Carolina, enjoying sunsets, walks in the woods, movies, boating, gardening, and nine grandchildren. With a constant load of eight doctoral advisees and full-time teaching, Jane reports that life after 50 is the best ever! I had the good fortune of beginning my tenure as ACA executive director in 1990, the year that Jane Myers was president of ACA. We attended numerous meetings, traveled throughout the country, and worked together for the benefit of the counseling profession the entire time I was at ACA. Jane and I had been full-time doctoral students during the 1977–1978 academic year at the University of Florida, but both of us were very busy with our assistantships and classes and had never met until the late 1980s when we were in various ACA leadership roles.

Before I got to know Jane personally, I was very impressed that a contemporary of mine was such an accomplished scholar and recognized professional leader. I was familiar with Jane's work in the area of gerontological counseling and knew that she was a respected counselor educator. But after I began to interact with Jane on a personal basis, I realized that she had a vision for the profession that was exciting and dynamic. I also came to understand that Jane's effectiveness as a leader was the result of her ability to create strategies for success in a political environment, her unwillingness to give up on ideas she knew were important for the profession, and her comprehensive understanding of what was best for our profession.

Because I participated in many of the meetings and was personally involved in the decision-making, I believe that Jane Myers deserves credit for the following events:

- changing ACA's name from the American Association for Counseling and Development, to the clear and recognizable, American Counseling Association;
- helping the American College Personnel Association disaffiliate from ACA and form a separate organization (the American College Counseling Association) so that ACA could clearly focus on representing members of the counseling profession;
- creating a category of membership in ACA for professional counselors to distinguish professional members from those who simply hold an interest in counseling;
- reinstituting the ACA Advocacy Committee, which addressed the goals of promoting the counseling profession and ensuring jobs for professional counselors;
- moving the ACA Foundation from its separate agenda for the use of ACA financial resources to its current clear position of supporting ACA directly; and
- insisting that the *Journal of Counseling & Development* provide scholarly leadership for the counseling profession that is separate and apart from the profession of psychology.

The important lesson I learned personally from Jane Myers was that one dynamic professional can make a substantial positive impact on the counseling profession and that we should never give up when we believe in something.

## REFERENCES

Goldenson, R. M., Dunham, J. R., & Dunham, C. S. (Eds.). (1978). *Disability and rehabilitation handbook.* New York: McGraw-Hill.

Locke, D. C., Myers, J. E., & Herr, E. L. (Eds.). (2001). *The handbook of counseling.* Thousand Oaks, CA: Sage.

Myers, J. E. (1989). *Adult children and aging parents.* Alexandria, VA: American Counseling Association.

Myers, J. E. (1990). *Empowerment for later life.* Greensboro, NC: ERIC/CASS.

Myers, J. E., & Schwiebert. V. L. (1996). *Competencies for gerontological counseling.* Alexandria, VA: American Counseling Association.

Myers, J. E., Sweeney, T. J., & Witmer, M. (2000). Counseling for wellness: A holistic model for treatment planning. *Journal of Counseling & Development, 78,* 251–266.

Wright, G. N. (1980). *Total rehabilitation.* Boston: Little Brown.

# CHAPTER 24

# Merle M. Ohlsen

Reece Chaney

*All my research and writing was focused on becoming a better counselor.*

Merle M. Ohlsen currently lives in Savoy, Illinois. Even though he has been retired for 20 years, he continues to maintain an active interest in the counseling profession. Merle was born on March 3, 1914 to Nick and Dora Ohlsen, a few miles north of Willow Lake, South Dakota. He had two younger sisters, Audrey and Marjorie. Five feet tall, weighing 80 pounds in the ninth grade and suffering from rheumatic fever and poor health in general, Merle's education seemed in doubt. Because of poor crops, his parents lost their two family farms and could no longer afford the room and board in town for his education. Charles Stewart, Superintendent of Schools in Willow Lake, took young Merle into his home so he could complete high school. Stewart became a lifelong mentor, especially encouraging Merle through graduate school.

In 2002 Merle and his wife, Helen, celebrated their 58th wedding anniversary. Four children, Marilyn, Linda, Barbara, and Ronald, have blessed them with ten grandchildren. Merle and Helen have maintained a unique partnership as devoted spouses, parents, and grandparents. Helen's contribution to Merle's professional work and writing was enormous, and he has always proudly acknowledged it.

## CAREER DEVELOPMENT

After a brief interruption for a year of teaching in a rural school, Merle completed his bachelor's degree at Winona State University in 1939. From 1939 to 1941 he taught math in the Champaign Public Schools while he earned a Master of Arts degree from the University of Illinois. He was a senior high school principal in Sioux City, Iowa (1941–1943), a math instructor at the University of Iowa (1943–1944), and a chemistry teacher for Iowa City High School (1944–1945). In August 1945 Merle completed his Ph.D. at the University of Iowa.

During his career Merle was actively involved in many organizations. He served three national organizations as president:

- 1959–1960, SPATE (Student Personnel Association for Teacher Education)
- 1969–1970, APGA (American Personnel and Guidance Association, currently the American Counseling Association, ACA)
- 1977–1978, ASGW (Association for Specialists in Group Work)

Merle is particularly proud of two honors, the APGA Professional Development Award, 1978, and the Association for Counselor Education and Supervision (ACES) Distinguished Mentor Award, 1987.

In a short statement prepared by Merle for this chapter, several factors were identified as having professional as well as personal significance. Factors he included are summarized below:

- During his first year at Washington State University as an assistant professor of education in 1945, Merle was elected to the Faculty Executive Committee and two years later served as chairperson.
- In 1961, Merle was elected by the APGA (ACA) Board of Directors to serve on a highly prestigious committee, the Commission on Guidance in American Schools. C. Gilbert Wrenn was the chairperson of that commission and published a book on the report in 1962 (Wrenn, 1962). That report served as a landmark for school counseling for many years and was one of the most cited and utilized documents at that time.
- In 1963 the U.S. Office of Education sponsored a workshop on improving research in group counseling at the governor's home in New York. Merle was one of three consultants and presented his approach to group counseling for participants. Ben Cohn, a well-known writer in group counseling, published a book on that conference (Cohn, 1967). Rudolph Dreikurs, psychiatrist and well-known founder of the

Adlerian Institute in Chicago, was also a presenter. Dreikurs, who was a highly skilled therapist and group leader, showed great interest in Merle's approach and encouraged him to provide additional demonstrations during the workshop and later at the annual Adlerian conference. Always up for a challenge, Merle did so and was greatly praised for his efforts.

- In 1963, Merle was invited to give a series of lectures at Cornell University concerning his approach to group counseling. The proceedings from that series were published as *Evaluation of Group Counseling Techniques in the Secondary Schools* (Ohlsen, 1963).
- In 1964, Merle was elected as chairperson of the Educational Policy Committee by the University of Illinois Senate (a body made up of full professors), whose task it was to evaluate all new proposed changes in curricula.
- Merle has been eternally grateful for fabulous mentors beginning with Charles Stewart, Superintendent of Schools; Roy Tozier, Professor of Economics at Winona State University; J. Murray Lee, Dean of the College of Education at Washington State University; Willard Spalding, Dean of the College of Education at the University of Illinois, who edited Merle's first book (Ohlsen, 1955); Lee Cronbach (colleague at Washington State University and University of Illinois, who provided feedback with research grants); and Vernon Price, professor of mathematics at the University of Iowa (who hired Merle in 1943 to assist him in constructing mathematics tests for the Armed Forces Institute). Other colleagues/mentors included John Clawson, psychiatrist at Washington State University (from whom he obtained marvelous counseling supervision), Ed Borden and Howard Pepinski (Washington State University), and Fred Proff (University of Illinois), all of whom provided peer supervision.

Merle was an early pioneer in guidance and this is clearly reflected in his first book, *Guidance: An Introduction* (Ohlsen, 1955), which was one of a very few books available at the time reflecting a futuristic perspective of things to come in the profession. For many years, guidance and counseling was fashioned on the general principles outlined in his book and a few other texts. Merle made a significant contribution to the development of elementary school counseling preparation programs. He was chairperson of the ACES committee that developed standards for the preparation of elementary school counselors (Ohlsen, 1968). The standards have endured and closely resemble the Council for Accreditation of Counseling and Related Educational Programs (CACREP) standards today.

Merle designed one of the nation's first 3-year-long National Defense Educational Act (NDEA) Counseling and Guidance Institutes for the preparation of elementary school counselors (Faust, 1968). According to Faust, Merle demonstrated unusual courage and, again, a determination to promote elementary school counseling as involving more than individual testing, as the program model at the University of Illinois emphasized. He took a training position that deemphasized vocational information for elementary counselors and crisis intervention while emphasizing a more developmentally oriented and learning climate design.

Group counseling is undoubtedly Merle's greatest contribution to the profession. He published his first article on groups in 1941 (Ohlsen, 1941). His book *Group Counseling* (Ohlsen, 1970) appeared with two revisions (Ohlsen, 1977; Ohlsen, Horne & Lawe, 1988). A highly successful text, it was very readable and highly practical and relatively brief as such texts go. He reached a large audience through workshops and presentations. Merle utilized demonstration as a way to teach new counseling techniques and skills. More than anything else, he loved to develop an idea and then demonstrate it either in therapy or role-play situations. His great passion was to conduct group therapy and/or to provide supervision of students who were involved in it. Professionals came from around the country to take his courses or participate in popular summer group counseling workshops. George Gazda, an early student of Merle's, said it best in the Foreword to his 1988 text (Ohlsen, Horne & Lawe, 1988): "Ohlsen's enthusiasm for his profession and especially group counseling has motivated me and countless other students to become counselors and educators of counselors, and especially group counselors" (p. v). Perhaps the greatest contribution to group counseling was made by Merle's commitment to the preparation of counselor educators, who have continued the group tradition.

Merle recognized the value of mentorship early in his career, even among colleagues. He was highly involved with students in advising, guiding, supervising, and providing a swift metaphorical kick when they needed it to move along in the program. He steered students and other professionals to available positions, and after he retired, I spoke with him about several openings. As was his practice, Merle sent me several faculty names of the most qualified people he knew with a summary of the merits of each. It didn't matter if the person wasn't actively interested in changing positions. Merle seemed to think that a good position might be an opportunity too good to pass up. On more than one occasion I have received the following response from a nominee, "Thanks but I am very happy in my present position. It looks like Merle is at it again!"

Merle was a very committed, active professional at the local, state, and national levels. He received great satisfaction from presenting at conferences and workshops and even more from socializing with colleagues and old friends. He was eager to meet new colleagues and quick to befriend them. Merle's leadership role in professional organizations is reflected in the important positions he held, including serving as president of APGA, SPATE, and ASGW. He also served as the chairperson of several committees for divisions of APGA including ACES, the National Vocational Guidance Association, and the American College Personnel Association. An active writer and scholar, Merle published 12 professional texts and close to 120 journal articles. He was invited to serve on the editorial boards of several professional journals, including *Elementary School Guidance and Counseling, Journal of Individual Psychology*, and *Personnel and Guidance Journal.*

## WORKING WITH MERLE OHLSEN

Working with Merle for 12 years before his retirement gave me the opportunity to know him as a seasoned professional long after he established himself as a national figure. His role as Holmstedt Distinguished Professor at Indiana State University (one of only two such professorships on campus) placed him in elite company. It was not unusual for the university president to seek Merle's audience. He remained a true and loyal colleague and friend in spite of his status and position.

Merle came to Indiana State University in 1969 as Holmstedt Distinguished Professor of Guidance and Psychological Services one year after I arrived as a new assistant professor. He was selected based on his national reputation, experience, professional status, and wisdom to support a newly established doctoral program in counselor education. Merle greeted us each morning with a big smile, a story or two (most with a slightly naughty flavor, but certainly not vulgar), and a sincere interest in faculty and students. He was available to discuss what we each were doing and was always available for reactions, support or advice, or a good story. I came to the department to develop a master's degree program in elementary school guidance. As one of the pioneers in elementary school counseling, Merle was a wonderful mentor. He recognized in me my need to establish my own professional identity. He understood what it meant for a new professional to develop independence and to find my own way. He also knew how to be available and supportive without being meddlesome or intrusive. I was very proud and appreciative when Merle was awarded the ACES Mentor

Award in 1987. It has been my goal to provide the same caliber of mentoring for students with whom I work.

Immediately upon his arrival at Indiana State University, Merle invited all faculty to join him for peer supervision of group counseling. Several faculty members joined him and participated by running groups, participating in peer supervision, and meeting with him for individual supervision. In a short time, faculty and students were heavily engaged in the group counseling process using the "Ohlsen Model." Research related to group counseling increased greatly and continued during Merle's stay at Indiana State University, resulting in many doctoral dissertations and publications.

On reflection, Merle had a significant impact on my way of understanding clients and conceptualizing the needs of clients and supervisees. I learned from him the great value of the use of intuition as a therapeutic, teaching, and leadership method. He had an excellent way of exciting students while encouraging and motivating them. His means of engendering mutual respect with students and colleagues placed him in an enviable position of leadership and high respect.

As a long-time member of ACA, Merle knew virtually every leader in the profession. He was naturally gregarious, with a high altruistic bent. He also was inclined to get involved at all levels of professional activity. He listened carefully and always, even to this day, responded when others asked for help, especially in hiring faculty. He is highly opinionated, but more importantly, his opinions were the result of thorough study and research intermixed with considerable experience. Students were quite impressed and sometimes dismayed by his great breadth and depth of knowledge, which supported his opinions.

His remarkable career in guidance and counseling, beginning in the 1940s, naturally put him in the midst of an evolving, rapidly developing profession. Being an individual who wanted to be on the cutting edge and shape the future of the profession, Merle took advantage of many opportunities to provide leadership in carving out the profession. It was his vision, insightfulness, and keen intellect that set him apart from many others. A strong preparation in mathematics and statistics coupled with a commitment to scholarship aided Merle in being well prepared and always thorough. There were only a few areas of counselor education and supervision that Merle had not researched or been actively involved with at some level.

A few years ago I approached Merle about the possibility of establishing an endowed award in his name for the benefit of doctoral students in the counseling program at Indiana State University. Although many former students and friends contributed, Merle personally increased the endowment considerably. When asked what the criteria should be, he quickly responded by suggesting that we should help a financially strapped student for whom the award could make a difference in helping him or her complete the program. He has not strayed far from his roots. As one who was able to overcome great physical and financial difficulties through hard work, perseverance, and a little help from mentors, Merle never forgot, nor did he allow students and colleagues to forget, those ingredients necessary for achieving success, providing effective leadership, and reaching one's goals.

## REFERENCES

Cohn, B. (Ed.). (1967). *Guidelines for future research on group counseling in the public school setting.* Washington, DC: American Personnel and Guidance Association.

Faust, V. (1968). *History of elementary school counseling.* Boston: Houghton Mifflin Company.

Ohlsen, M. M. (1941). Group guidance through pupil forum. *The Clearing House, 15,* 529–530.

Ohlsen, M. M. (1955). *Guidance: An introduction.* New York: Harcourt Brace.

Ohlsen, M. M. (1963). *Evaluation of group counseling techniques in the secondary schools.* Ithaca, NY: Cornell University Press.

Ohlsen, M. M. (1968). Standards for the preparation of elementary school counselors. *Counselor Education and Supervision, 7,* 172–178.

Ohlsen, M. M. (1970). *Group counseling.* New York: Holt, Rinehart & Winston.

Ohlsen, M. M. (1977). *Group counseling* (2nd ed.). New York: Holt, Rinehart & Winston.

Ohlsen, M. M., Horne, A. M., & Lawe, C. F. (1988). *Group counseling* (3rd ed.). New York: Holt, Rinehart & Winston.

Wrenn, C. G. (1962). *The counselor in a changing world.* Washington, DC: American Personnel and Guidance Association.

# CHAPTER 25

# Theodore P. Remley, Jr.

Mary A. Hermann

*The formula for success for counselors includes a strong professional
identity and a dedication to quality services.*

Theodore (Ted) Phant Remley, Jr., was born in Eustis, Florida, on February
7, 1947. Ted's father was from Charleston, South Carolina, and his mother,
Era Forehand Remley, was from Bonifay, Florida. Ted has one older half-
brother, Henry Jesse McVay.

Ted grew up in Florida and graduated from Tavares High School. He
received a B.A. degree in English from the University of Florida in 1969.
He was awarded a fellowship for preparing community college counselors and earned M.Ed. and Ed.S. degrees in Counselor Education from
the University of Florida in 1971. In 1980, he completed both a J.D.
degree at Catholic University in Washington, DC, and a Ph.D. degree in
Counselor Education from the University of Florida. Ted's advisor and
mentor at the University of Florida was Robert O. Stripling, the major
initiator of counselor education program accreditation and former President of the Association for Counselor Education and Supervision
(ACES). Stripling established the University of Florida's Counselor Education program as one of the leading programs in the United States. Ted
is a licensed professional counselor in Louisiana, Mississippi, and Vir-

ginia, and is a member of the Bar in Virginia and Florida. He is also a National Certified Counselor.

## CAREER HIGHLIGHTS

Ted's career has included providing professional counseling services in a number of settings, serving as a professional association staff member, and teaching counseling as a university faculty member. He has been a member of the American Counseling Association (ACA) since 1969 and has maintained membership throughout his career in the American School Counselor Association (ASCA), the American Mental Health Counselors Association (AMHCA), ACES, and the Association for Spiritual, Ethical, and Religious Values in Counseling (ASERVIC). After completing counseling internships at Santa Fe Community College in Gainesville, Florida, from 1970 to 1971, Ted's first professional position was as a counselor at Orange Park High School in Clay County, Florida, during the 1971–1972 academic year.

He then entered the United States Army as a 2nd Lieutenant for three months of active duty. While at Ft. Sam Houston in San Antonio, Texas, Ted was assigned to teach psychiatric technicians for the Army. He completed 6 years of military service and received an honorable discharge as a captain after serving as the executive officer of a medical unit in the Virginia Army National Guard in Charlottesville. Ted was Student Activities Director and Counselor at Blue Ridge Community College in Weyers Cave, Virginia, from 1972 through 1974 and began to attend meetings of the Virginia Counselors Association (VCA) during that period of time.

From 1974 through 1983 he was a counselor and a professor at Northern Virginia Community College (NVCC), Alexandria Campus. During that 9-year period, he served in counseling association leadership positions including president of the Virginia College Personnel Association, Government Relations Committee Chairperson, and president of the VCA, and chairperson of the ACA Southern Region Branch Assembly. Ted took a leave of absence from NVCC during the 1977–1978 academic year and completed a year of law school and the residency for his doctoral program at the University of Florida. He was a half-time graduate assistant in the Career Resource Center for that year. During the 1979–1980 academic year, and another leave of absence from NVCC, Ted was a paid half-time lobbyist for the American Bar Association. In 1976, Ted participated in the legislative effort under the leadership of Carl Swanson, a counselor educator at James Madison University. This legislative effort resulted in the passage of the first counselor licensure bill in the United States.

Ted had a part-time law practice and a part-time private practice in counseling in Alexandria, Virginia, from 1981 through 1987. In his law practice, he represented criminal clients as well as individuals in divorce, child custody, and other types of civil proceedings. Ted was the attorney for a number of mental health professionals and assisted them in managing their private practices, serving as expert witnesses, and avoiding unwanted court appearances. In his counseling practice, Ted provided individual, group, and family counseling to clients and supervised counselors in preparation for licensure. During that period, Ted also taught graduate courses for Radford University in Radford, Virginia; George Mason University in Fairfax, Virginia; and George Washington University in Washington, DC.

From 1983 through 1987, Ted was assistant professor and coordinator of the Counseling and Development Graduate Program at George Mason University. While there, he was appointed by the Governor of Virginia as a member of the Licensed Professional Counselor Board and served as chairperson. Ted was also the founding president of the American Association of State Counseling Boards (AASCB).

Ted was an associate professor and chairperson of the Counselor Education Department at Mississippi State University from 1987 through 1990. In 1990, he was promoted to full professor. During the time Ted was at Mississippi State University, the graduate program in counseling received accreditation by the Council for Accreditation of Counseling and Related Education Programs (CACREP). He also served as executive director of the AASCB, ASCA parliamentarian, and chairperson of the ACA Counseling Advocacy Committee. Ted was also appointed by the Governor of Mississippi to be on the Licensed Professional Counselor Board, was elected chairperson of that Board, and served as the ASCA representative to the CACREP Board.

Ted was ACA executive director from 1990 through 1994. During this time, he worked with the District of Columbia Counseling Association to pass a counselor licensure law and was appointed by the Mayor of DC to serve on the first Licensed Professional Counselor Board. As ACA executive director, Ted was also a Board member of the ACA Governing Council, the ACA Insurance Trust, and the ACA Foundation. Ted's major focus as ACA executive director was to present the profession of counseling to its members and to the public as a unified profession that was stronger as a whole than it would be if fragmented by its many specialties.

Ted has been professor and coordinator of the CACREP-accredited Counseling Graduate Program at the University of New Orleans since 1994. In 2000, he was appointed chairperson of the Department of Educational Leadership, Counseling, and Foundations in which the Counseling Graduate Program is located. Since 1997, Ted has been a part-time counselor at Family Service of Greater New Orleans, a community mental health center. He has served on the Louisiana Licensed Professional Counselor Board since he was appointed by the governor of Louisiana in 1998. During the time he has been at the University of New Orleans, Ted has taught graduate courses at the Puerto Rico Campus of Mississippi State University, the University of Maine in Orono, the University of Mississippi in Oxford, and Lyndon State College in Lyndonville, Vermont. He is a frequent workshop presenter and expert witness in mental health practitioner malpractice cases throughout the United States.

Throughout Ted's career as counselor, he has performed community service. In New Orleans, he is a member of the Tulane University Hospital Ethics Committee and the Volunteer Information Center Board of Directors. He has also chaired the Trinity Counseling and Training Center Board in New Orleans and the Voluntary Action Center Board in Harrisonburg, Virginia, and he served on the Oktibbeha County Association for Retarded Citizens in Mississippi. Ted currently serves on the Board of Trustees of Divine Word College in Epworth, Iowa.

The professional identity development of counselors became a concern for Ted in 1976 when he was lobbying for passage of the first counselor licensure law in the United States. Recognizing that legislators and the general public had little information about the quality of the academic preparation of counselors and the important services they were providing to society, Ted began to reflect upon the lack of clear statements about the identity of counselors in the professional literature. As ACA executive director from 1990 through 1994, Ted published monthly columns in the ACA newsletter, often focusing upon the uniqueness of counselors and how they related to other mental health professionals. His strongest and most comprehensive statement regarding counselor professional identity appears in chapter 2 of the book *Ethical, Legal, and Professional Issues in Counseling*, coauthored with Barbara Herlihy (Remley & Herlihy, 2001).

Ted has become a noted authority in the area of legal issues in counseling and mental health. Many of his 31 refereed journal articles, 9 book chapters, and 3 books focus on that topic. Ted also wrote the first volume (Remley, 1991) and edited the entire 12-volume *The ACA Legal Series* (Remley, 1991–1994), a collection of monographs designed for counseling practitioners. He has presented numerous local, regional, state, national, and international workshops in the area of legal and ethical issues in counseling and provides expert witness testimony in that area in lawsuits throughout the United States.

Ted has been honored as the recipient of the following awards: the Southern ACES Individual Achievement Award in 1999; the Joe Wittmer Distinguished Professional Service Award at the University of Florida in 1993; the John R. Cook Award for Outstanding Service to the Counseling Profession at Virginia Commonwealth University in 1992; the AASCB Leadership Award in 1992; and the Outstanding Scholar Award in Family Law at Catholic University in 1979. Ted is also the only counselor to have served on more than one state licensure board for counselors. He has served on four. As a board member, Ted's contributions have been in the areas of drafting reasonable and understandable regulations for licensed professional counselors on each state board and chairing disciplinary committees that review and process complaints against licensees.

Ted has provided substantial leadership for the profession of counseling. Leadership opportunities seem to gravitate toward him. He seems to emerge as a group leader without really looking for such opportunities. He usually works within organizations and groups where a shared vision exists. He excels at negotiating and finding compromises with people who have differing views and is skilled at organizing and delegating—cornerstones of good leadership ability.

As soon as Ted chose counseling as a profession, he felt a strong responsibility to promote the profession. He has always been certain that the counseling philosophy, which emphasizes wellness and prevention and considers most problems to be normal and developmental in nature, is the best philosophy for mental health practitioners. Ted has spent his counseling career implementing this philosophy as a mental health practitioner, counselor educator, and leader in the counseling field.

## TED REMLEY, THE PROFESSOR

I first heard about Ted Remley when I was finishing law school. The counselor at the school where I taught commented that he thought I would enjoy being a school counselor and, considering my background in law, he suggested that I speak with his major professor, who was an attorney and a counselor. After the rigors of law school, I wasn't interested in pursuing any more education. Instead, I went to work as an attorney. Fortuitously, in the next year, I saw my counselor friend several times and my friend always reminded me to contact Ted Remley.

When I decided to return to teaching and pursue a master's degree in school counseling, I did contact Ted. One of my first questions to him was how he integrated his knowledge of law in his career as a counselor educator. He didn't just tell me, he showed me. While I was still a master's degree student, he invited me to give presentations with him at local and national conferences. We also worked as coauthors on several projects. After completing my master's degree, I was planning to work as a school counselor in another state, but Ted convinced me to stay and work on my doctorate under his supervision.

Working with Ted has been one of the best learning experiences I have ever had. As my professor and mentor, he has generously shared his extraordinary knowledge of research, writing, and publishing. Not only have I learned from observing his mentoring and leadership activities, but he also encouraged me and all of his students to become leaders in counseling. Thus, Ted is not only a leader in the counseling profession today; his legacy of leadership is extending to generations of counselors and counselor educators.

## REFERENCES

Remley, T. P., Jr. (Ed.). (1991). *The ACA legal series, Volume 1: Preparing for court appearances.* Alexandria, VA: American Counseling Association.

Remley, T. P., Jr. (Ed.). (1991–1994). *The ACA legal series.* Alexandria, VA: American Counseling Association.

Remley, T. P., Jr., & Herlihy, B. (2001). *Ethical, legal, and professional issues in counseling.* Upper Saddle River, NJ: Prentice-Hall.

# CHAPTER 26

# Bruce Shertzer

Kenneth L. Miller

*Helping others is a worthy goal, but at its best, it represents an enlight-
ened self-interest at work.*

Bruce Shertzer was born on January 11, 1928, in Bloomfield, Indiana. The
fifth of eight children born to Edwin Franklin and Lois B. Shertzer, his
childhood and early adolescent years coincided with the stock market
crash of 1929 and the Great Depression of the 1930s. In these social and
economic contexts, Bruce's most significant childhood experience surrounded his father's accidental fall from the third story of a house in 1933.
A house painter by trade, Edwin Shertzer suffered two broken legs and
pulverized bones in both ankles. Although doctors told the elder Shertzer
that he would neither walk nor work again, his tenacity eventually proved
doctors wrong on both counts. Bruce recalled his father's courage in a
vivid memory of a bright November day when his father, still on crutches
and with a gun slung over his shoulder, prepared for a quail hunt.

The most significant event of Bruce's early adolescent years was the bombing of Pearl Harbor on December 7, 1941. Returning home from playing basketball that Sunday morning, he found his mother crying. She explained what had happened and her fears for Bruce's older brother, Clifford, who was serving in the U.S. Army. Although Clifford did serve in the Pacific theater, he returned home safely in 1945.

One week after high school graduation in May 1946, Bruce enlisted in the U.S. Army. He was promoted first to corporal and then to sergeant in 14 months while serving at Fort Sam Houston in San Antonio, Texas. After discharge, he enrolled at Indiana University in September of 1948. In 1952, he earned a B.S. degree in secondary education (social studies). One year later, he earned an M.S. degree in guidance, followed by an Ed.D. in counseling and guidance in 1958.

In November 1948, Bruce married Carol Rice, who worked at an RCA factory and provided financial support while he earned his bachelor's degree. In 1953, Carol gave birth to their first child, Sarah, and 16 months later, a son, Mark, was born. During these years, the Shertzers lived in Martinsville, Indiana, where Bruce worked as a teacher and counselor at Martinsville High School.

Sarah earned bachelor's and master's degrees in education and is currently a kindergarten teacher in Anchorage, Alaska, where she lives with her husband and their two children. Mark Shertzer earned an M.D. degree from Indiana University and completed a four-year residency in pathology at Bowman-Gray Hospital, affiliated with Wake Forest University in Winston-Salem, North Carolina. He is married and currently lives in Dothan, Alabama, where he is a senior partner in a pathology laboratory.

## CAREER PATH

Bruce's career path began as a teacher and counselor at Martinsville High School (1952–1956), where he was appointed director of guidance and testing for the school district. From 1956 to 1958, he was appointed and served as director of the Division of Guidance and Pupil Personnel for the State of Indiana. Between 1958 and 1960, Bruce served as associate director, Project for the Guidance of Superior Students. This research and training program, which included some 100 secondary schools, was conducted under the auspices of the North Central Association of Colleges and Secondary Schools.

In 1960, Bruce was appointed as assistant professor in counselor education at Purdue University. He was promoted to associate professor in 1962 and to professor in 1965. During the 1960s, he taught in seven aca-

demic-year and summer National Defense Education Act (NDEA) Counseling and Guidance Institutes. In 1968, he was appointed chairperson,
Counseling and Personnel Services, at Purdue University. He held this post
until 1989, when he was appointed head, Department of Educational Studies, and served in that position until his retirement in 1994.

All of these appointments were instrumental in Bruce's professional development. Of particular importance was his appointment as a Fullbright
Senior Lecturer during the 1967–1968 academic year at the University of
Reading, England. This sabbatical enabled his family's first visit to Europe.
In 1969, he returned to Europe for two weeks as a consultant in counseling
to the Minister of Education of Cyprus. Additional valuable cultural experiences were obtained from visiting professorships in the summer of 1967 at
the University of Hawaii, from January through June of 1975 at the University of Southern California Overseas Program (Germany) and again, from
January through June in 1982 (Germany and Spain).

Bruce has been a productive and impressive leader in counseling professional associations. In 1961, he was instrumental in developing the Indiana Personnel and Guidance Association (IPGA). Two years later, he was
elected president of IPGA. In 1968, Bruce was elected president of the
North Central Association for Counselor Education and Supervision
(NCACES). From 1970 through 1971, he served as president of the Association for Counselor Education and Supervision (ACES), a division of the
American Personnel and Guidance Association (APGA), and from 1973
through 1974 he served as president of APGA (currently the American
Counseling Association).

Bruce's term as APGA president was strengthened measurably by the
help of then APGA executive director, Charles Lewis. With Lewis's able
assistance, the following goals were achieved: (a) a severe budget deficit
was erased, (b) the American College Personnel Association (ACPA)
elected to remain a division of APGA, (c) the APGA ethical code was revised for the first time since 1952, and (d) four position papers were prepared, including one on career education.

In 1976, Bruce was appointed chairperson of a committee (the product
of which became known as the "Shertzer White Paper"), which made the
following recommendations to the American Association for Counseling
and Development (AACD): (a) establish an accrediting body for counselor
preparation programs, (b) create a national registry of counselors, (c) vigorously pursue counselor licensure laws, and (d) expand its efforts to
advance professional development. The association's governing council
adopted these recommendations, and through the leadership of national,

divisional, and regional presidents and officers, AACD created (a) the Council for Accreditation of Counseling and Related Educational Programs (CACREP), (b) the National Board for Certified Counselors (NBCC), (c) information and financial support for states seeking to establish licensure laws, and (d) opportunities to obtain continuing education credits at pre-convention workshops.

In 1986, Bruce was appointed to a 3-year term as trustee of the AACD Foundation and served for 1 year as its chairperson. In the same year, he was awarded the Distinguished Professional Service Award by AACD. To honor his many accomplishments in the profession of counseling, he has been inducted as an honorary life member of Chi Sigma Iota, Counseling Academic and Professional Honor Society International.

During his tenure at Purdue University, Bruce served as major professor and chairperson for 85 Ph.D. degrees, 326 M.S. degrees, and 25 educational specialist degrees. He was elected and served on the School Senate and University Senate, department and school tenure and promotion committees, the University Graduate Council, and search committees for department heads and deans.

Bruce's leadership to the counseling profession through scholarly contributions is legendary. These include 12 textbooks (Shertzer, 1960, 1976, 1985a; Shertzer & Stone, 1970; Stone & Shertzer, 1972) and the Professional Guidance Monograph Series (Stone & Shertzer, 1979), which he authored or coauthored and edited or coedited with S. C. Stone. This series included 10 sets of monographs with some 10 monographs per set. Two texts, *Fundamentals of Guidance* (1981) and *Fundamentals of Counseling* (1980), coauthored with S. C. Stone, were widely adopted by counselor education programs. The wealth of research-based information on counseling theory, knowledge, and skills contained in these textbooks provided, and continues to provide, a foundation upon which counselor education programs have flourished. An immensely prolific writer, Bruce also authored or coauthored 52 articles in professional counseling journals that include Shertzer (1984, 1985b), Shertzer and Stone (1963a, 1963b, 1965, 1972), Stone and Shertzer (1963, 1964, 1967, 1971), as well as 5 book reviews, 14 booklets, pamphlets, and other chapters.

Bruce's phenomenal record of achievement reflects a leadership style characterized by perceptiveness, hard work, and perseverance. His ability to identify situations requiring leadership is based on keen observation, careful listening, and the capacity to discriminate solvable from intractable problems. His skill in resolving problems derives from his knowledge of human dynamics and systems, in concert with an unrelenting drive to achieve the achievable. His ability to succeed stems from an unshakable capacity to persist, even in the face of overwhelming obstacles. Although the calculus of leadership may never be fully explicated, Bruce's style, skills, and achievements contribute substantially to the equation.

## MEMORIES OF MY WORK WITH BRUCE SHERTZER

I met Bruce Shertzer for the first time in November 1983. While applying to the doctoral program in counselor education at Purdue University, I thought that a discussion with the department chair would answer many of my questions. The man who greeted me warmly that November morning had a weathered yet kind face, obvious intelligence, a serious nature, a keen sense of humor, and a quiet grace. Before leaving the meeting, I knew that this was a man from whom I could learn much.

During the following years, I had many opportunities to benefit from Bruce's leadership. As an instructor in several of my doctoral courses, he consistently communicated high performance expectations, developed rigorous assignments, generated opportunities for dissent and discussion, and provided meaningful evaluative feedback. I vividly recall Bruce's challenges to my all-too-common vague responses, unparsimonious use of language, and lack of clarity in written assignments. His straightforward and rigorous teaching style motivated me to learn and greatly influenced my later work with students in classroom and clinical settings.

While serving a one-year internship as coordinator of the Purdue Counseling and Guidance Center, I consulted Bruce on many occasions regarding a wide range of administrative and clinical issues. Despite the frequency and often inopportune moments of my visits, Bruce always made time to answer questions or provide assistance. His wealth of clinical knowledge, expertise in human dynamics, and calm demeanor in the face of difficult decisions served as a model that I attempt to emulate in my work with clients, colleagues, and staff.

Through my work with Bruce, I came to understand the fundamental dynamics of leadership. They include an uncommon caring for people, strong commitments to one's work and profession, an intelligent application of knowledge, and a ceaseless striving for quality. Bruce's contributions as a leader, scholar, mentor, and teacher have shaped the personal and professional lives of thousands of people. I am deeply honored to be among them.

## ACKNOWLEDGMENTS

The author gratefully acknowledges significant contributions by Bruce Shertzer in the preparation of this manuscript.

## REFERENCES

Shertzer, B. (Ed.). (1960). *Working with superior students.* Chicago: Science Research Associates.

Shertzer, B. (1976). *Career exploration and planning* (2nd ed.). Boston: Houghton Mifflin.

Shertzer, B. (1984). An examination of the proposed measurement preparation standards. *Measurement and Evaluation in Counseling and Development, 17* (3), 161–165.

Shertzer, B. (1985a). *Career planning: Freedom to choose* (3rd ed.). Boston: Houghton Mifflin Company.

Shertzer, B. (1985b). Integrating computer assisted testing and counseling: A reaction. *Measurement and Evaluation in Counseling and Development, 19,* 27–28.

Shertzer, B., & Stone, S. C. (1963a). Administrative deterrents to guidance program development and management. *Theory into Practice, 2,* 24–32.

Shertzer, B., & Stone, S. C. (1963b). The counselor's publics: Problems in role definition. *Personnel and Guidance Journal, 41,* 687–693.

Shertzer, B., & Stone, S. C. (1965). Challenges confronting counselors. *The School Counselor, 12,* 235–241.

Shertzer, B., & Stone, S. C. (Eds.). (1970). *Introduction to guidance: Selected readings.* Boston: Houghton Mifflin.

Shertzer, B., & Stone, S. C. (1972). Myths, counselor beliefs and practices. *The School Counselor, 19,* 370–377.

Shertzer, B., & Stone, S. C. (1980). *Fundamentals of counseling* (3rd ed.). Houghton Mifflin Company.

Shertzer, B., & Stone, S. C. (1981). *Fundamentals of guidance* (4th ed.). Boston: Houghton Mifflin.

Stone, S. C., & Shertzer, B. (1963). The militant counselor. *Personnel and Guidance Journal, 42,* 342–347.

Stone, S. C., & Shertzer, B. (1964). Ten years of personnel and guidance journal. *Personnel and Guidance Journal, 42,* 958–969.

Stone, S. C., & Shertzer, B. (1967). A confrontation and a challenge. *The School Counselor, 5,* 262–267.

Stone, S. C., & Shertzer, B. (1971). Counselor Education: Retrospect and prospect. *Hawaii Personnel and Guidance Journal, 1,* 26–40.

Stone, S. C., & Shertzer, B. (1972). *Careers in counseling.* Boston: Houghton Mifflin.

Stone, S. C., & Shertzer, B. (Eds.). (1979). *Professional guidance monograph series.* Boston: Houghton Mifflin.

# CHAPTER 27

# Robert O. Stripling

Donald A. Haight

*A leader in accreditation and standards of preparation
in counselor education.*

Robert O. Stripling (Bob) was born in 1915 in Lower Peach Tree, Alabama, the youngest of eight children. His father, a Methodist circuit rider in the West Florida–South Alabama Conference, died when Bob was a year old. When he died, his mother moved the family to Montgomery, Alabama, where he was raised until attending college. Bob attended the University of Alabama for 1 year and then transferred to the University of Florida, where he received bachelor's and master's degrees. He started his career as a social studies and English teacher and later switched to teaching geography. He then became a school counselor and a counselor in the undergraduate counseling office in the College of Education at the University of Florida. Following these experiences he attended Teachers College, Columbia University, where he received his Ed.D. degree in 1952. He served as a faculty member in the College of Education at the University of Florida for 37 years, chairing the Department of Counselor Education for 13 years. He retired from teaching in 1980, but continued to assist in the profession for years after his retirement until his death in the spring of 1991.

Bob was married to Dorothy (Dot) Claire Atkinson in 1940. Dot attended Florida State College for Women and taught kindergarten and elementary grades. She is an artist who paints with oils, and most of her paintings are of flowers and nature scenes. They have two children, Robert, Jr. (Bob) and Carolyn. Bob, Jr., resides in Gainesville with his wife, Sylvia, and they have three sons—Robert Scott, Clifford Britt (Casey), and John William (Jack). Bob is the senior member of his own law firm and is a past president of the Florida Trial Lawyers Association and a former member of the Board of Governors of the Florida Bar Association. Bob, Sr., and Dot's daughter, Carolyn, is a former teacher. She and her husband, Albert B. Jolly, Jr., live in Spartenburg, South Carolina, where he owns a very successful architectural firm. Carolyn and Albert have two daughters, Elizabeth Claire and Catherine Hollingsworth.

## MAJOR CAREER ACCOMPLISHMENTS

Robert O. Stripling made contributions to the counseling profession primarily through his writing, his leadership in professional counseling associations, and his leadership of the Counselor Education Department at the University of Florida. He authored more than 70 articles, book chapters, and books, and would often describe himself as a writer. His major written contributions, however, might best be reviewed as part of his leadership in the counseling profession. Therefore, the focus of this presentation will be on his leadership in the counseling profession and his leadership at the University of Florida.

Shertzer and Stone (1980) cited Bob as influential in the achievement of four milestones in the history of the counseling profession, sponsored primarily by the Association for Counselor Education and Supervision (ACES). They were: (a) the 5-year grassroots study of counselor education, which started in 1959; (b) the approval in 1964 by the American Personnel and Guidance Association (APGA) of the *Standards for Counselor Education in the Preparation of Secondary School Counselors (ACES, 1964);* (c) the approval in 1972 by ACES and APGA of the *Standards for the Preparation of Counselors and Other Personnel Services Specialists* (ACES, 1977); and (d) the approval by ACES in 1978 of the *ACES Guidelines for Doctoral Preparation in Counselor Education* (ACES Committee, 1978). This author would add to the list the following three milestones in which Bob was influential: (a) the publication of *Standards for Preparation in Counselor Education* (ACES & APGA, 1979), the first standards published by the new profession for entry-level and advanced programs in counselor preparation; (b) the publication in 1978 by APGA of the *Accreditation Procedures Manual for Counselor Education* (Stripling & Sheeley, 1978); and (c) the establishment of the ACES National Committee on Accreditation (now Council for Accreditation of Counseling and Related Educational Programs or CACREP).

ACES launched the 5-year grassroots study of counselor education, entitled the Planning Cooperative Study of Counselor Education, in 1959 (as noted above) (Stripling, 1965). The committee directing the study was lead initially by cochairpersons Willis Dugan and Bob. Bob assumed the chair of the Standards Committee in 1962 and he was the one who saw an opportunity for counselor educators around the country to meet and plan a program of counselor education. Funding made available through the Guidance and Counseling Institutes Program of the National Defense Education Act (NDEA) was used to pay for some of the meeting expenses. The directors of the Institutes met twice a year, once at the time of the APGA convention and at one other time. The directors' travel expenses were paid through the NDEA Institute Program and Bob saw an opportunity to schedule meetings of the ACES Counselor Education Standards Committee around the directors' meetings, thus eliminating travel expenses for ACES.

During the 5-year work of the committee, 12 different individuals served on the committee at the national level and involved over 700 professional persons on 150 grass-roots committees in 50 states (Stripling, 1965; Stripling & Dugan, 1961). This study led directly to the adoption by ACES of the "Standards for Counselor Education in the Preparation of Secondary School Counselors" (ACES National Committee on Counselor Education Standards, 1964). These standards were the first ever prepared under the sponsorship of the emerging profession. They served as the first major step toward the development of what is now CACREP.

Bob continued to work with several APGA and ACES national committees and commissions on standards and accreditation during the next few years. As a result of his leadership, ACES and APGA approved in 1973 the "Standards for the Preparation of Counselors and Other Personnel Services Specialists" (ACES Commission on Standards and Accreditation, 1977). This was the first set of entry-level standards for preparation adopted by the profession to prepare counselors for all levels of education as well as for other settings in our society. Bob served as chairperson and principal author for the national committee that prepared the standards over a 3-year period.

In 1977, ACES approved the "ACES Guidelines for Doctoral Preparation in Counselor Education" (ACES Committee to Develop Guidelines for Doctoral Preparation in Counselor Education, 1978), the first official adoption by the profession of advanced preparation standards in counselor education. Bob served as chairperson and principal writer for this committee during a 3-year period. In 1979, he served as the editor of *Standards for Preparation in Counselor Education*, published by APGA (ACES & APGA, 1979). This was the first official publication of the profession that provided a set of standards for preparation in counselor education at both the entry level (master's degree and educational specialist degree levels) and the advanced level (doctoral degree level).

From 1978 through 1980 Bob served as chairperson of the newly organized ACES National Committee on Accreditation. This committee organized and conducted accreditation visits to the first four institutions accredited by ACES. It later became CACREP (in affiliation with the American Association for Counseling and Development [AACD]). During this time, Bob also served as coauthor and editor of the *Accreditation Procedures Manual for Counselor Education* (Stripling & Sheeley, 1978), the first accreditation manual used by the new profession (Haight, 1988).

During the more than 20 years that Bob assumed national leadership responsibilities for the counseling profession, he was also establishing a counselor education program at the University of Florida that has become preeminent in the United States (Ralph C. Bedell, personal communication, February 23, 1973). He was the first chairperson of the Counselor Education Department and served from 1955 through 1968 in that capacity. During this period of time he was directly involved in securing outside funds amounting to $2,201,645 for support of research, program development, and professional development in counselor education. A significant proportion of these funds were from the NDEA Counseling and Guidance Institute Program (noted above) and from the Education Professions Development Act. Bob, in his role as department chair, was able to secure regular appointments to the University of Florida's counselor education faculty for some NDEA Institute staff members, and as a result, he was able to help build the regular counselor education program faculty. These appointments helped the University of Florida develop counselor education programs with strong practicum and internship components, a significant sense of community among a sizeable proportion of full-time students, a significant scholarly tradition, and a depth of preparation beyond the nationally recognized minimum levels. The Department of Counselor Education at the University of Florida is consistently ranked as one of the top counselor education departments in the country. In addition, Bob was chairperson of the building committee that was largely responsible for the $7 million addition to the College of Education at the university known as the "back porch."

## LEADERSHIP STYLE

Bob Stripling had a clear vision that there were some issues that he should do something about and he described it as an "intuitive feeling." It related to his goals and what he wanted to accomplish over a period of time. Bob also noted that, in the counseling profession, there were some issues where other people were taking the leadership, and these were issues in which he would not become interested. He noted that he enjoyed the challenge of trying to accomplish certain things in his life, even though not all his friends and colleagues were unanimous in their opinions about whether or not they should be accomplished (Haight, 1988).

Bob was a gentle, yet persuasive individual who constantly led by example. He was a person of action who was involved as a leader in the counseling profession for his entire life. This author remembers him saying, "It is usually better to do something, even when you're uncertain, than do nothing." He used encouragement frequently, suggesting to others that they become involved. Bob himself noted that he had some capacity to sense the things that others wanted to do. "I've always enjoyed trying to help them [others] achieve their goals," he said (Haight, 1988, p. 324). Helping others contributed significantly to the high esteem in which Bob was held. It drew people to him and kept them motivated while working toward a shared vision. Bob was also known to share the recognition of achievements with others and rarely sought recognition for himself.

Joe Wittmer, a colleague and close personal friend of Bob's for 23 years, did not remember Bob giving a lecture on leadership. However, he noted the following:

> Bob often told me that our profession needed people with a sense of commitment, a deep appreciation for counseling, and most importantly, individuals who were not afraid to become "active" and to take a stand. That is, where action is absent, so is leadership! He would remind me that "leader" is an entity, leadership is an action! And, he was a master at taking the appropriate action to get things done. (J. Wittmer, personal communication, August 15, 2001)

## AUTHOR'S MEMORIES OF WORKING WITH DR. STRIPLING

My own experiences with Robert O. Stripling include his work as my doctoral advisor, a month sabbatical leave I spent with him, and the five weeks he spent on our campus in 1989 as a Distinguished Visiting Professor. It is this latter experience that I will address below.

Bob and Dot Stripling spent 5 weeks on our campus in 1989. My experiences with Bob during this time were some of the most rewarding of my career. Bob's primary role was to assist us in our accreditation efforts. I learned a great deal from him about curriculum development and about working with faculty and college administration. Bob and I discussed how to approach individual faculty members who were wary about accreditation. I wrote many memos to the faculty and to the college administration and many program proposals after consulting with Bob. This was a highly rewarding and productive time for me. One of the major understandings I gained from this period was that one could push ahead with programmatic changes even when faced with opposition and be successful at having those changes adopted.

It was also exciting for me to learn that a year later, in 1990, our institution received 2-year accreditation for all three of our preparation programs. In 1991, Plattsburgh State University selected Bob to receive an honorary Doctor of Humane Letters degree at its spring graduation. I called Bob to inform him of our college's decision, knowing that this was a complete surprise to him. Here was a man I admired, a person very articulate and able to think quickly, who was speechless. I remember him asking me if he could get Dot on the phone and if I would start all over again as if I hadn't said anything to him. This was one of the most rewarding experiences of my life. Unfortunately, Bob died shortly before graduation that spring. But he did know he would receive this degree. His wife, son, and daughter traveled to Plattsburgh to receive it and his son presented a statement that Bob had written before he died.

In the above paragraphs, a brief description of the life of Dr. Robert O. Stripling was presented, including biographical information and major accomplishments. Bob Stripling was a prince of a person and the impact of his work in the profession will continue into the future. CACREP has referred to him as the "Father of Accreditation" in counselor education, a fitting reference to a man who dedicated much of his professional life to standards and accreditation in the counseling profession. Indeed, his work has contributed significantly to the development of counseling as a profession.

## REFERENCES

Association for Counselor Education and Supervision and American Personnel and Guidance Association. (1979). *Standards for preparation in counselor education.* Washington, DC: American Personnel and Guidance Association.

Association for Counselor Education and Supervision, Committee to Develop Guidelines for Doctoral Preparation in Counselor Education. (R. O. Stripling, Chairperson and Principal Writer). (1978). ACES guidelines for doctoral preparation in counselor education. *Counselor Education and Supervision, 17,* 163–166.

Association for Counselor Education and Supervision, Commission on Standards and Accreditation, and American Personnel and Guidance Association. (R. O. Stripling, Chairperson and Principal Writer). (1977). Standards for the preparation of counselors and other personnel services specialists. *Personnel and Guidance Journal, 55,* 596–601.

Association for Counselor Education and Supervision, National Committee on Counselor Education Standards. (R. O. Stripling, Chairperson and Principal Writer). (1964). Standards for counselor education in the preparation of secondary school counselors. *Personnel and Guidance Journal, 42,* 1060–1073.

Haight, D. A. (1988). Robert O. Stripling: A man dedicated to standards and accreditation in counselor education. *Journal of Counseling & Development, 66,* 317–325.

Shertzer, B., & Stone, S.C. (1980). *Fundamentals of counseling* (3rd ed.). Boston: Houghton Mifflin.

Stripling, R. O. (1965). Standards for the education of school counselors. In J. W. Loughary, R. O. Stripling, & P. W. Fitzgerald (Eds.), *Counseling, a growing profession* (pp. 19–30). Washington, DC: American Personnel and Guidance Association.

Stripling, R. O., & Dugan, W. E. (1961). The cooperative study of counselor education standards. *Counselor Education and Supervision, 0,* 34–35.

Stripling, R. O., & Sheeley, V. L. (1978). *Accreditation procedures manual for counselor education.* Washington, DC: American Personnel and Guidance Association.

# CHAPTER 28

# Thomas J. Sweeney

J. Melvin Witmer

*First, teach them to believe in themselves. (Martin Luther King, Jr.)*[1]

Tom Sweeney was born and educated in Akron, Ohio, where he earned his bachelor's degree from the University of Akron in social studies and education. He began teaching in the Akron public schools in the fall of 1958 and continued his studies toward a master's degree in school guidance. In the meantime, he was selected to receive a National Defense Education Act (NDEA) fellowship in school guidance from the University of Wisconsin (Madison) and completed his master's degree there in 1960 with Gail Farwell as Institute Director and adviser. Upon graduation, he completed 6 months of military active duty as a lieutenant at Fort Sam Houston, San Antonio, Texas, where he was an instructor/trainer in the U.S. Army Educational Services Unit until February 1961. Prior to accepting a graduate associateship with an NDEA Guidance Institute at The Ohio State University under Herman J. Peters, he returned to the Akron public schools to complete another semester of teaching that resulted in a total of 2 years of public school teaching experience.

---

[1]Quote from Martin Luther King, Jr., taken from Gardner (1990, p. 195).

During his doctoral studies at Ohio State (1961–1964), Tom had opportunities to study and interact with scholars and leaders in counseling, teacher education, and student development, across departments and throughout the country as a part of the institute's programs under Herman Peters. While majoring in counselor education, he completed minor areas of study in teacher education, student development in higher education, and counseling psychology. Tom credits the education he received at Ohio State for his early knowledge about the hallmarks of a profession and the need for counseling to acquire them in order to earn the respect that it deserved. National preparation and ethical standards, accreditation, professional membership associations, and credentialing were central to these hallmarks. To help support the costs of a graduate education, Tom used his musical talent to sing professionally on a Columbus television station, the Jack Denton Morning Show, featuring live audience interaction and light comedy.

Internships per se were not part of counselor education requirements at that time. Tom decided to delay his graduation, however, in order to work as a school counselor full-time for one year (1963–1964) in Southwestern City Schools in Grove City, Ohio, because of its proactive, comprehensive pupil personnel programs and excellent curriculum for a wide variety of students. Bill VanHoose was the director who helped create this exemplary pupil personnel program, and it was he who hired Tom as a high school counselor. Years later their paths would cross again in the move to create national accreditation.

## CAREER DEVELOPMENT

Tom was recruited to the University of South Carolina in 1964. Serendipity played a role. When his major professor at Ohio State, Herman Peters, was invited to speak at the South Carolina Guidance Annual Conference in the summer of 1963, he invited Tom and another of his doctoral students to join him in leading small groups. Herman Peters also let it be known that Tom sang. As a consequence, he entertained the participants in addition to leading the groups. Participant response to Tom's group facilitation and openness to sharing his other talent led to an invitation to apply for the position of the director of the Guidance Center (university and community based) and assistant professor for counselor education.

He taught at the University of South Carolina for 8 years, where he developed their counselor education program from a faculty of one and a quarter persons to eight faculty, four secretaries, and a modern counselor education laboratory and faculty suite. From what was solely a school counselor education program, Tom developed rehabilitation, community, and college counseling, as well as a doctoral program for counselor educators, supervisors, and those seeking advanced counseling competencies. This was possible because of a variety of grants that he authored, including those in vocational education, rehabilitation, and elementary and secondary school guidance. Probably the most notable experiences for Tom were associated with the General Electric (GE) Foundation–funded institutes for counselors and, ultimately, teachers, administrators, and public representatives. GE was interested especially in career guidance for non-college-bound youth and, more particularly, minorities and girls.

During his entire career, Tom was successful in getting corporate and government grants. Starting in 1968, GE funded one of several summer institutes for school counselors. Without fanfare, Tom's institutes integrated the summer residence halls of the University of South Carolina with 50 school counselors from 13 southeastern states. African-American, Asian-American, Latino, and White counselors, male and female, were integrated. A key staff member was John McFadden (University of South Carolina), one of Tom's doctoral advisees, who helped shape an atmosphere of diversity with dignity, caring with respect, and honesty with compassion.

Tom continued his work with the GE Foundation for 18 years, 14 of them after he had moved to Ohio University. The Educators in Industry programs sponsored by GE were possibly among the most successful of any outside of government-supported career education. Literally thousands of educators throughout the nation and hundreds of thousands of young people were touched by the GE poster campaigns (e.g., "If You Can Dream It, You Can Do It!"). Academic year programs with local plants as well as summer programs were sponsored by GE in conjunction with universities, school systems, local and state chambers of commerce, and other businesses and industries. Tom attributes his own deep commitment to career education as a motivating factor in his long-term relationship with these programs.

Tom was recruited by Ohio University at an interesting transition in its history in 1972. George E. Hill, Distinguished Professor of Education, was retiring. Our department head, Don Green, had died suddenly of a heart attack earlier in the year. With George's political influence, the Dean of the College of Education agreed to allow us to recruit not one but two full professors! As department chairperson at the time, I called then assistant executive vice president of the American Personnel and Guidance Association (APGA), Pat McDonough, about possible candidates for our positions. Pat named Tom as one of the "rising stars" in the profession. As a faculty, we had been and were committed to leadership within the profession. This was one of George Hill's legacies to our program. We wanted our faculty and students to see themselves helping to shape the future of the profession.

I remember that Tom was well liked at the University of South Carolina and seemed content with the work and lifestyle that he had there. In fact, he refused to come for a visit until we persisted in asking and, out of curiosity, finally agreed to a Mother's Day weekend visit. Circumstances could have been better, as the campus was flooded with families visiting, the phone lines were overloaded, and parking was worse than usual. To top it off, I missed getting Tom and his family back to the airport in time for their flight! Nevertheless, he decided it was time to shift from heavy administrative duties in South Carolina to re-network with old friends in Ohio and pursue the opportunities afforded by being on the faculty at Ohio University. This was the beginning of a collegial and enriching personal relationship that has continued for almost 30 years. Tom's commitment to the profession, his striving for excellence, and loyalty to our program have been greatly valued by me and an inspiration to my career. Any differences we've had were momentary and limited to such incidents as my encroachment upon his office space.

Ultimately, he became program coordinator of Counselor Education and Director of the School of Applied Behavioral Sciences and Educational Leadership at Ohio University. He was instrumental in helping to get the support from the Dean of the College of Education to start a rehabilitation program, initially without external funding, and to create what became the George E. Hill Counseling and Research Center. His leadership within the profession that began early in his career in South Carolina blossomed in Ohio. He may be the only Southern Association for Counselor Education and Supervision (SACES) president (1972–1973) who served while living and working in another region!

## CAREER ACHIEVEMENTS

As president of SACES, Tom was the first to fund the Committee on Women (Sheeley, 1977) in keeping with an expectation that it provide leadership in this important area of counselor education. It was during his past-president's year (1973–1974) that he presented what became the issue of licensure for the counseling profession based upon the Ohio Board of Psychology's aggressive implementation of its new law (Sweeney & Sturdevant, 1974). As a result of the immediate response in the business meeting at the conference, Tom was asked to become the chairperson of the first SACES Committee on Licensure for the profession. He was subsequently asked to write a position paper for the APGA Governing Council on the issue and it was adopted and still stands as the policy guiding the licensure efforts of the profession. He also chaired the first APGA Commission on Licensure that began work on model legislation for the states' consideration.

Election to the presidency of the Association of Counselor Education and Supervision (ACES, 1976–1977) resulted in Tom shifting from primarily licensure efforts to those of standards and accreditation as well. His education at Ohio State had clearly left a mark on the importance of these hallmarks of a profession. During his presidency of ACES, he asked Bob Stripling (University of Florida) to chair a committee to develop doctoral standards because none existed and without them any effort to include doctoral preparation in the scope of national accreditation would be deficient. Contextually, it was also helpful to know that psychology accredits only doctoral programs, and counseling psychologists were gaining ground in counselor education because graduates could be licensed as psychologists and still teach in counselor education.

George Hill, Bill Dugan (University of Minnesota), and Bob Stripling had been striving for some years to have preparation standards adopted not only by ACES but APGA. APGA had "received" them as a matter of record. Nevertheless, Tom asked Bill VanHoose (University of Virginia) to chair a committee on "Standards Implementation" for ACES. The name was chosen because there was opposition to accreditation and Tom wanted the committee to have time to respond to objections and prepare a suitable rationale. VanHoose's committee did so, and 2 years later ACES approved the proposed plan and appointed the ACES Committee on Accreditation.

Also during his ACES presidency (1976–1977), Tom worked with John McFadden (University of South Carolina) and Ron Quinn (South Carolina State University) to coauthor an ACES position paper on "NonWhite Concerns in Counselor Education." He again actively supported the Committee on Women among counselor educators and supervisors and sought to insure equity among those in appointed positions.

As president of APGA (1980–1981), Tom was able to have the Governing Council adopt the ACES preparation standards, establish a committee to study accreditation (which he chaired), fund the Registry Committee chaired by Lloyd Stone (Emporia State University) in order to conduct a survey of membership regarding the need for a national certification of counselors, and create a fund to assist state organizations working on counselor licensure. The position paper on accreditation that he wrote on behalf of his committee was adopted by APGA and was the basis for establishing the Council for Accreditation of Counseling and Related Educational Programs (CACREP).

Few members will remember that even Bob Stripling (Stripling, 1978) had serious doubts about APGA creating its own accrediting agency and preferred instead to consider the National Council on Accreditation of Teacher Education (NCATE) as the best choice for counselor accreditation. Bob's public and private efforts are notable because of his considerable presence in standards development. He noted later, however, that his colleague and first executive director of CACREP, Joe Wittmer (University of Florida), and Tom Sweeney were correct in the course that was finally taken.

Tom served for 6 years as the first chairperson of CACREP. These were years of formulating policies and procedures and establishing credibility in an otherwise hostile higher education environment. The issues before the council ranged from demands by the American Mental Health Counselors Association (AMHCA) and ACES for higher standards (more credit hours and supervised experiences) to greater inclusiveness of language related to special topics. Perhaps the most important objective was the ultimate approval of the Council for Post Secondary Accreditation (COPA), whose endorsement at the time was essential to continued success. This was attained through Tom and Joe Wittmer's efforts in 1987. According to Joe Wittmer, CACREP may not have succeeded without Tom's hard work and perseverance in those early years (J. Wittmer, personal correspondence, April 2001).

Before completing his leadership with CACREP, Tom saw a need for a new type of association within counseling. He noted that in his early days as a student in counseling, Gail Farwell and Herman Peters expected their advisees to be members of the counseling profession's associations. It was a clear and positive message, "You need this to remain current and professional" (T. Sweeney, personal correspondence, April 2001). Since the early 1970s with psychologists' licensure efforts, marriage and family changing its name from "counseling" to "therapy" (American Association of Marriage and Family Counseling vs. American Association of Marriage and Family Therapy), and texts being written to serve an increasingly diverse population of "mental health providers," identity with and pride in the choice of counseling as a career seemed to have been lost in many counselor education programs. There seemed to be an obvious need for more mentors with a clear vision and identity for the counseling profession such as Gail Farwell and Herman Peters presented. With a hope of reaffirming such an identity, Chi Sigma Iota (CSI) came into being in McCracken Hall of Ohio University.

Tom became the founding president of the CSI Counseling Academic and Professional Honor Society International in 1985 and, 2 years later, its executive director. Since its inception with Alpha Chapter at Ohio University, it continues to grow by approximately 3,000 new initiates each year and a dozen new chapters in each of the last several years. There are currently over 30,000 members initiated, 217 chapters in this country and abroad, and over 8,000 active members including almost 700 life members.

## CAREER LEGACY

Tom's scholarship, leadership, and service vita reveals a long and distinguished career. To summarize his many contributions, Tom was president of six state, regional, and national/international organizations and founding president of two of them. Ten other positions requiring leadership include department head, school director, and chairperson or coordinator of a professional organization or group. Two position papers authored by Tom, one on licensure and the other on accreditation, were adopted by APGA and used for implementing action plans. Tom became the first chairperson of these two national professional credentialing committees. Two notable leadership accomplishments in career development are the Educators in Industry programs with the General Electric Foundation (1968–1986) and a special career education project with the National Aeronautics and Space Administration (NASA).

Over a 15-year period (1973–1998), Tom was in the top 5% as a contributor to the *Journal of Counseling & Development* (Weinrach, Lustig, Chan, & Thomas, 1998). Two of his publications, *Coping With Kids* (1979) and *Adlerian Counseling* (1998), have been popular with counselors as well as teachers and parents. Tom's application of counseling theories is an integrated one with the Adlerian philosophy as the basis for conceptualizing the life situation of the person. He is the recipient of numerous state, regional, and national awards, including three national awards from ACA and two from ACES. More recently, two leadership awards have been established in his name, one by the faculty at Ohio University and the other by CSI.

In addition to over 80 refereed articles, books, monographs, chapters in books, and research reports, Tom has created both training videos and an award winning telecourse, *Coping With Kids* (1979), distributed worldwide and broadcast on local, state, and regional television. He has helped pro-

duce a series of nationally distributed training videos and guides on counseling older persons and directed a project for ACA (funded by NASA)
that produced career education materials and video for fourth to sixth
grade students. He is currently working on the fifth edition of his book,
*Adlerian Counseling*. Tom has been a keynote speaker, presenter, workshop director, and consultant in this country and abroad.

## LEADERSHIP STYLE AND ATTRIBUTES

The style and substance of Tom's leadership in counselor education over
37 years have been greatly admired by colleagues and graduate students.
Words describing his leadership range from visionary to caring and com-
passionate. One colleague and mentee has described it as like fine wine:
smooth, mellow, and delightful to experience. I have been a colleague of
Tom's for almost three decades. I have seen him use all the attributes of an
outstanding leader who has been driven by a desire to make counseling a
unique profession worthy of respect. In committees and organizational
sessions, I have seen him share his vision for the profession or the task, express his ideas with passion, listen to the ideas of others, demonstrate his
knowledge of the issues, and advocate a plan of action.

To challenge him conceptually or factually, you need to do your homework. More than once I have noticed him drop out of a discussion, be silent
while drafting a position statement that captured the essence of an emerging consensus, then present it to the group for review. Usually the statement was adopted. In addition to all the above qualities, Tom networks
extensively to educate and gain support, anticipates potential opposition,
foresees tasks needed to accomplish a goal, and has a good sense of
timing. He has people skills, political savvy, and a sense of humor, and understands how one must work within the policies and procedures of an organization in order to accomplish change. He can be challenging in the
debate of ideas, but with his diplomatic skills and positive approach, he is
able to attain the support of others to pursue common objectives. To assist
in doing this, he is a catalyst in getting others to take leadership responsibility. I have never seen Tom seek leadership for the sake of position or
prestige. Always it has been because his colleagues recognized his talents
and believed he had the vision and skills to accomplish the goals of the
group. Besides his contributions as a leader, he has mentored numerous
doctoral students and colleagues who have become leaders in their own
right, thus leaving a legacy that will continue long after his retirement.

## REFERENCES

Gardner, J. W. (1990). *On leadership*. New York: The Free Press.

Sheeley, V. L. (1977). *Presidential review: ACES leaders create ties, 1940–77*. Falls Church, VA: Association for Counselor Education and Supervision.

Stripling, R. O. (1978). Standards and accreditation in counselor education: A proposal. *The Personnel and Guidance Journal, 56*, 608–611.

Sweeney, T. J. (1979). *Coping with kids*. Award-winning series of twelve half-hour public broadcast programs designed as a telecommunications course using Adlerian theory, methods and research for teachers, parents, and others who guide young people. Alexandria, VA: American Association for Counseling and Development (Films and Study Guide).

Sweeney, T. J. (1998). *Adlerian counseling: A practitioner's approach* (4th ed.). Philadelphia: Accelerated Development, Taylor & Francis.

Sweeney, T. J., & Sturdevant, A.D., (1974). Licensure in the helping professions: Anatomy of an issue. *The Personnel and Guidance Journal, 52*, 575–580.

Weinrach, S. G., Lustig, D., Chan, F., & Thomas, K. R. (1998). Publication patterns of *The Personnel and Guidance Journal/Journal of Counseling & Development*: 1978 to 1993. *Journal of Counseling & Development, 76*, 427–435.

# CHAPTER 29

# Joe Wittmer

Larry C. Loesch and M. Harry Daniels

*Put the swing where the children want it. The grass will grow back.*

Paul Joseph ("Joe") Wittmer was born in southern Indiana into a world almost unimaginable to most of us, that of the Old Order Amish. German was his first language during much of his childhood, and after beginning school, he experienced the difficulties of learning English as a second language. However, those difficulties paled in comparison to the complex psychosocial issues he encountered during the transition from being a member of a truly unique American subculture to finding a unique identity in a strange new culture. From it he emerged to have a strong work ethic, sense of self, and compassion for the human condition, and a great love for humankind expressed as many forms of helping.

Joe received his B.S. and M.S. degrees in education from Indiana State University. He achieved school counseling certification from St. Francis College, Indiana, and a sixth year diploma from Michigan State University. He received his Ph.D. degree from Indiana State University in 1968 and has been a counselor education faculty member at the University of Florida (UF) since that time. He and his wife, Sue, reside in Gainesville, Florida. They have two sons and a daughter, a daughter- and son-in-law, and three grandchildren.

## CAREER PATH

Fresh out of his doctoral program and filled with seemingly unbounded energy, Joe raced full ahead into professional research and writing, at least in part because he realized that UF was and is a "publish or perish" institution. In addition to his own efforts, Joe often teamed with other highly productive faculty and thus soon gained wide respect for his contributions to the professional literature. This recognition in turn led to many invitations for many types of consultations, both in the United States and in other parts of the world. Concomitantly, he was developing and honing his excellent teaching skills. In addition to his own high standards for personal performance, underlying this activity and success level was a growing love for and commitment to UF.

Joe holds several unique distinctions at UF, including being a co-holder of the record for shortest time (5 years) from assistant to full professor. The same year he became a full professor (1974), he was selected by his peers as department chairperson, a position in which he served for 15 years. During that time the department expanded and then reorganized the number of programs it offered; increased the number of students in its programs; achieved all programmatic accreditations it sought; was home to faculty who achieved and received numerous professional positions, awards, and recognitions; served as the initial home for the Council for Accreditation of Counseling and Related Educational Programs (CACREP); assisted in the evolution of the National Board for Certified Counselors (NBCC); facilitated the start of Chi Sigma Iota (CSI, Counseling Academic and Professional Society International); was recognized for excellence by numerous professional organizations and publications; and generally achieved a high level of prominence and respect in the counseling profession. Joe was the catalyst for it all, sometimes at the head of the pack when it needed leadership and sometimes at the back when it needed pushing, but always in the thick of things when good work was being accomplished.

Joe took a brief hiatus from being department chairperson, only to return for another 3-year stint beginning in 1993. During this second term, the department was first recognized by *U.S. News & World Report* as among the best counselor preparation programs in the country. Although certainly not the most objective or strongest indicator of the department's professional accomplishments, it is nonetheless a public recognition of what can happen when a program has positive and directed leadership for a long time.

But why all these words about the department when this is supposed to be about Joe? Because as chairperson he always took more pride in the accomplishments of the department as a whole or of other faculty members than he did of his own. And that is what Joe is about: concern for others before concern for self. For example, he often worked on obtaining grant funds for department faculty members when he could have been seeking funds for himself; he excluded himself from receipt of merit monies so that it would be distributed to and among other department faculty members, and he used personal funds for professional travel so that available travel funds could be used by department faculty members.

Despite his "other orientation," his personal accomplishments should not and must not be overlooked. For example, rather than shun his background, Joe embraced it (from a perspective few will ever know). He used this love of heritage as impetus to champion several religious freedom law suits on behalf of "defensive Christian" Amish who "turn the other cheek" and will not defend themselves. While Amish parents were being given jail sentences for refusing to send their children to public high schools, Joe, as vice-chairperson of the National Committee for Amish Religious Freedom, marshalled a lawsuit on behalf of Amish children all the way to the U.S. Supreme Court. As a result, Amish children are no longer required to attend public high schools and instead attend parochial ones through the eighth grade. That case was the first time compulsory education (through high school) had been challenged successfully in the United States, and it halted a massive emigration of Amish to South American countries in their search for religious freedom.

Joe has authored or coauthored more than 90 journal and magazine articles, five monographs, six book chapters, and 13 books, including *The Gentle People: Personal Reflections on Amish Life* (Wittmer, 1990), *Managing Your K-12 Counseling Program* (Wittmer, 2000), *The Teacher as Facilitator* (Wittmer & Myrick, 1980), *The Peace Train: A School-Wide Violence Prevention Program* (Wittmer, Thompson, & Sheperis, 1999), and *Classroom Guidance Activities: A Sourcebook for Elementary School Counselors* (Wittmer, Thompson, & Loesch, 1997). He has held a wide variety of appointed professional positions and been recognized by local, state, national (including a distinguished service award from the American Counseling Association [ACA]), and international professional organizations for his numerous contributions to the counseling profession. He also has received awards and recognitions from civic organizations for his service activities. Along the way, he established a laudable teaching record that has been recognized on several occasions, including the awarding to him of the Wolfson Award, which is given to only one UF faculty member per year for excellence in teaching. His cumulative professional accomplishments led to him being awarded the rank of UF Distinguished Service Professor (DSP) in 1996, making him now one of only 67 DSPs from among more than 4,500 UF faculty. His career at UF has been stellar, to say the least.

From among his many publications, Joe perhaps received the most attention, both positive and negative, for his writings on the distinctions between counseling and counseling psychology (e.g., "CACREP or APA: A Counselor Educator's Personal Views," Wittmer, 1988). A staunch supporter of the position that counseling is a profession unto itself (and therefore distinct from counseling psychology), Joe wrote and talked about the distinction in both friendly and unfriendly environments, which stands as testimony to his unwavering commitment to both the counseling profession and his own personal values.

During the late 1970s and early 1980s, Joe and Robert O. (Bob) Stripling were among the leadership professionals in Florida championing a state licensure law for mental health counselors in Florida. Both became "card-carrying" lobbyists and spent innumerable hours, as well as personal resources, to lobby state representatives and senators on behalf of the licensure bill. The results of their efforts did not go unnoticed because both were invited to attend the ceremony when the Governor of Florida signed the bill into law.

Among the many contexts from which Joe has become widely known and respected in the counseling profession, his work with CACREP and NBCC has perhaps been the most significant. His work with professional "standards of preparation" for counselors, and the then remote possibility for a procedure to accredit programs based on those standards, began soon after he got to UF (or, soon after he met Bob Stripling). Astute enough to realize that the "standards movement" was actually going to go somewhere in the profession, he became integrally involved early on in its many aspects. For example, he was instrumental in the development of the standards themselves as well as the initial plans for how to implement them.

These early involvements led to the first CACREP headquarters being housed in the UF Department of Counselor Education, and directly under Joe's leadership. Joe convinced two different UF education deans that this was a good thing, and thus garnered financial and other support from them. He also gathered support and resources from other places, both inside and outside UF. Such activity was crucial to the early functioning of CACREP because it was insufficiently funded and unable to generate sufficient self-sustaining funds. One of the least known aspects of Joe's career is how much he did to enable CACREP to function initially.

Joe has written and consulted extensively about facilitating human communication and positive behavior. His early work with CACREP was a tribute to his skills in that regard. Back then, everyone had an idea about what the standards ought to be. It fell upon Joe and his good friend Tom Sweeney (then CACREP Chairperson) to bring the disparate parties together, and they did so with a minimum of political bloodshed. There also were innumerable perspectives about how the accreditation process ought to be implemented, who should be involved in it, and how much it ought to cost. Again, Joe (and Tom) steered the ship through those turbulent waters. When in 1987 CACREP moved to ACA headquarters, with 52 programs already accredited, it did so in good stead, both financially and professionally, in large part because of Joe's efforts.

Joe's leadership style reflects his life outlook and the behaviors associated with it. He has an exceptionally high level of personal integrity, a strong work ethic, and an unshakable belief in the basic goodness of humankind. These qualities are well respected, even among those whose opinions differ from his. Because of these characteristics, people are moved to work with, not against, him for the common good.

## PERSONAL GLIMPSES

The first author, Larry, has worked with Joe for over 28 years, while the second author, Harry, has worked with him for about 6 years. Thus, we have experienced Joe in dramatically different ways. In what follows each of us provides a personal glimpse of our experience, beginning with the senior author.

In the early years of his career as a counselor educator, Joe was fortunate to work with Bob Stripling, one of the truly great early leaders in our profession. Bob was a mentor to Joe, and they developed an enduring friendship based on deep personal and professional respect for each other. Among other things, Bob was a "doer," a person who could not only "see" the future (in particular, of the counseling profession), but also one who could make it happen. Joe was an ardent student of Bob's skills and strategies and developed the same talents for vision and accomplishment. Joe is a person of many and diverse abilities, but elaboration of only a few illustrates some of the reasons for his inclusion in this volume.

Bob and Joe were chief among several counseling professionals responsible for the start-up and success of the Association for Counselor Education and Supervision (ACES) Committee on Accreditation and the initial success of CACREP; to say otherwise would be to do them both a disservice. This ACES committee, first chaired by Bob and then by Joe, was housed in the UF Department of Counselor Education and was the first national organization to accredit counselor preparation programs. Joe also enabled CACREP to be housed in our department for its first 7 years, and he served notably as its first executive director. One of the major tasks of that period was to get CACREP accredited by the Council on Professional Accreditation (COPA). In spearheading this effort, Joe, working closely with Tom Sweeney, was masterful in both planning the application strategy and in fending off "attacks" by those persons and organizations that opposed CACREP being in COPA. A long, 6-year effort was finally successful. Afterward, Joe commented, "It's easy to walk across water if you know where the stumps are."

Not too long after I began working with the NBCC in the early 1980s, I walked into Joe's office one morning and said, "You need to be an NCC." He replied, "Okay, and what's an NCC?" I replied, "It's gonna be a big deal in our profession, you should be a part of it, and I have to go to class." A few months later he told me he was studying for the NCE, *which at the time had no criterion score.* Joe works exceptionally hard at whatever he does and always gives his best effort, regardless of the circumstance. Who can't learn from that type of modeling?

In the mid 1980s, I said to Joe one morning, "Tom Sweeney and Jane Myers are starting up an organization for counselors called Chi Sigma Iota, and I am involved, too. We need money from you." Joe wrote a (substantial) check right then. Several days later, he asked me, "So what is this Chi Sigma Iota thing?" Providing support and encouragement and facilitating positive action are among Joe's finest talents; he always helps others feel good and do well.

Unlike Larry, who has had the good fortune of being one of Joe's colleagues for over 25 years, the majority of my (Harry's) experience with Joe has been vicarious in nature. Yet he has exerted a considerable influence over my views about counseling and counselor education. I was one of the fortunate ones who attended graduate school at the time when the distinctions between counseling and counseling psychology were being hotly debated in many academic departments. I guess that was the first time that I read about Joe's ideas, because he was right in the middle of that debate. But I did not realize the strength of his position until after I had graduated and had taken a faculty position at Southern Illinois University at Carbondale. As the newest member of the faculty I was invited to join my colleagues in the local discussion about the counseling–counseling psychology distinction. I can remember feeling lost in the discussion and looking for some distinctive event that would draw attention to counseling as a profession.

I am pleased to say that Joe provided the event that I was looking for when he returned his license to practice psychology in Florida to the state licensing board because the board was actively lobbying against legislation that provided for the licensing of mental health counselors. I can remember as if it were yesterday the faculty meeting in which Mike Altekruse told about Joe's decision. Although I did not know him, I had the utmost respect for Joe and thought that he was very courageous. By demonstrating his commitment to counseling as a profession through this particular action, Joe greatly influenced an entire generation of counselor educators.

As I have come to know him over the last six years, I recognize that Joe did not view his decision to return his psychologist license as being particularly courageous. I think the word that he would prefer might be "congruent." He was acting in a manner that was consistent with his beliefs! I recognize that now, just as I recognize that being congruent is the cornerstone of his professional and personal life. It is, as we described above, a lesson that he first learned in the Amish community of his youth, and one that he has applied again and again throughout his life. I am delighted to call him a colleague and friend.

## REFERENCES

Wittmer, J. (1988). CACREP or APA: A counselor educator's personal views. *Counselor Education and Supervision, 27,* 291–294.

Wittmer, J. (1990). *The gentle people: Personal reflections on Amish life.* Minneapolis, MN: Educational Media Corp.

Wittmer, J. (Ed.). (2000). *Managing your K-12 counseling program* (2nd ed.). Minneapolis, MN: Educational Media Corp.

Wittmer, J., & Myrick, R. (1980). *The teacher as facilitator.* Minneapolis, MN: Educational Media Corp.

Wittmer, J., Thompson, D., & Loesch, L. (1997). *Classroom guidance activities: A sourcebook for elementary school counselors.* Minneapolis, MN: Educational Media Corp.

Wittmer, J., Thompson, D., & Sheperis, C. (1999). *The peace train: A school-wide violence prevention program.* Minneapolis, MN: Educational Media Corp.

# Part III

# Dimensions and Areas for Leadership

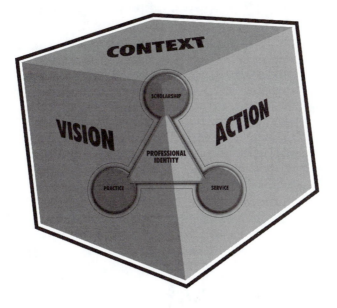

# CHAPTER 30

# Dimensions and Areas
# for Leadership

Cynthia J. Osborn, John D. West, Donald L. Bubenzer,
Jill D. Duba, and Seth D. Olson

In the first chapter of this book we discussed three dimensions of leadership: gaining an appreciation for the *context* in which leadership originates and is practiced, developing a *vision* for the future, and facilitating the dimension of *action* in order to help the vision come to life. These dimensions should not be considered as discrete and mutually exclusive but rather as interdependent components of leadership that inform one another. In this chapter we would like to review these three dimensions of leadership, in light of the individuals who were recognized in the second section of the book, and then spend time considering some possible areas for making contributions to leadership within the counseling profession.

## REVIEWING DIMENSIONS OF LEADERSHIP

The authors who wrote of the 23 leaders in the second section of this book appeared to offer observations and comments that were, in part, related to the previously mentioned dimensions of leadership. Miller, writing of

Bruce Shertzer noted, "His ability to identify situations requiring leadership is based on keen observation, careful listening, and the capacity to discriminate solvable from intractable problems." Marbley noted Loretta Bradley's "grassroots approach to leadership," which we interpreted as an interest in listening to and speaking with folks in the field, and Rawlins and Altekruse wrote of Michael K. Altekruse's ability "to create a vision that brings others on as partners in a project by listening to multiple viewpoints." Cormier wrote of wisdom in leadership she had gained from Harold L. (Dick) Hackney and mentioned "the value of humility" and, indeed, we see this as supportive of one's interest in listening to others. It is this receptiveness to hearing about current events in the lives of colleagues, students, and clients that we have previously described as gaining an appreciation for the *context*.

With time and reflection, this appreciation of context may lead to the generation of a *vision* for the future. Niles mentioned of Edwin L. Herr that, in part, he has drawn "upon the extant theoretical and research literature to formulate his vision for the future of the counseling profession" and "in addition to being able to understand future trends in counseling, a 'vision' for leadership emerges from an understanding of past and present factors influencing the profession." Henderson spoke of Samuel T. Gladding's "talent of open listening and wise synthesis" and she noted, "He has learned to search for possibilities and to find a mutual meeting place to start conversations." The components of listening and synthesizing of information with the help of others appear to us to be in the service of creating a vision. Likewise, comments by Briddick and Hayes, regarding Roger F. Aubrey, seemed to suggest how a vision is developed: "Roger's interactions with us were driven by an unselfish, humanistic philosophy of helping others, be they colleagues, friends, or clients." That is, for a vision to have meaning, it must avoid the feeling of being self-serving and it should show a concern for others. A similar ability to have concern for others was highlighted by Loesch and Daniels in remarks about Joe Wittmer. Being able to manage and arrange a variety of issues is also suggestive of creating a vision and this was noted in Witmer and Reardon's description of Harold F. Cottingham: "His vision of what could be and his ability to integrate an array of ideas and points of view gave clarity to the big picture and a focus on the issues at hand." The ability to integrate an array of ideas and points of view, so that they demonstrate a concern for others, seems crucial to developing a vision. Integrating ideas and points of view and demonstrating a concern for others may be facilitated by placing one's self in communication with others and Remley made a similar point when writing about Jane Myers: "She is not afraid to tackle difficult issues, but does so in a manner that involves others in a process of gathering information, discussing alternatives and the consequences of outcomes, and a shared process of decision making."

In the chapter on Robert O. Stripling (by Haight), the dimension of *action* in leadership is highlighted, "Bob often told me [Joe Wittmer] that our profession needed people with a sense of commitment, a deep appreciation for counseling, and most importantly, individuals who were not afraid to become 'active' and to take a stand. That is, where action is absent, so is leadership!" Writing of George E. Hill, Davis and Witmer noted, "He pursued his vision for the profession with a passion, believed greatly in its value to our educational system, and worked diligently to establish its credibility. His knowledge, . . . commitment to the profession, and dependability for getting a job done were hallmarks of his leadership qualities." Likewise, Engen commented on Kenneth B. Hoyt's interest in professional involvement and Chaney commented on Merle M. Ohlsen's professional commitment. Ginter wrote of David K. Brooks, Jr., "What made David unique was that he possessed talents that enabled him to lead through action—he made ideas work." Hermann appeared to be speaking of this action dimension when she noted, of Theodore P. Remley Jr., that he is skilled at both "organizing and delegating." Underwood mentioned of Thomas W. Hosie that "he leads by example" and that "Tom inspires by example." The importance of inclusiveness in action was supported on the first page of the chapter focusing on Don C. Locke (by Faubert) when it was noted that "Cultural diversity makes us strong." Similar perspectives were evident when reading the chapters on Judy Lewis (by Carlson, Cebuhar, and Goodman), Courtland Lee (by Herlihy and Brooks), John McFadden (by Jencius, Durant, and Hawley), and Thomas Sweeney (by Witmer). Nassar-McMillan mentioned of Mary Thomas Burke that, "She is not above any job, and can often be found working 'in the trenches,' all the while bringing along others with her optimism for life." The need for action in leadership was also pointed out in comments about Jane Myers (by Remley): "She believes that leaders should do their homework, always be prepared, . . . and, importantly, always seek consultation from multiple sources when dealing with decisions affecting the lives of others."

The description of these individuals, who have been recognized for their professional leadership, should in no way be seen as inclusive of all they have contributed. We believe, however, that counselors and graduate

students in counselor education programs can benefit from being introduced to some of the folks who have provided noteworthy leadership to the
counseling profession. When considering opportunities to offer professional leadership, counselors and graduate students will want to consider
the process of leadership, as perhaps suggested by the previously mentioned dimensions of leadership.

## PASSIONATE PRIDE IN THE PROFESSION

We hope it is clear that we have been inspired by the stories of those
individuals featured in this book. Their leadership and legacies in the
counseling profession make us extremely proud to be members of the
counseling profession. In many ways, their commitment to the advancement of counseling as a profession allows us all, as counselors, to do the
work for which we are prepared. We are therefore indebted to them for
their resolute vision, perseverance in the trenches over the years, accomplishments, and triumphs, as well as their preparation of current and
future leaders.

One of the aspects of leadership that is prominent for us as we reflect
on those who have "gone before," those who in many ways have fashioned
the profession we enjoy today, is the sense of pride in the counseling profession and the accompanying identity of being a counselor. This is evident
in Joe Wittmer's relinquishment of his psychologist license once he
learned that the state psychology board was actively lobbying against legislation for mental health counselors in Florida. This sense of pride also
seemed to be reflected in what we interpreted as Don C. Locke's message
to be proud of who we are as counselors, a message that we thought resem-
bled that given to his daughters to be proud of their identity as Lockes and
as African American women. And in a similar manner, Sam Gladding's oc-
casional salutation of "Hi, I'm Sam and I'm a counselor" conveys pride in
his clear professional identity.

This sense of pride is fitting for those who have heeded the call to be a
helping professional. The word *proud* is derived from Latin meaning *beneficial, advantageous*, and *to be useful*, indicating that pride has a purpose,
that of promoting beneficence and utility. We take this to mean that feeling
or showing pride, as in one's identity as a counselor, demonstrates one's
commitment to being helpful. Pride in the counseling profession, therefore, signifies one's desire to be of service and to be part of a cause or
a mission that provides advantages for persons who utilize our services

(e.g., clients and students). Inspired conviction is another way to view such pride.

In addition, pride suggests involvement in or the exemplification of something special or unique. For counselors, this may entail what Remley and Herlihy (2001) regarded as "a unique belief system regarding the best way to help people resolve their emotional and personal issues and problems" (p. 19). According to Remley and Herlihy, this philosophy of helping shared by counselors encompasses four belief systems: (a) wellness or health promotion, (b) developmental perspective, (c) prevention and early intervention, and (d) empowerment. We would add that an appreciation and intentional use of the client's resources, strengths, and capacities are integral to the focus and work of counselors and may represent a preferred paradigm or posture for the counseling profession.

Although other mental health professionals may endorse a similar philosophy, such a belief system is *primary* for counselors. Remley and Herlihy (2001) stated that "the key to a strong professional identity is the philosophy underlying the services, not the services being rendered" (p. 23). Pride in one's professional identity as a counselor, therefore, may originate and emanate from the primacy of this unique belief system, illustrating Kouzes and Posner's (1995) observation that "uniqueness fosters pride" (p. 99).

Passionate pride in the counseling profession reflects or exemplifies a unique identity, one emphasized among counselor education doctoral graduates now in private practice (Swickert, 1997), and an identity which Smith (2001) and others (e.g., Myers, Sweeney, & Witmer, 2000) have regarded as embracing a primary philosophy of wellness, one that comprises or includes a preoccupation with and cultivation of client strengths and resources. Not only does this unique identity for counselors foster pride, but pride, in turn, fosters loyalty. Kouzes and Posner (1995) noted, "The prouder we are of the place we shop, the products or services we buy, the school we (or our children) attend, the community in which we live, or the place we work, the more loyal we're likely to be" (p. 99). The pride of being a counselor and of providing service to the profession suggests a loyalty to the profession. And it is loyalty to the uniqueness of counseling, and to the health and endurance of the profession, that is evident in the work and lives of those who are recognized as leaders in this book. In a very real sense, leadership promotes and articulates the uniqueness of the organization or profession, and this uniqueness generates pride, which in turn fosters loyalty.

## THE "LEADERGRAM": A VISUAL DEPICTION OF LEADERSHIP

Informed by the work of these and other leaders, we have attempted to capture in a visual diagram what we believe are the primary expressions of leadership (i.e., scholarship, practice/teaching, and service) in and to the counseling profession today. This "leadergram" reflects our current understanding of and appreciation for expressions of leadership in counseling, which have been shaped by our own readings and conversations, as well as our reflections on the leadership styles of the 23 leaders included in this book. It is intended as a schema for students, faculty, practitioners, and counselor education programs alike as they consider ways in which to participate in and promote leadership in the profession. Although the "leadergram" certainly doesn't capture all the possible expressions of leadership, we trust that the illustration in Figure 1 and the corresponding text convey some sense of the essence of leadership.

Figure 1

## "Check Your Professional ID, Please"

Passion for the counseling profession and pride in one's identity as a counselor comprise what we believe is the capstone of leadership in and for counseling. That is, without a clear and certain identity as a counselor, as a committed member of this profession, leadership is inauthentic, unsteady, and misguided. A clear identity as a counselor shapes and informs all leadership activities in the profession, serving as a model and guide for those who work with us now and for those who are our future leaders. The placement of professional identity at the center of the leadergram is evidence of its importance and attests to its indispensability. Without a clear identity, one lacks the connection with and appreciation for the founders and visionaries of the profession. Indeed, we believe that leadership signifies one's indebtedness to the profession and its pioneers.

If professional identity implies uniqueness, then an understanding and promotion of that uniqueness appear warranted. For example, if you are a graduate student in a counselor education program, consider the following questions:

- What is it about the counseling profession that initially attracted you to a graduate program in counselor education?
- What is it about being a graduate student in a counselor education program that defines your identity?
- What sustains you in your role and work as a graduate student in a counselor education program?

In 2000, we in the Counseling and Human Development Services (CHDS) Program at Kent State University conducted a survey of those who had graduated from our master's and doctoral programs from 1990 to 1999. This was separate from the periodic survey administered to alumni for CACREP accreditation purposes (please contact the first author for a copy of the most recent Alumni Survey we distributed). Information obtained (e.g., current title and employment, address and phone number, license/certification held, and salary) from the 244 respondents (45% response rate) was used (with their permission) to compile an alumni directory, made available to current students. In addition, two wall maps (of the United States and Ohio) are now prominently displayed in the CHDS office, with colored dots corresponding to and identifying the location of CHDS alumni. Periodic surveys of new graduates (e.g., conducted every two years) and follow-up surveys of earlier graduates are planned in order to expand on and make current the alumni directory.

From such surveys, not only do current students gain an appreciation for the dispersion of graduates within Ohio and across the United States, but they also have access to what our alumni are doing now. Such a visual portrayal of the work and accomplishments of alumni (which, in a very real sense, represent the products of a counselor preparation program) can convey a message of unique identity and pride.

If you have graduated from a counselor education program, and are now working as a counselor or counselor educator, think about your own entrance into the counseling profession and ponder the following questions:

- "What drew you to the profession of counseling?" (This resembles the question referenced in Chapter 1 that was posed by Mary Jo Mason [1998] to graduate counseling students.)
- "What about the counseling profession today continues to be attractive or appealing to you?"
- "What about your identity as a professional counselor today generates pride?"

Your responses to questions such as these may help to add your own unique meaning to the philosophy of the counseling profession and may help to foster pride in your purpose and allegiance to the profession.

Revisit the leadergram in Figure 1. Not only is professional identity placed at the center of the diagram; its connection to the three areas of leadership—scholarship, practice/teaching, and service—are open, allowing dynamic and recursive interaction. One's practice and expression of leadership, therefore, is cultivated and guided by one's professional identity that, in turn, continually informs and refines one's professional identity. Leadership through supervision or teaching, for example, may challenge one to clearly articulate and convey to future counselors the essence, or at least the salient nuances, of one's counselor identity. Aspects of one's counselor identity may shift in emphasis or be more clearly defined in light of classroom or supervisory discussions related to such topics as consultation with other mental health professionals (e.g., multidisciplinary treatment team interactions), pursuing professional certifications, and striving for recognition from particular insurance companies.

## Scholarship

One of the areas or expressions of leadership depicted in the leadergram, an area that expresses and conveys one's professional counselor identity, is scholarship. By this we refer to somewhat systematic activities that challenge and probe; to circumscribed endeavors that investigate alternative methods or practices; and to opportunities to pursue and structure tasks to make sense of our observations and to apply and make public what we find useful, and to generate new understandings. In this manner, scholarship is an approach or an expression of leadership.

We believe that, by definition, scholarship is not an isolating or an exclusionary activity. Rather, it represents work that "none can accomplish alone" (Shulman, 1999, p. 15). Scholarship, therefore, can only be conducted in the company of others and for the benefit of others (e.g., the profession). This designates the person who engages in scholarship as an expression of leadership as a member of a community of learning, one who is a perpetual learner, who learns from and with others. Scholarship, therefore, is a cooperative effort, and the dissemination (or test) of one's scholarship takes place within a community. Shulman (1999) noted that the list of references at the end of any publication represents "a set of thank-you notes . . . acknowledging that, without the people whom we reference, we could not have done the work we did" (p. 15). In this same manner, leadership as scholarship builds on the work of others, those who have gone before, and have allowed us to ponder and generate ideas for future consideration.

Consequently, we regard the activity and all forms of scholarship as subject to peer review. Indeed, the expression of leadership in the area of scholarship implies that one's work has been made public in some manner and is held out for review and critique by members of one's intellectual and professional community. In this manner, the process and products of scholarship are

> acts of mind and spirit that have been made public in some manner, have been subjected to peer review by members of one's intellectual or professional community, and can be cited, refuted, built upon, and shared among members of that community . . . [and represent] the building block[s] for knowledge growth [understanding] in a field. . . . (Shulman, 1998a, p. 5)

Examples of scholarship that represent expressions of leadership in the counseling profession include:

- regular attendance at professional counseling gatherings (i.e., workshops and conferences), both as a presenter and as an active participant;
- regular investment in writing projects and the submission of one's written work for review by one's peers, with the intentions of such work being published for wider dissemination and critique; and
- active engagement in research investigations for the purpose of identifying both common and idiosyncratic observations and reflections, as well as synthesizing ideas, and generating new questions for consideration.

Examples of consistent and high-quality expressions of scholarship are certainly evident in the work of the leaders featured in this book. In many ways they have set the standard for and defined active and productive scholarship in the counseling profession. We can, and perhaps must, continue to learn from them and others, by participating as active readers and consumers of their ideas, their observations from applied research, their reflections, and their recommendations. It behooves us to build on the work of others and to also participate in scholarship activities for the purpose of maintaining a community of counseling learners, upholding the integrity and credibility of the profession, and promoting the benefits of counseling to the public at large.

### *Questions for Reflection*

Perhaps you had not considered the practice of scholarship as a form of leadership. What are the current scholarship activities you are involved in? In what ways can these (even one or two examples) be viewed as expressions of leadership on your part? Describe the processes and products of your scholarship. From these, what would you hope to (a) make public, (b) obtain feedback on from your peers, and (c) pass on to others, as a means of participating in leadership within the counseling profession? Using the leadergram as a guide, jot down some of your responses and consult with a trusted colleague and/or mentor about ways in which your scholarship activities could exemplify one or two of the dimensions of leadership (i.e., appreciating context, generating vision, and facilitating action) discussed earlier.

### Practice/Teaching

The practice of counseling, supervision, and teaching represent for us a second expression of leadership. Although teaching is regarded as a form of scholarship (Boyer, 1990; Shulman, 1998a), in discussing leadership in the counseling profession, we have elected to include teaching in the practice area of leadership, along with counseling and supervision. Active involvement in these activities indicates a desire to help shape the profession of counseling through direct contact and interaction with clients, supervisees, and students. As opposed to "sitting on the sidelines," continued involvement in such "front line" and "hands on" activities suggests a willingness to "work in the trenches," "get dirty with constituents," and remain directly immersed in the challenges and rewards of the provision of care associated with the profession of counseling. In addition, this expression of leadership involves not only the facilitation of learning for others, but the pursuit of one's own learning and professional development. This is particularly true if we believe that our clients, supervisees, and students can represent great sources of learning (Skovholt & Ronnestad, 1995), assuming on occasion the role of teacher for us.

Remaining active in the practice of counseling and the intentional use and refinement of one's counseling skills across a variety of roles and tasks (e.g., conducting a faculty meeting, coordinating a series of in-service training workshops) support and strengthen one's identification with and appreciation for all practicing counselors. Furthermore, these activities serve to reinforce and promote one's counselor identity, through the active use of one's counselor license or credential, thereby reminding the counselor of his or her unique philosophy of helping. This can, as noted earlier, foster a sense of pride, as well as generate and sustain a sense of gratitude to those who have made it possible to practice as a licensed and/or certified counselor.

The provision of supervision to those in training and those working toward licensure, is an aspect of leadership, particularly in light of Bernard and Goodyear's (1998) elucidation of supervision's simultaneous purposes:

> (1) enhancing the professional functioning of a more junior person(s), (2) monitoring the quality of professional services offered to the client(s) she, he, or they see(s), and (3) serving as a gatekeeper of those who are to enter the particular profession. (p. 6)

Assisting in another's professional identity development (i.e., beyond skill acquisition) and being able to protect the profession by exercising care regarding who is to be recommended for graduate degree conferral and licensure are certainly examples of leadership in action. This is why we support rules and guidelines in several states that counselor trainees be supervised only by members of their same profession (i.e., licensed counselors), rather than persons from other mental health disciplines. In the process of supervision, one serves as a role model for current and future counselors and leaders in the profession, a (hopefully) humbling, daunting responsibility of leadership that cannot be taken lightly.

As an area of leadership in the counseling profession, the practice of teaching is more than the transmittal of information through the use of carefully prescribed techniques. Rather, teaching is the thoughtful embodiment and expression of one's identity and integrity (Palmer, 1998). By this we infer that leader-as-teacher is one who maintains a clear counselor identity and conveys this strong identity and pride in the profession to one's students. This supports our belief that faculty charged with the responsibility of preparing future counselors and members of the counseling profession themselves be licensed and/or certified as counselors and, preferably, hold doctoral degrees from counselor education programs. As the leadergram suggests (see Figure 1), identity is central to leadership, nourishing the expressions of leadership. In the role of teacher, advisor, and mentor, therefore, active and current identification with the counseling profession is essential.

The expression of leadership in teaching also suggests a commitment to the process of learning and the benefits of education. The leader-as-teacher is a perpetual student, one who challenges himself or herself to continually make sense of and derive meaning from theory and research, implementing newly-derived concepts to one's own current professional practice. This also means that, in the practice of leadership, the teacher is willing to take certain risks, such as using one's self to demonstrate in the classroom a particular counseling approach, correcting inappropriate student conduct in the classroom, and making appropriate references to one's own experience as the provider and/or recipient of counseling services.

Because the purpose of one's teaching is to facilitate student learning, one's teaching style and methods need to continually be relevant to the students' learning needs and preferences so that the material can come to life for students. In this regard, teaching as leadership is open to innovation, challenging a no-longer-useful status quo (see Kouzes & Posner, 1995), and staying clear of the susceptibilities Shulman (1999) termed the "pathologies of learning" that both students and teachers experience periodically: amnesia, fantasia (i.e., illusory understanding or persistent misconceptions), inertia (i.e., material lacking purpose or utility), and nostalgia (i.e., "more of the same" thinking). Pursuing a critically reflective stance, as Brookfield (1995) recommended, assists in this process, allowing the expression of leadership in teaching to assume an authentic flavor, a credible disposition, one which integrates and honors the goals and aspirations of student, teacher, and profession.

### Questions for Reflection

Reflect on your own current practice, be it counseling, supervision, teaching, or a combination of these two or three. In what ways are these activities expressions of leadership? How are these illustrative of your own counselor identity? Who in your life (be it a teacher, mentor, colleague, supervisor, or counselor) serves as a model for such leadership practices? How might you continue to build on his or her efforts and follow in his or her steps in order to further a vision and mission of relevant practice? In what ways would these continued efforts benefit your own clients, supervisees, and students, as well as the counseling profession as a whole?

## Service and Stewardship

If an important characteristic of any profession is the obligation to be of service or to provide service to others (Shulman, 1998b), it is certainly appropriate to consider service as an expression of leadership within the counseling profession. By service we mean the various ways a counselor makes himself or herself available to be of help for a specific cause or mission, particularly one that has direct implications for the counseling profession at local ("grassroots"), regional, state, national, and perhaps even international levels. Although the word *service* and related terms corresponding to persons who engage in or perform service activities (e.g., *servant*, *serf*, and even *slave*) are not always heralded or received in a positive light, our use of the word *service* emphasizes and brings attention to its connotation of *devotion* and *stewardship*. That is, the provision of service emanates from and exemplifies one's devotion and commitment to the good of a particular cause, such as the pursuit of counselor licensure, establishing national standards for counselor preparation, successfully managing the editorial demands of a counseling journal, fulfilling the duties of a counseling association president, and supporting efforts to unify various divisions within the parent organization (the American Counseling Association). In these and other expressions of leadership through service, the sacrifice of one's time, talent, and resources for the good of the profession clearly exemplify the positive intent of service and stewardship. This is evident in reference to Mary Thomas Burke (see Chapter 11) as a "professional servant."

Examples of leadership expressed through service are replete throughout the 23 chapters in part II of this book. All of the noted leaders featured in that section have been active in service activities for the benefit of the counseling profession. We have been impressed by the willingness of some of these folks to be of service, sacrificing time and energy perhaps originally allocated to or intended for other investments, such as family, scholarship, and recreation. Some have demonstrated not only a keen sense of perception and timing, but also a true grit to see projects through to completion, "stepping up to the plate" when others may have shied away or tired of the task.

Service to and for the profession, therefore, is typically not undertaken for acclaim or to relish the limelight. Rather, leadership as service originates from a genuine desire to be helpful and often an unselfish inclination to "give away" one's knowledge, ideas, vision, and creativity for the benefit of a larger good. This is not to say that service activities are for the naïve or "pushovers." To the contrary, those who have consistently participated in professional service are often the prescient ones, those who have configured a vision, have dreamed a dream, and have subsequently paved the way and set the standards for excellence in the counseling profession. In addition, they can be said to be the cultivators and keepers of the "family name," promoting the primary philosophy of counseling and protecting the unique identity of counselors. In this sense, they represent the epitome of devotion and loyalty.

Leadership as service demonstrates good citizenship, which can often "begin at home." This means looking for and actively seeking opportunities for service and volunteerism within one's local community. The phrase "bloom where you are planted" comes to mind, conveying the sentiment that opportunities and resources abound within our midst to contribute to one's immediate surroundings and participate in helpful ways within the community.

### Questions for Reflection

Refer to the leadergram in Figure 1. In what ways has your devotion to the counseling profession been demonstrated? What needs and opportunities for improvement have you observed in your current work and surroundings that could benefit from your leadership? In what ways would you like to be involved for the good of the larger counseling profession? What initial steps and strategies can you envision and devise for participating in what can be challenging yet immensely rewarding service?

## CONCLUSION

We have offered three dimensions of leadership, context, vision, and action, and three areas or expressions of leadership, scholarship, practice/teaching, and service, all informed and guided by a clear professional counselor identity in the hopes of capturing what we believe are some essential aspects of leadership for the counseling profession today. The "leadergram" has been presented in this concluding chapter as a visual depiction of leadership and is intended for your use as you consider ways in which your own leadership as a counselor can be furthered and refined.

We are immensely proud of the 23 leaders featured in this book, individuals who have devoted themselves to the unique philosophy, mission, and identity of the counseling profession. Their lives and legacies comprise the foundation and building blocks of our own work and, we believe, the continued strength and relevance of the profession.

In light of their investments, we are encouraged by reports that attest to the growth of the counseling profession, as well as the apparent satisfaction of counselors with their career choice. In a document published by the Department of Health and Human Services, West et al. (2001) reported that of eight mental health disciplines surveyed from 1998–2000, counseling boasts the largest number of practitioners: 108,104 in 2000. This figure is almost double that of the next two highest disciplines surveyed, psychology and social work. In addition, in a survey of randomly selected Association for Counselor Education and Supervision (ACES) members (Parr, Bradley, Lan, & Gould, 1996), respondents revealed a strong satisfaction (81%) with a career in counseling and would select it again if given a choice (88.6%).

Although reports such as these certainly do not present a complete picture of the profession, they do reinforce our view of a strong, vibrant, and relevant profession, one steered by devoted and competent "servant leaders" such as the 23 featured in this book. We hope the testimonies given to their captivating vision for the profession, their persistent and untiring contributions to worthy pursuits, their nurturing and mentoring of future leaders, and their dedication and loyalty to the counseling profession provide fuel and sustenance for continued participation in leadership activities for the profession. May their lives and legacies steer all of us in due course. They and you—you who share a passionate pride in the profession of counseling—have our sincerest gratitude.

## REFERENCES

Bernard, J. M., & Goodyear, R. K. (1998). *Fundamentals of clinical supervision* (2nd ed.). Boston: Allyn and Bacon.

Brookfield, S. D. (1995). *Becoming a critically reflective teacher*. San Francisco: Jossey-Bass.

Boyer, E. L. (1990). *Scholarship reconsidered: Priorities of the professoriate*. New York: Wiley.

Kouzes, J. M., & Posner, B. Z. (1995). *The leadership challenge: How to keep getting extraordinary things done in organizations.* San Francisco: Jossey-Bass.

Mason, M. J. (1998). *The development of counselors: A study of professional socialization through graduate school.* Unpublished doctoral dissertation, Kent State University, Kent, Ohio.

Myers, J. E., Sweeney, T. J., & Witmer, J. M. (2000). The wheel of wellness counseling for wellness: A holistic model for treatment planning. *Journal of Counseling & Development, 78,* 251–266.

Palmer, P. J. (1998). *The courage to teach:* Exploring the inner landscape of a teacher's life. San Francisco: Jossey Bass.

Parr, G. D. Bradley, L. J., Lan, W. Y., & Gould, L. J. (1996). The career satisfaction of the Association for Counselor Education and Supervision members. *Journal of Employment Counseling, 33,* 20–28.

Remley, T. P., Jr., & Herlihy, B. (2001). *Ethical, legal, and professional issues in counseling.* Upper Saddle River, NJ: Prentice-Hall.

Shulman, L. S. (1998a). Course anatomy: The dissection and analysis of knowledge through teaching. In P. H. Hutchings (Ed.), *The course portfolio: How faculty can examine their teaching to advance practice and improve student learning* (pp. 5–12). Washington, DC: American Association for Higher Education.

Shulman, L. S. (1998b). Theory, practice, and the education of professionals. *The Elementary School Journal, 98,* 511–526.

Shulman, L. S. (1999, July/August). Taking learning seriously. *Change,* 11–17.

Skovholt, T. M., & Ronnestad, M. H. (1995). *The evolving professional self: Stages and themes in therapist and counselor development.* Chichester, England: Wiley.

Smith, H. B. (2001). Professional identity for counselors. In D. C. Locke, J. E. Myers, & E. L. Herr (Eds.), *The handbook of counseling* (pp. 569–579). Thousand Oaks, CA: Sage.

Swickert, M. L. (1997). Perceptions regarding the professional identity of counselor education doctoral graduates in private practice: A qualitative study. *Counselor Education and Supervision, 36,* 332–340.

West, J., Kohout, J., Pion, G. M., Wicherski, M. M., Vandivort-Warren, R. E., Palmiter, M. L., Merwin, E. I., Lyon, D., Fox, J. C., Clawson, T. W., Smith, S. C., Stockton, R., Nitza, A. G., Ambrose, J. P., Blankertz, L., Thomas, A., Sullivan, L. D., Dwyer, K. P., Fleischer, M. S., Goldsmith, H. F., Henderson, M. J., Atay, J. E., & Manderscheid, R. W. (2001). Mental health practitioners and trainees. In R. W. Manderscheid & M. J. Henderson (Eds.). *Mental Health, United States, 2000* (pp. 279–315). Washington, DC: Center for Mental Health Services [DHHS Pub. No. (SMA) 01–3537].

# Contributors

Michael C. Altekruse, Ph.D., Psychologist, University of Wisconsin Oshkosh Counseling Center, Oshkosh, WI.

L. DiAnne Borders, Ph.D., Professor and Chair, Department of Counseling and Educational Development, University of North Carolina at Greensboro, Greensboro, NC.

William C. Briddick, M.Ed., Instructor, Counseling and Human Resource Development South Dakota State University, Brookings, SD.

Morgan Brooks, Ph.D., Assistant Professor, Department of Education and Counseling, Niagara University, Niagara, NY.

Donald L. Bubenzer, Ph.D., Professor, Counseling and Human Development Services Program, and Chair, Department of Adult, Counseling, Health, and Vocational Education, Kent State University, Kent, OH.

Jon Carlson, Psy.D., Ed.D., Professor, College of Education, Governors State University, University Park, IL.

John Cebuhar, B.A., AIDS Advocate and Consultant and Master's Student, Governors State University, University Park, IL.

Reece Chaney, Ph.D., Professor of Counseling Psychology, Department of Counseling, Indiana State University, Terre Haute, IN.

Sherry Cormier, Ph.D., Professor, Department of Counseling, Counseling Psychology, and Rehabilitation Counseling, West Virginia University, Morgantown, WV.

Jane A. Cox, Ph.D., Assistant Professor, Department of Educational Psychology and Special Education, Southern Illinois University at Carbondale, Carbondale, IL.

M. Harry Daniels, Ph.D., Professor and Chair, Department of Counselor Education, University of Florida, Gainesville, FL.

Thomas E. Davis, Ph.D., Professor, Counselor Education, and Chair, Department of Counseling and Higher Education, Ohio University, Athens, OH.

Jill D. Duba, M.A., Doctoral candidate, Counseling and Human Development Services Program, Kent State University, Kent, OH.

Chas Durant, Ph.D., Senior Research Associate, Center for Literacy Studies, University of Tennessee, Knoxville, TN.

Harold B. Engen, Ed.D., Professor Emeritus, Counselor Education, University of Iowa, Iowa City, IA.

Marie Faubert, CSJ, Ed.D., a member of the Congregation of the Sisters of Saint Joseph, and Director, Counselor Education Program, University of Saint Thomas, Houston, TX.

Earl J. Ginter, Ph.D., Professor, University of Georgia, Division of Academic Assistance, Athens, GA.

Samuel T. Gladding, Ph.D., Professor, Counselor Education, Wake Forest University, Winston-Salem, NC.

Jane Goodman, Ph.D., Associate Professor of Counseling, Oakland University, Rochester, MI.

Donald A. Haight, Ed.D., Professor and Chair, Counselor Education Department, Plattsburgh State University, Plattsburgh, NY.

Lisa D. Hawley, Ph.D., Assistant Professor, Department of Counseling, Oakland University, Rochester, MI.

Richard L. Hayes, Ed.D., Professor, Counseling and Human Development Services, The University of Georgia, Athens, GA.

Donna A. Henderson, Ph.D., Associate Professor, Counselor Education Program, Wake Forest University, Winston-Salem, NC.

Barbara Herlihy, Ph.D., Professor, Counselor Education Program, University of New Orleans, New Orleans, LA.

Mary A. Hermann, J.D., Ph.D., Assistant Professor, Department of Counselor Education and Educational Psychology, Mississippi State University, Mississippi State, MS.

Marty Jencius, Ph.D., Assistant Professor, Counseling and Human Development Services Program, Kent State University, Kent, OH.

Judith A. Lewis, Ph.D., Professor, Division of Health Administration and Human Services, Governors State University, University Park, IL.

Larry C. Loesch, Ph.D., Professor, Department of Counselor Education, University of Florida, Gainesville, FL.

Aretha Marbley, Ph.D., Assistant Professor and Clinical Director, Educational Psychology and Leadership, Texas Tech University, Lubbock, TX.

Kenneth L. Miller, Ph.D., Assistant Professor, Department of Counseling, and Director, University Counseling Center/Community Counseling Clinic, Youngstown State University, Youngstown, OH.

Sylvia C. Nassar-McMillan, Ph.D., Assistant Professor, Department of Counseling, Special Education, and Child Development, University of North Carolina at Charlotte, Charlotte, NC.

Spencer G. Niles, Ed.D., Professor of Education and Professor-in-Charge of Counselor Education Programs, Penn State University, University Park, PA.

Seth D. Olson, M.A., Doctoral Candidate, Counseling and Human Development Services Program, Kent State University, Kent, OH.

Cynthia J. Osborn, Ph.D., Assistant Professor, Counseling and Human Development Services Program, Kent State University, Kent, OH.

Gerald Parr, Ph.D., Professor and Chair, Educational Psychology and Leadership, Texas Tech University, Lubbock, TX.

Melanie Rawlins, Ph.D., Professor and Chair, Counselor Education and College Student Personnel Department, Western Illinois University, Macomb, IL.

Robert C. Reardon, Ph.D., Professor, Department of Human Services and Studies, and Director of Instruction, Research, and Evaluation in the Career Center, Florida State University, Tallahassee, FL.

Theodore P. Remley, Jr., Ph.D., J.D., Professor, Counseling Graduate Program and Chair, Department of Educational Leadership, Counseling and Foundations, University of New Orleans, New Orleans, LA.

Susan Jones Sears, Ph.D., Associate Professor, Counselor Education, The Ohio State University, Columbus, OH.

Marie F. Shoffner, Ph.D., Assistant Professor and Coordinator of the School Counseling Program, Department of Counseling and Educational Development, University of North Carolina at Greensboro, Greensboro, NC.

Holly A. Stadler, Ph.D., Professor and Head, Department of Counseling and Counseling Psychology, Auburn University, Auburn, AL.

Thomas J. Sweeney, Ph.D., Professor Emeritus, Counselor Education, Ohio University, Athens, OH.

Joe Ray Underwood, Ph.D., Professor and Coordinator, School Counseling Program, Department of Counselor Education and Educational Psychology, Mississippi State University, Mississippi State, MS.

Laura J. Veach, Ph.D., Assistant Professor, Counselor Education Program, Wake Forest University, Winston-Salem, NC.

John D. West, Ed.D., Professor and Coordinator, Counseling and Human Development Services Doctoral Program, Kent State University, Kent, OH.

J. Melvin Witmer, Ph.D., Professor Emeritus, Counselor Education, Ohio University, Athens, OH.

# Index